# Music and the sociological gaze

MANCHESTER
1824

Manchester University Press

Music and society

*Series editors*    Peter J. Martin and Tia DeNora

*Music and Society* aims to bridge the gap between music scholarship and the human sciences. A deliberately eclectic series, its authors are nevertheless united by the contention that music is a social product, social resource, and social practice. As such it is not autonomous but is created and performed by real people in particular times and places; in doing so they reveal much about themselves and their societies.

In contrast to the established academic discourse, *Music and Society* is concerned with all forms of music, and seeks to encourage the scholarly analysis of both 'popular' styles and those which have for too long been marginalised by that discourse – folk and ethnic traditions, music by and for women, jazz, rock, rap, reggae, muzak and so on. These sounds are vital ingredients in the contemporary cultural mix, and their neglect by serious scholars itself tells us much about the social and cultural stratification of our society.

The time is right to take a fresh look at music and its effects, as today's music resonates with the consequences of cultural globalisation and the transformations wrought by new electronic media, and as past styles are reinvented in the light of present concerns. There is, too, a tremendous upsurge of interest in cultural analysis. *Music and Society* does not promote a particular school of thought, but aims to provide a forum for debate; in doing so, the titles in the series bring music back into the heart of socio-cultural analysis.

Peter J. Martin

# Music and the sociological gaze
## Art worlds and cultural production

Manchester University Press
Manchester and New York

distributed exclusively in the USA by Palgrave

*Published by* Manchester University Press
Oxford Road, Manchester M13 9NR, UK
*and* Room 400, 175 Fifth Avenue, New York, NY 10010, USA
http://www.manchesteruniversitypress.co.uk

*Distributed exclusively in the USA by*
Palgrave, 175 Fifth Avenue, New York,
NY 10010, USA

*Distributed exclusively in Canada by*
UBC Press, University of British Columbia, 2029 West Mall,
Vancouver, BC, Canada V6T 1Z2

*British Library Cataloguing-in-Publication Data*
A catalogue record for this book is available from the British Library

*Library of Congress Cataloging-in-Publication Data applied for*

ISBN   0 7190 7216 6 *hardback*
EAN    978 07190 7216 1

ISBN   0 7190 7217 4 *paperback*
EAN    978 07190 7217 8

First published 2006

14  13  12  11  10  09  08  07  06      10  9  8  7  6  5  4  3  2  1

Typeset in Great Britain
by Northern Phototypesetting Co Ltd, Bolton
Printed in Great Britain
by Biddles Ltd, King's Lynn

# Contents

# Acknowledgements

Chapter 2 of this book, 'Music and the sociological gaze', is based on a paper originally presented to the Colloquium on 'Musicology Beyond 1999' held in August of that year at the University of Gothenburg. I am grateful to Professor Olle Edström for inviting me to the Colloquium, and to Professor Anders Carlsson for allowing me to reprint an edited version of the article which appeared in *Svensk Tidskrift for Musikforskning* (The Swedish Journal of Musicology), Volume 82, 2000.

Chapter 3 'Over the rainbow?' is an edited version of the review article which appeared in the *Journal of the Royal Musical Association*, Volume 127, 2001. I have to thank Professor David Charlton for the original invitation to write the piece, and Professor Nicholas Cook for permission to reprint it here.

Chapter 4 'Music and manipulation' is based on a paper presented to the International Conference on Music and Manipulation, organised by the Karolinska Institute, and held in Stockholm in September, 1999. I have to thank the organisers for inviting me to speak at the Conference, and to Steven Brown and Ulrik Volgsten for permission to reprint a revised version of the article which has appeared in *Music and Manipulation* (Berghahn Press, 2006).

Chapter 7 'Spontaneity and organisation' is a revised version of the article which appeared in *The Cambridge Companion to Jazz* (Cambridge University Press, 2002). I have to thank David Horn and Professor Mervyn Cooke for inviting me to contribute this piece, and Linda Nicol and Vicki Cooper of Cambridge University Press for permission to reprint it here.

Chapter 8 'Hear me talkin'' is based on a paper presented at the conference on 'Musicology and Sociology' held at the University of

Gothenburg in August, 2002. Once again, I am grateful to Professor Olle Edström and his colleagues for inviting me to the conference.

Chapter 9 'Text, context and the cultural object' is based on a paper presented at the ISA/ESA International Conference on the Sociology of the Arts held at the Ecole Nationale des Beaux Arts in Paris during April 2003.

Much of the material for this book has been presented at various conferences and seminars. I am particularly grateful to participants at the ASA Conference on Social Theory and the Arts at Vanderbilt University, Nashville, in October 1999, and those at the ESA Culture and the Arts Network Conference held in Exeter in August, 2000, for their comments and suggestions. My thanks are also due to members of seminar groups in the universities of Southampton, Sheffield, Leeds, Edinburgh, Glasgow, Bolton, Oxford Brookes, at University College Worcester, and the Manchester Ethnography Group.

Many individuals have contributed in all sorts of ways to the production of this book, though I should emphasise that they should not be held responsible for the outcome. I am particularly grateful to Tia DeNora, with whom I have been discussing the music–sociology interface for quite a few years now, and Howard Becker, whose work across a range of fields is exemplary and inspirational, and whose sociological imagination is matched only by his good nature. I thank him for all that (and for an invaluable CD-Rom). I also appreciate greatly various conversations and discussions with Paul Atkinson, Andy Bennett, Alf Björnberg, Allison Cavanagh, Nick Cook, Sarah Daynes, Alex Dennis, Olle Edström, Vic Gammon, Will Gibson, Penny Gouk, Antoine Hennion, David Horn, Jina Kim, Tony King, Richard Leppert, Lars Lilliestam, Richard Middleton, Pete Peterson, Dave Russell, Derek Scott, Wes Sharrock, Ola Stockfelt, Rod Watson, Bob Witkin, the Manchester Music in Culture group and all members of the Grafton Seminar. I am greatly in debt to Ted Cuff for his close reading and many helpful suggestions. I also have to record with sadness the death in 2003 of Wilf Allis, whose fascination with the social history of music in Manchester contributed much to the discussion in Chapter 6.

At Manchester University Press, Kate Fox, Matthew Frost and Tony Mason have been not only supportive and extremely tolerant, but invariably cheerful too. I am greatly in debt to all of the above, and others, but most of all to Yvonne, Tom and Claire, who were kind enough to put up with me while all this was going on.

# 1

# Introduction

It is now more than ten years since the appearance of my previous book on music, *Sounds and Society*. It would have been appropriate to follow it with a substantial study which aimed to demonstrate the utility of the sort of sociological perspective on music which was developed in the book; that this project did not come to fruition was largely due to the demands of various university management roles which then occupied me for several years. (I even spent some time as Dean Martin.) However, during that period I was able to produce a series of papers, articles and conference presentations which dealt in various ways with the sociological analysis of musical activities, and it is a selection of these that forms the basis of this book.

Moreover, and this is one of the themes which I hope to develop in the pages that follow, since the mid-1990s the distinctiveness of a sociological approach to music has become increasingly apparent. That is, it has become far clearer how sociology can offer perspectives which differ from, and yet may be complementary to, those emerging from musicology, cultural and media studies, history, philosophy, and psychology. At the risk of oversimplifying a complex situation, it may be asserted that the primary focus of this specifically sociological 'gaze' is a concern to examine the various ways in which music is *used* in a whole range of social situations, and the consequences of this. Just as in the study of language, sociologists have with increasing confidence investigated the *use* of music by real people in real situations, thus moving away from a concern with revealing the meaning of musical texts. This approach does not invalidate the textual 'readings' produced by musicologists or cultural theorists, which can tell us much, for example, about how pieces of music or other cultural objects are constructed, or about their history – but a sociological concern with the uses of music seeks to return such cultural objects to the social contexts in which they are produced and experienced. (Inevitably, this invites interesting sociological questions about the claims to authority of the expert analysts who presume to determine the 'real' meaning of 'works' from the security of the study, and the nature of the 'art worlds' which their activities help to constitute). It follows that this focus on the *uses* of music greatly broadens the range of music encompassed by the analysis because, as Richard Leppert has suggested, even now those musicologists who have been concerned with popular music tend to analyse and 'valorise' the exceptional rather than the routine (2002: 345), finding little of interest in the latter. Yet, as I argued in *Sounds and Society*, it is precisely the ordinary, prosaic, music which becomes part of people's everyday lives that may be of greatest interest from a sociological point of view.

Indeed, while critical reaction to *Sounds and Society* was mostly positive, one reviewer took the book to be a polemic against textual 'interpretation' as traditionally practised in the humanities, while granting 'radical autonomy' to listeners in terms of the meanings they may extract from musical experiences. Needless to say, although I believe this reading to be radically misguided, indeed per-verse – and I'm encouraged that no other reviewer read it in this way – such comments do nevertheless serve to illustrate some of the ways in which the sociological gaze may illuminate aspects of musical activity which are of little concern to those engaged in text-based interpretations. One way of putting this would be to say that socio-logical analysis simply takes seriously Herbert Blumer's well-known proposition that meanings are not inherent in objects; indeed, *all* objects of human consciousness are ' . . . formed and transformed by the defining process that takes place in social interaction' (1969: 69). Analytical interest thus shifts to the 'defining process' and to 'social interaction' rather than seeking the essential qualities of objects; concern is with the ways in which, for example, cultural objects such as 'the blues', 'Beethoven', 'South Pacific' or 'Elvis' are constituted and represented through the collaborative social inter-action of real people in real situations. This does *not*, of course, mean that people are free to define objects as they choose; on the contrary, the achievement of orderly social life depends greatly on a tacit consensus among individuals on what they are to 'take for granted', and much sociological work is concerned to illuminate ways in which people are constrained and influenced by what Blumer himself called the 'obdurate character' of the social world (1969: 22).

Yet some remain troubled by this emphasis on the social constitution of cultural objects, the 'social construction' of the world of everyday experience. Nicholas Cook, for example, while accepting that meaning cannot be inherent in music, nevertheless worries that . . . ' . . . then there is nothing in music that can constrain interpretation' (2001: 173), and seeks to retain the notion that there must be some sort of identifiable relationship between the 'structural properties' (*ibid.*: 174) of music and 'the meanings ascribed to it' (*ibid.*: 171). Cook quotes Johnson's example of the ' . . . insistent oboe playing the dotted eighth-sixteenth note pattern in Haydn's Symphony No. 83', which is ' . . . the image of a hen to some, the expression of merriment to others, and an essential thread in a web of indescribable content to others. But it would be hard to argue credibly that it is a funeral dirge, or paints the storming of the Bastille, or promotes slavery' (Johnson, 1995: 2). A similar issue is raised by Fish in his discussion of contrasting interpretations of William Blake's poem 'The Tyger'. For some critics the tiger is 'unambiguously and obviously evil', while for others the poem 'celebrates the holiness of tigerness' (Fish, 1980: 339). Indeed, it has been argued that the very ambiguity or 'indistinctness' of literature is its great glory (Carey, 2005: 214). So the question, as Cook puts it, is what is there to constrain or limit the interpretations placed on cultural objects? 'After all', as Fish says in a passage that anticipates Johnson's example from Haydn, 'while "The Tyger" is obviously open to more than one interpretation, it is not open to an infinite number of interpretations . . . no one is suggesting that the poem is an allegory of the digestive processes or that it predicts the Second World War . . . ' (Fish, 1980: 341–342). But this is exactly what Fish then does, outlining (in one of the very few academic discussions that have made me laugh out loud) a way of reading 'The Tyger' which *does* render it as 'an allegory of the digestive processes' (Fish, 1980: 348–349). I am tempted to go further, using Chomsky's famous example of a sentence which, although grammatically correct, is 'senseless' (Harrison, 1979: 170): 'Colourless green ideas sleep furiously'. Since Chomsky invented the sentence, of course, the concept of 'green ideas' has become widely understood, and 'colourless green ideas' might easily be taken to refer, for example, to environmentalist thinking which lacks radical bite. Moreover, if one can sleep 'soundly' or 'peacefully', then we can't rule out the possibility of sleeping 'furiously'. So it is not at all impossible to image a context in which Chomsky's sentence *does* make sense – for example, as a newspaper headline to an article about a conference of environmentalists.

I don't want to push this too far, but such examples show how interpretations need *not* be constrained or limited by texts. Neither, however, are they random or uncontrolled: the whole point of Fish's discussion is to emphasise the influence of 'interpretive communities' and the 'authority' which they may confer or withhold. Thus

> the literary institution . . . at any one time will authorise only a finite number of interpretive strategies. Thus, while there is no core of agreement *in* the text, there is a core of agreement (though one subject to change) concerning the ways of *producing* the text. Nowhere is this set of acceptable ways written down, but it is a part of everyone's knowledge of what it means to be operating within the literary institution as it is now constituted. (Fish, 1980: 432).

Two points deserve emphasis here. First, as Fish suggests, 'texts' are *consequences* of interpretation, not *vice-versa*. Texts cannot be described neutrally or objectively, but only within the parameters of particular 'interpretive strategies'. And so it is with music, perhaps even more so. An example from Chapter 3 may serve to illustrate the point: while the composer Harrison Birtwistle explained that one of his pieces is built around 'six mechanisms', Robert Adlington observes that 'the three writers who have analysed the piece in detail have arrived at different conclusions as to the identity and location of each mechanism' (Adlington, 2000: 141). Secondly, Fish's discussion of 'interpretive communities' emphasises the fundamentally collective, public, in a word *social*, aspects of processes of interpretation. All too often, in music as in literature, discussions of 'meaning' and 'interpretation' seem to presuppose that those deriving meanings or engaging in interpretation are atomised social isolates, individual 'subjects' somehow removed from their cultural environment. This is not a credible view of the social world inhabited by real people: whereas the terms used by Fish are consistent with a view of social life as constituted in and through processes of collaborative interaction. Thus he speaks of authoritative 'communities', and draws attention to the 'institution' of the literary world and its established procedures, which 'everyone' knows, or must learn about if they wish to operate in it.

So an answer to Cook's question is that 'while there are always mechanisms for ruling out readings, their source is not the text but the presently recognised interpretive strategies for producing the text' (Fish, 1980: 347). In other words, the constraints on the interpretation of cultural objects are to be found neither within the objects nor 'hard-wired' into the individual's psyche. Rather, they are *social* processes in which, as I argue in Chapter 9, individuals come to share definitions of what constitutes the cultural object, to 'take for granted' the conventions and rules of the game, to accept or challenge interpretive strategies, and so on. With this in mind, it is significant that Cook appears to accept the importance of these processes:

> it is central to my argument that music never *is* 'alone', that it is always received in a discursive context, and that it is through the interaction of music and interpreter, text and context, that meaning is constructed, as a result of which the meaning attributed to any given material trace will vary according to the circumstances of its reception. In this way it is wrong to speak of music *having* particular meanings; rather it has the potential for specific meanings to emerge under specific circumstances. (Cook, 2001: 180).

The crucial phrase here, I suggest, is 'discursive context', in other words the cultural environment in which music is heard, not by an isolated 'interpreter', but by real people who have *already* been imbued with what Alfred Schütz called 'a scheme of reference for [the] interpretation of its particularity' (1964: 168). Nevertheless, Cook still wants to find a way to hold on to the idea that there are specifiable limits to the range of meanings or emotions which any given music can 'afford', and even speculates on the possibility of cross-cultural concurrence on these matters (2001: 187). These notions cannot be pursued here, other than to say that sociological interest is in *actual* associations between music and meaning, and the uses of music in real situations, rather than in philosophical speculation about its potential significations for hypothetical 'subjects'. This reorientation of analytic attention – away from both the idea of inherent meanings and a preoccupation with individual subjectivities, and towards the social processes which sustain the intersubjective world of everyday appearances – is consistent with much work in contemporary sociology. In particular, it is a perspective which is developed in Howard Becker's *Art Worlds* (1982), a work which, as will become evident, I believe to be an enormously fruitful source for the sociology of cultural production.

Sociologists who have pursued these matters in recent years have come to converge on an approach that is not primarily concerned with the deciphering of texts, or with the 'style', or indeed with deciding the 'quality', of the music in question. Rather, their main interest is in what people do with it, and what it enables them to do. As Simon Frith has put it: 'The critical issue . . . is not meaning and its interpretation – musical meaning as a kind of decoding – but experience and collusion: the "aesthetic" describes a kind of self-consciousness, a coming-together of the sensual, the emotional and the social *as* performance' (1996b: 272). As I suggested above, we are thus led to consider the fundamental, but normally taken-for-granted, realm of the intersubjective realities which are the source of all human experience, and the part that music can play in constituting and sustaining it.

However, it is clear that the analysis of intersubjectivity and everyday experiences in social situations are well beyond the field of academic musicology, and quite properly so. What should also be apparent, though, is how the disciplinary concerns of sociologists generate a distinctly different perspective on music. Once again, the comments of an earlier (and rather more sympathetic) reviewer may serve to make the point. As suggested above, and as I argued in *Sounds and Society*, it is not the business of the sociologist of music to make value judgements about it. For some, especially those committed to textual interpretation, this is an evasion of responsibilities, a presumption, even, of 'Olympian detachment' (Middleton, 1996: 656). I submit, however, that there is no evasion, but simply a difference between the discourses of musicology and sociology, with their divergent disciplinary commitments, assumptions and procedures. For sociologists, the collaborative practices through which social order is achieved and sustained are of prime concern. These practices include music. As Tia DeNora has put it, in some sociological studies 'we can see music providing a resource in and through which . . . agency and identity are produced' (2000: 5).

In recent years, then, the nature of the differences between musicological and sociological discourses has become clearer. Up to this point, however, I have been speaking as though 'musicology' and 'sociology' were unified, coherent enterprises – which is, of course, completely untrue. Like all academic specialisms, indeed like all organisations, they are in the end constituted by individual people collaborating, competing and colliding, with the appearance of unity sustained mainly by various rhetorical devices and symbolic representations. Yet the latter do make possible the appearance of 'movements' and 'schools of thought' – such as the emergence of the 'new' musicologists in the 1990s, and the disputes and debates which ensued. If anything, sociology is an even more fragmented field, although as I argue in Chapter 2, just as people attach themselves (and others) to 'old' and 'new' musicological work, so there are old and new sociologies, with the latter tending to reject 'structural' explanations in favour of approaches which understand patterns of social organisation – or 'the human world' (Jenkins, 2002) – as the outcome of collaborative interactional practices (Martin, 2004: 34–35; see also Dennis and Martin, 2005).

As I suggest in Chapter 3, it is somewhat ironic that some of the 'new' musicologists (taking their cue from that 'grand theorist' Adorno), have adopted a distinctly 'old' version of sociology, in which musical forms somehow articulate or represent ideological formations. One of the problems inherent in such analyses, as Cook has put it, is that ' . . . it is hard to put your finger on exactly how the linkage between musical and social structure is meant to work' (2001: 172). Moreover, despite their fondness for the 'social' analysis of music, the work of the 'new' musicologists shows little awareness of the contours of the contemporary sociological landscape: their studies show few, if any, signs of an engagement with such basic texts as (among others) those of Mead (1934), Goffman (1959), Cicourel (1964), Schutz (1964 and 1972), Berger and Luckmann (1966), Garfinkel (1967), Blumer (1969), Weber (1978), Becker (1982), or the important collections edited by Rose (1962), Douglas (1971), Sudnow (1972) and Button (1991). There is much of interest in the revived concern with the 'social' analysis of music, but the new musicologists should be aware of the very considerable gap between their work and the discourse of contemporary sociology. This theme is developed in Chapter 3, originally written for the *Journal of the Royal Musical Association*, in which I attempt to consider three recent musicology books from a sociological point of view, and to suggest some of the ways in which the two fields have different analytical concerns. Chief among these, as I suggested above, is the contrast between efforts to specify the meaning of musical 'texts' (whether or not they are held to 'articulate' ideological elements), and the ways in which music is used by real people in actual situations. For example, several sociologists have examined ways in which music (irrespective of its 'style' or 'quality') may be used by people to assert a certain kind of identity; some implications are considered in Chapter 4 on music and the idea of manipulation. My sociological conclusions are that, theoretically, the 'meanings' of music must be understood as embedded in more general configurations of social activity, and methodologically that ethnographic research, rather than the production of decontextualised 'readings', is more likely to elucidate these meanings.

In Part II, attention turns to another way in which music has been used, and one which has attracted a certain amount of attention among sociologists – the supposed relationship between social class position and musical tastes. The topic presents another clear example of the divergence between musicological and sociological concerns. For musicologists, quite understandably, much of the sociological work is deficient since it says little or nothing about the music. Sociologists, on the other hand, are not greatly concerned about the nature or alleged quality of the music in question; their primary interest is in the ways in which, as Richard Peterson puts it, musical taste may serve as a 'status marker'. Indeed, for Bourdieu, there is a close relationship – important to his theory of cultural transmission – between musical taste and a person's position in the socio-economic hierarchy, and it has been argued that this is because styles of music symbolically represent class values. However, it is suggested in Chapter 5 that empirical evidence provides little support for the assumption of a tight class–music nexus. At best, the relationship is much 'looser' than is often supposed, and it is proposed that studies of the ways in which music is used and defined by social groups offer a better way of understanding it that the assumption of a 'homology' between them.

Moreover, rather than examining the conscious activities of real people in different musical worlds, Bourdieu's emphasis on cultural differences in fact presupposes the operation of underlying 'structural', class-based, processes. This topic is pursued in Chapter 6, in relation to the development of musical institutions during the period of European industrialisation, with particular reference to the 'bourgeoisie' in nineteenth-century Manchester. Here, the emergence of

Charles Hallé's orchestra and its symphonic concerts are not seen as the inevitable outcome of class-based ideology, but as a consequence of the successful promotion of a relatively new discourse of aesthetic appreciation by various 'cultural entrepreneurs' (of whom Hallé was one), and the establishment of a 'classical' music art world. Indeed, the evidence provided by the history of the Gentlemen's Concerts suggests strongly that many of the legendary 'Manchester men', the thrusting entrepreneurs who made the city emblematic of capitalist modernity in the nineteenth century, had relatively little interest in the 'serious' music promoted by Hallé.

It might seem that the movement from a concern with processes of social stratification in Part II to the examination of the practice of musical improvisation in Part III represents a shift form a 'macro' to a 'micro' level of analysis. However, I would strongly resist such an interpretation. This opposition raises a wide range of issues, which cannot be pursued here (see Dennis and Martin, 2005); suffice it to say that from a broadly interactionist perspective, the very distinction between 'macro' and 'micro' is itself problematic (Atkinson and Housley, 2003: 174), as is the dualism of 'structure' and 'agency'. So while the topics considered here may differ, the focus of the analysis remains concentrated on the actions and interactions of real people in particular social contexts, each with its taken-for-granted rules, norms, understandings and conventions. Once again, Becker's concept of the art world not only provides a link between this and previous topics, but allows an understanding of the ways in which the constraints, conventions and affordances of the art world enter into the thinking of participants and, indeed, may become 'embodied' in their habitual practices. It is in such ways that the 'individual' and the 'social' are fused in the ongoing flow of activities in everyday life; the focus is not on subjectivity but the achievement of intersubjectivity.

The relevance of the art world perspective to an understanding of jazz improvisation is considered in Chapter 7, which draws on Paul Berliner's (1994) authoritative research, and uses the career of Charlie Parker as an illustration. Chapter 8 develops the idea that musical improvisation within stylistic contexts can be understood as a kind of natural language – but as such must be seen in social, rather than an individual, terms. Thus approaches which decontextualise individuals and concentrate on their assumed innate capacities, or on their cognitive processing abilities, can get at only a part of the story. Performances are instances of collaborative social practices, not the output of isolated brains. It has been pointed out to me that the perspective developed here has something in common with Albert Lord's classic discussion of oral poetry traditions. 'The singer of tales', wrote Lord, 'is at once the tradition and an individual creator. His [sic] manner of composition differs from that used by a writer in that the oral poet makes no conscious effort to break the traditional phrases and incidents; he is forced by the rapidity of composition in performance to use these traditional elements. To him they are not merely necessary, however; they are also right' (Lord, 2000: 4). This sort of perspective, as I have suggested, not only gives a sense of how cultural and stylistic traditions are fused with individual creativity in the process of performance, but allows an insight into *what* gets played or sung – in other words to under-stand the process of constituting cultural objects. Consequently, as is argued in Chapter 9, the familiar distinction between 'text' and 'context' is also rendered problematic, as is the suggestion that a sociological approach to art is unable to say anything about artworks themselves. On the contrary, the suggestion here is that a sociologi-cal approach is essential to an understanding of the activities through which artworks, indeed any cultural objects, are created; such an approach will not be concerned to decontextualise them so as to decipher their essential 'meaning', but to examine how they were created, interpreted and used in real social situations.

Finally, I return to a consideration of the uses of music in every-day situations in Chapter 10. Some recent ethnographic studies have examined the ways in which people use music as part of their every-day lives, and suggested how it is effective for them irrespective of its style or 'quality' as judged by others. It is argued that Alfred Schütz's ideas concerning mutual 'tuning-in' and the synchronisa-tion of individuals' experience offer a strong theoretical foundation for further studies of how music 'works' for people. It is also clear, however, that such sociological investigations take us a long way from the discipline of musicology and its established concerns.

Part I

# Musicology and sociology: the interface

## 2

# Music and the sociological gaze

### Introduction

'The history of musicology and music theory in our generation', write Cook and Everist, 'is one of loss of confidence: we no longer know what we know' (1999: v). The reasons for this widely acknowledged crisis of confidence need not be rehearsed, but clearly arise from a series of challenges to the established discipline – from, for example, the critical and feminist theories of the 'new' musicologists, from various claims about the proper relation of musicology to ethnomusicology, from the emergence of popular music studies, and so on. In this chapter I will be concerned with one aspect of these challenges and the response to them – an aspect which could be succinctly, if rather inadequately, characterised as a 'turn to the social' in the study of music. Some authors have brought new life to a tradition of analysis which has come to be identified with Adorno, arguing that music inevitably bears the imprint of the societal conditions in which it was created. For John Shepherd,

> because people create music, they reproduce in the basic structure of their music the basic structure of their own thought processes. If it is accepted that people's thought processes are socially mediated, then it could be said that the basic structures of different styles of music are likewise socially mediated and socially significant. (1987: 57)

For Shepherd, therefore, it is not accidental that the conventions and procedures of functional tonality have achieved virtually hegemonic status in Western societies, since in them is encoded a representation of the dominant ideology of industrial capitalism (Shepherd, 1991: 122). Similarly, for Susan McClary, specific 'gender/power relationships [are] already inscribed in many of the presumably value-free procedures of Western music' (1991: 19). For these authors, musical analysis must go beyond the notes themselves to elicit the fundamentally social meanings which they convey.

Others have agreed with the proposal that musical works must be understood in terms of the social contexts from which they have emerged, but rather than seeking social meanings within the texts, so to speak, have sought to explore issues concerning the social circumstances of their production, performance and reception. An insistence on the fundamental importance of context, for example, permeates Olle Edström's discussion of the approach developed by the 'Gothenburg School', specifically as a result of its members' reading of Adorno: 'we gradually gained a deeper insight', he writes, 'into the pointlessness of instituting theoretical discourses on music without a solid ethnomusicological knowledge of the everyday usage, function and meaning of music' (1997: 19; see also Tagg, 1998: 228).

For present purposes, my initial concern is simply to suggest that, whether the focus is on music as a 'social text' (Shepherd, 1991), or on the societal contexts of its production and reception, the proposed analytical reorientation necessarily leads musicologists to engage with issues which are also of fundamental concern to sociologists, and have been so for many years. This much I take – perhaps optimistically – to be uncontentious. What I would argue, rather more polemically, is that in general this 'turn to the social' in musicological studies has not led to a sustained engagement with the themes and traditions represented within the established discourse of sociology. In so saying, I do not intend either to reify or to ascribe a spurious unity to sociology – which, like musicology, has its warring factions, its doctrinal disputes, and a constant tendency towards fragmentation. Nevertheless, there are various ways in which sociological insights can illuminate all kinds of musical practices in their various contexts, so sociologists may therefore have a legitimate interest in such practices. Sociological concerns, however, arise from a rather different disciplinary discourse, and may well diverge from those of musicologists, whether old or new.

Put more simply, music, like any other phenomenon, may be approached from various different perspectives, of which the sociological is one. Yet whereas studies of music by historians, philosophers, psychologists and, to a lesser extent, economists, using their distinctive skills and insights, have apparently been quite acceptable to musicologists, the interface with sociology appears problematic, certainly when viewed from the sociological side of the fence. Part of the difficulty may well be that most sociologists lack the technical and theoretical knowledge required to undertake musicological analysis; but the same point could be usually be made about historians, philosophers, and the rest. In fact, it could be argued that a similar lack of awareness – this time of the discourse of sociology – has hindered musicologists in their efforts to make the 'turn to the social'. It seems appropriate, therefore, to suggest some of the ways in which the agenda of the sociology of music may differ from that of musicology, but yet make a distinctive contribution to the understanding of musical practices in their cultural contexts.

## Problems at the interface

That the relations between musicologists and sociologists of music remain problematic is evident in their mutual responses. Indeed, for sociologists such responses usefully demonstrate the extent to which their efforts may be subject to misunderstanding and misapprehension. By way of illustration it may be useful to focus on two related issues here, both of which have been raised by musicologists in relation to my own work, but (I am encouraged to note!) have also been seen as troublesome elements in other sociological studies.

### The myth of value-freedom

This myth arises out of the quite fundamental contention that (despite all Adorno's arguments) it is not the business of the sociologist of music to make aesthetic judgements concerning music or its performers. To many musicologists and others with a background in the humanities, this position has on occasion been interpreted as a quite unworthy abdication of serious responsibilities, as a quite futile effort to achieve 'value freedom', or even (as has been said of some work of mine) a presumption of 'Olympian detachment' (Middleton, 1996: 656). In fact, the position entails none of these criticisms. It is insufficiently appreciated that the approach, far from being value-free, derives from a different, but specific and identifiable, set of assumptions and values. The principle of 'sociological indifference' is itself one of these values. It should also be emphasised that this principle is not a further example of superficial postmodern relativism, since those familiar with the sociological literature recognise it to be a methodological precept elaborated by

Max Weber nearly a century ago. Weber distinguished between sociology as a science concerned with 'the interpretive understanding of
social action', i.e. it formulates explanations of action based on 'subjective meaning', whereas other 'dogmatic disciplines . . . such as
jurisprudence, logic, ethics, and aesthetics . . . seek to ascertain the
"true" and "valid" meanings associated with the objects of their
investigation' (1978: 4). More concretely, the aim of the sociological exercise is not to decide on the justness of a law, or the rightness
of a principle, or indeed the 'real' meaning of a piece of music, but
to understand the beliefs held and meanings taken by real people in
actual situations, in order that their actions may be explained, and
the course of events understood. To this end, it is essential that the
sociologist attempts to remain indifferent to the claims and counter-
claims made by the protagonists who are the subjects of the research:
to take sides or to intervene would be to compromise the investigation itself – we would not, for example, expect a racist bigot to
produce a credible study of inter-ethnic relations.

Sociologists' perspectives on these matters, then, are no more
detached than those of musicological analysts – but the object of
their studies, and their methodology, may be very different. In this
context it is instructive to recall the remarks of Howard Becker on
the relations between ethnomusicology and sociology, in which he
points out that contemporary sociologists of art are no longer
primarily concerned with the (often speculative) grand narratives
relating art and society produced by European theorists of Adorno's
generation, but focus on the collective activity through which things
like music-making get done: 'Sociologists working in this mode',
says Becker, 'aren't much interested in decoding art works, in finding the works' secret meanings as reflections of society. They prefer
to see those works as the result of what a lot of people have done
jointly'. It is worth emphasising this point, for as Becker himself suggests, the notion of investigating 'what a lot of people have done
jointly' is 'deceptively simple' (1989: 281–282). It's too simple in
one sense, because as every sociologist knows, and a moment's
reflection will confirm, the scientific analysis of the collaborative
interactions which are the essence of human social life is an
immensely difficult and complex undertaking. Earlier I referred to
the 'technical and theoretical knowledge' which is rightly regarded
as essential if a person is to operate as a professional musicologist.
At this point, it is worth noting that there is also an extensive domain

of 'technical and theoretical knowledge' which has been developed by sociologists concerned with the analysis, in various ways, of the routine accomplishment of orderly patterns of social organisation. Without some awareness of that domain, it may be hard to grasp what the sociologists' purposes are, and I strongly suspect that this is the source of some of the misapprehension of sociological work by some musicologists. I will consider below a few of the ways in which this sociological concern with the technical (and normally taken-for-granted) aspects of social organisation may illuminate aspects of musical activity.

*Social constructionism*
This second issue concerns the implications of the contention that the meaning of cultural objects is not inherent in the objects themselves. Neither does their meaning somehow exist independently of social life. Rather it is constituted in and through the interactional processes of real people in real situations. What is entailed, of course, and what some authors have considered a radically new idea, is that 'pieces' of music do not have a single or unambiguous meaning which it is the business of the analyst to decipher. Instead, meanings are created, sustained and challenged in processes of collaborative interaction; indeed, from this perspective, cultural objects may be said to be *constituted* through such processes. Far from being a novel suggestion, however, the theme of the 'social construction of reality' has been (or should have been) familiar to every undergraduate student of sociology since Berger and Luckmann's book of that title was published in 1966 (Berger and Luckmann, 1991: 27). Moreover, the book itself draws its main inspiration from the work of Alfred Schütz,whose *Phenomenology of the Social World* (1972) first appeared in Germany in 1932. In the present context, it is worth noting that the German title of the book was *Der sinnhafte Aufbau der sozialen Welt* ('The meaningful construction of the social world'), which in many ways conveys a better sense of its main theme. In it, Schütz drew heavily on Husserl's phenomenology, in particular the notion of the *Lebenswelt* – the 'lifeworld' – which is fundamental to human experience, and in which the unique subjectivities of individuals come together to generate a shared sense of taken-for-granted reality. Another influence on Berger and Luckmann was the work of G. H. Mead and the sociological tradition of symbolic interactionism (Berger and Luckmann, 1991: 29), which

drew on elements of American pragmatism rather than European phenomenology and investigated patterns of social organisation as the dynamic outcome of what has been called 'collective action' (e.g. Becker, 1974). From this perspective too, the aim of analysis is not to establish whether people's assumptions, beliefs and ideas are objectively correct, morally right or aesthetically good, but to determine the ways in which such beliefs – whatever they may be – influence the processes of collaborative interaction which are basic to any human organisation. Indeed, the words of the early Chicago sociologist W. I. Thomas have long been adopted as a slogan for this approach as a whole: 'If men define situations as real', wrote Thomas, 'then they are real in their consequences'. And in another classic statement, Herbert Blumer concisely outlined the implications of Mead's thought for sociologists, emphasising, *inter alia*, not only that meanings do not inhere in objects, but also that *all* objects ' . . . are social products in that they are formed and transformed by the defining process that takes place in social interaction' (1969: 69).

I have dwelt on the idea of the 'social construction of reality' in order to confirm that the idea is far from new to anyone familiar with the sociological literature, but more importantly to suggest, once again, that its utility for the sociologist arises in the context of a specific area of research interest, where we ask how the remarkable phenomenon of normatively organised social order is brought about in an everyday, taken-for-granted manner by those people we are studying. Seen from this perspective, many all-too-familiar criticisms appear to miss the point. Social constructionism does not, for example, give licence to an unbridled relativism, since firstly, as I have said, it is itself rooted in a particular academic discourse, and secondly it is concerned, not to adjudicate between competing claims about facts, values or meanings, but to take the whole process of claims-making – and the ensuing conflicts, debates, negotiations and their outcomes – as its topic. Moreover, as this implies, it is not the case that a constructionist view (or interactionism more generally) neglects phenomena of power and conflict (Dennis and Martin, 2005). On the contrary, attempts to achieve, defend or challenge positions of advantage are precisely what motivate individuals and groups in the social arena: the 'social structure', with its huge inequalities of wealth, power and symbolic resources, is simply the outcome at any moment of this perpetual struggle for advantage. So it is also a great mistake to write of social reality as being 'only' or 'merely' a social construction – anyone who has the least acquaintance with Berger and Luckmann's book will be aware of the attention they pay to the 'objective facticity' of social institutions (1991: 30) and their lengthy consideration of 'society as objective reality' (*ibid.*: 63ff). Moreover, unless we are prepared to accept the claims of such now-discredited approaches as instinct theory, genetic determination, or operant conditioning, there would appear to be no other way in which human social life could be carried on, so it would seem reasonable to view this field as being of some scientific interest.

## Contrasting approaches

Just as, therefore, there are now 'old' and 'new' musicologies, so there have been older and newer sociological approaches. In sociology, the older ones are generally concerned with 'structural' phenomena and 'macro' social processes which, as in the grand schemes of Marx, Durkheim and Parsons, are held to operate independently of real people, the newer ones starting from the fundamental reality of individuals in collaborative interaction, and examining the ways in which the social order is built up from that. And just as in musicology, the old and the new remain in uneasy coexistence. However, I think it is reasonable to detect in recent years a general drift away from 'structural' approaches (on the grounds that they reify collective phenomena, and entail deterministic explanations of human behaviour). Certainly most theoretical sociologists have left behind them the conceptual baggage of structural and post-structural approaches, and seek to develop an understanding of social life in terms of practical action in interactional contexts. In such contexts, as Giddens puts it, 'meaning is produced and sustained through the use of methodological devices' (1987: 214–215). Significantly, too, the work of Bourdieu, who explicitly saw his task as an 'effort to escape from structuralist objectivism without relapsing into subjectivism' (1990: 61) has attracted criticism precisely because he did *not* succeed in detaching his analyses from 'structuralist' presuppositions, thereby failing to capture 'the emergent processes inherent in the production and reproduction of the structure of daily life reasoning, language use, and practical action' (Cicourel, 1993: 112). In general, then, and with varying emphases, much recent sociology has focused on the ways in which the 'objective facticity' of the intersubjective world is produced, reproduced, and changed through organised practices which, however routine and regularly occurring, must nonetheless be enacted by real people in real situations.

What I wish to suggest, therefore, is that the application of this particular sociological 'gaze' to the field of musical practices generates a rather different kind of discourse to that of musicology. As Becker suggested, the sociologist will not be concerned to decode or decipher the meaning of musical 'texts', however defined, either from a syntactic or a semantic point of view. Nor, as argued above, is it any business of the sociologist to take sides in the inevitable and perpetual debates about their meaning or value. What will be of interest, however, are the many and varied ways in which such cultural objects are constituted and defined, the uses that are made of them, and the consequences of these activities, for it is through this sort of investigation that we may arrive at an understanding of the social organisation of the musical 'worlds' (Becker, 1982) in which all production, performance and reception take place.

One of the important contributions of Leonard B. Meyer was the recognition that aesthetic experience not only depends fundamentally on the kind of expectations the listener brings to the music, but that such expectations themselves are derived from particular kinds of cultural learning and experience. Individuals' responses and reactions, which are experienced as right and 'natural', are nonetheless shaped by prior processes of social learning (Meyer, 1970: 43). This is not quite as 'paradoxical' as Meyer suggests, if we accept the point above that inculcation into the everyday intersubjective world *is* in fact the 'natural' way in which human beings acquire the capacity to have any kind of experience, and so to engage in organised social life. But for present purposes the essential point is simply to emphasise the implications of the idea that the ways in which we hear music are profoundly influenced by our cultural experience, which varies both between and within societies: as Edström has put it 'the significance and meaning of music is created, like everything else, in its social environment' (1997: 16). What this has been taken to mean, quite properly, is that the production, performance, and reception of music are 'socially mediated', to use Shepherd's term, and in specific ways, so that – for example – styles of music are held to be capable of 'implicitly coding an explicit world-sense'

(Shepherd, 1991: 85), which is then assumed to be characteristic of specific social groups. Now there are some general theoretical problems with this sort of analysis, and I have discussed these elsewhere (Martin, 1995: 160ff). At present what I wish to suggest as an extension of the points made above, and Becker's (1989) distinction between the old and the new sociologies of art, is that the things which are taken to constitute the 'social environment' – such things as 'societies', 'social classes', musical 'styles' and so on – are not entities 'out there', so to speak, whose relationships can be unambiguously defined by the analyst. Rather, they are to be conceived as entities whose reality is constituted – and whose existence is normally taken for granted – through collaborative social interaction in specific situations. We need only reflect on the enormous range of actual sounds and musical styles which have been referred to as 'jazz', for example, to realise the extent to which the meaning of the term – that is, what it signifies at any particular moment – is context-dependent.

It should be said straight away, in order to anticipate a frequent set of misunderstandings, that this sort of perspective does not commit us to philosophical idealism, to subjectivism or solipsism, or to a denial of the massive inequalities of wealth and power in societies. This theme cannot be pursued here, but is developed by Berger and Luckmann in their discussion of objectification and the consequent 'coercive power' of institutions (1991: 78); Blumer, too, asserts that any denial 'of the existence of structure in human society . . . would be ridiculous' (1969: 75). What I do wish to consider briefly, though, is the emerging importance of the social situation for the study of music as social practice. Again, Edström rightly includes the 'situation' in considering the mutual interrelations of the factors involved in reception (the others being the 'individual', the 'music', and the 'performance'). But the implication of the present argument is that we must go beyond a conception of the 'situation' as, for example, 'when and where music is performed' (Edström, 1997: 64). Rather we must consider the social situation much more fundamentally as the focal point where all other factors – not least, the unique subjectivity of each individual – are brought together to constitute what Schütz called a 'vivid present' through the interactional 'work' (DeNora, 1986) of participants. As Goffman pointed out, perhaps because of its very ordinariness, the importance of the social situation is often neglected. All of us, as human beings operating in specific cultural contexts, constantly experience the world not as 'social structures' or 'institutions' but in terms of the exigencies and constraints of a succession of social situations. All of what we call 'experience' is mediated in some way or other by social situations, from earliest infancy right through life; they, not 'social facts', are ' . . . a reality *sui generis*, as He used to say' (Goffman, 1964: 136; the He in question is, presumably, Durkheim). Moreover, the dynamics of social life – from momentous political projects to tiny conversational details – do not consist in the operation of disembodied social processes: they must be *enacted* by culturally competent individuals. Again, Goffman made the point succinctly, by contrasting the vast amount of attention given to the study of 'language' with the infinitely smaller number of studies of its actual use by speakers. However, asks Goffman, 'where but in social situations does speaking go on?' (*ibid.*). In short, *from a sociological perspective* it is through the analysis of actual situations (rather than musical 'works') that we will come to understand something of what Edström terms 'the everyday usage, function, and meaning of music' (1997: 19).

Consequently, studies of the reception, as opposed to the production or performance, of music assume a much greater significance, as Edström has also argued, in relation to Cook's distinction between the 'ways of hearing' characteristic of musicologists and non-specialists (Edström, 1997: 58; Cook, 1990). Once it is accepted that the meaning of music is not to be found 'within the text', so to speak, the analytical focus moves to concentrate on the meanings generated in the context of particular encounters, for they – and not the stipulations of some theoretician – will inform the subsequent conduct of the individuals concerned. (As Wittgenstein put it: 'You cannot prescribe to a symbol what it *may* be used to express. All that it CAN express, it MAY express' [quoted in Monk, 1991: 165].) Furthermore, I suggest that the term 'reception' is inadequate to convey what is involved here. The notion of reception is too passive, having the connotation of receiving a message which has been transmitted, as with radio and TV signals. What must be emphasised is the active and engaged process through which people 'make sense' of their cultural environment. Something of this process may be found in the discussions of popular music which criticise mass-society theorists for their assumption of a homogeneous aggregate of docile consumers, and examine instead the active 'appropriation' of music, and the ways in which consumer goods may be ' . . . taken over, transformed, reinterpreted, inserted into new contexts [and] combined to form a new style' (Middleton, 1990: 157). But the implications of the view I am exploring go even further, in the sense that, as Blumer suggested, all cultural objects are themselves constituted in the constant process of collaborative interaction. Mundane as it may seem, it is through talk that we create, sustain – and change – the taken-for-granted world of commonsense reality, learning, using and arguing about concepts such as 'the symphony', 'bebop', 'the orchestra', 'delta blues', and so on. Of course, we do not have the freedom to define situations however we wish, precisely because of the 'facticity' of institutions and cultural constraints. To paraphrase Marx, people make sense, but they do not make it as they please. Indeed, and I will return to this point, there is a 'political' dimension to all this: such concepts and the meanings associated with them are constantly open to renegotiation, as when we argue against others' interpretations and advocate our own, or – often more significantly – as when organised interest groups attempt to impose authoritative 'ways of hearing'.

These and other considerations arise from the apparently straightforward, but still problematic, suggestion that the sociologist of music may be primarily concerned with the uses to which music is put, as much as the qualities or characteristics of music itself. Even phrasing the matter in this way can cause difficulties: many listeners, most musicologists, and – almost by definition – all 'music-lovers' find it difficult or inappropriate to consider music in such prosaic, utilitarian, terms. Yet, quite apart from the process of demystification which is likely to result from any properly conducted sociological analysis, it is surely incontestable that music is 'used' for various purposes in a whole range of social settings and occasions: to yield a profit or earn a wage, to sell commodities, to create a desired atmosphere, to project an image of one's self, to work, exercise, or make love to, to form part of a ritual, and so on. The list could be extended, but already what is evident is that, particularly in the electronic age, music's effectiveness in these sorts of circumstances does not necessarily depend on the 'performance' of a 'work', a dedicated setting, an 'audience', or indeed attentive 'listening'. And while all such events can be of interest to the sociologist, the musicologist may, or may not, share this concern. That is to say, in each of these settings music plays a part, perhaps an important part, in the constitution of normatively organised social situations. Yet precisely because they *are* normatively organised and normally experienced as unproblematic, the organisational features through which this sense of order is created are simply taken for granted. As I have suggested, however, orderly collaborative interaction does not just happen; it involves, in Schütz's terms, the mutual orientation of the participants so as to secure a sense of intersubjective correspondence within an unproblematic 'world' (Schütz, 1972) and, further, the enactment of appropriate talk, gestures, actions, and so on in order to accomplish the event. These, I have argued, are matters of great technical interest to the sociologist who is concerned to understand the achievement of social order. But they may not be matters of much technical interest to the musicologist.

## Sociological studies of music

I have suggested that it is not part of the sociologist's task to make normative judgements about the aesthetic value of music, in large part because it is the normative organisation of social life that should be the central topic for sociological investigation. We study a war, and its contending armies, their resources, their generals and their tactics, their feuding factions and so on, in order to understand its outcome, rather than join the partisans on one side or another. This position is not therefore 'value-free' but derives from the discourse of scientific sociology, which from the outset has been influenced by a concern with the problem of 'social order' (Hughes, Sharrock and Martin, 2003: 10). It remains to suggest, albeit briefly, some of the ways in which sociological studies can contribute to our understanding of music 'in its socioeconomic context' (Edström, 1997: 62).

### Musical styles

It follows from what has been said above that the sociology of music is in principle concerned with all 'kinds' of music, which means in practice that popular music will be a topic of particular interest, since it is the music of most people, who both use it in a wide range of social settings (in the utilitarian sense mentioned above), and 'listen' to it in the more musicological sense of knowledgeable and active engagement. It goes without saying that this is another source of divergence between sociological and musicological concerns, with the latter until recently concerned primarily with Western 'art music'. Of course, there is no such entity as 'popular music', but the enduring use of the concept is suggestive of the power relations that obtain in this particular discourse – it is a 'catch-all' term for a vast array of heterogeneous styles and traditions which have not been classified authoritatively as 'serious' or 'art' music, and provides a means of demarcating an important symbolic boundary. Indeed, the concept itself may serve as an example of the way a taken-for-granted cultural object ('popular music') may be *constituted* in the context of a struggle to assert and defend cultural legitimacy.

Consequently, both the distinction between 'serious' and 'popular' music, and prevailing definitions of particular types or styles, are themselves to be seen as 'socially constructed'. They are, that is, not simply ways of registering evident differences (though they may do so) but are ways in which a 'conceptual map' of the cultural environment has evolved out of the claims and counter-claims of interested parties. Of particular interest in this context are studies which have examined the processes through which the notion of music as 'high culture' was institutionalised in the nineteenth century, and the cultural consequences of the resulting opposition between 'serious' and 'popular' music in the twentieth (e.g. DiMaggio, 1982; Bourdieu, 1984; Levine, 1988). Similarly, efforts to identify the essential qualities of a style often revolve around debates concerning 'authenticity' – as in the cases of, for example, 1950s rock 'n' roll, traditional jazz, or 'early music' – and lead to the definition of 'ideal-typical' stylistic paradigms which are then available to be used as criteria for the evaluation of particular performances. Simon Frith has discussed the ways in which musical, marketing, ideological and performance criteria, rather than simply 'the text itself' are all involved in the designation of popular music genres, noting that these criteria are constantly dynamic (Frith, 1996b: 93–4). More recently, Negus has examined the ways in which record company staff seek to impose stylistic definitions and create genre distinctions within the volatile field of music production on the basis of cultural preconceptions and the selective gathering of information about the presumed market for their products. He concludes that ' . . . while market research gives people within the corporation a sense of certainty and security, in the process it does not so much understand the world of musical culture and consumption but invents one' (Negus, 1999: 60).

*The 'politics of meaning'*

Just as 'types' of music as cultural objects may be socially constructed, so their meaning and value are the subject of perpetual
debate, negotiation and conflict. It is in this context that it is useful
to speak of the politics of meaning, as an (admittedly inadequate)
way of referring to the perpetual barrage of claims and counter-
claims that constitutes a discourse at any given moment. Once more,
Edström provides a good example when he speaks of the way in
which Kramer's analyses are based on specific '*claims* about the way
the inner meaning of music is constructed' (1997: 57, emphasis
added). There is thus not simply a technical, but a rhetorical aspect
to Kramer's discussion – he is saying 'Hear it this way', and by implication not another way, and trying to persuade us of the rightness of
his version of things. A great deal of talk and writing about music
operates in this way, providing us with possible ways of hearing the
sounds, suggesting what it is about, and arguing for (or against) its
aesthetic value.

Moreover, in the sociological gaze the making of such claims, and
the variety of perspectives revealed by, for example, composers,
members of audiences, critics of various persuasions, musicians, promoters, sponsors, and so on, appear not as positions to be argued
with, but as data which, in the aggregate, can display the *realpolitik*
of a particular art world. Whose claims will be accepted, and why?
Who has the most effective symbolic resources, or the greatest material ones? What sort of contingencies will affect the outcome? And
so on. From the point of view of social organisation, these matters
are important, since they determine the pattern of 'facticities' and
consequent constraints which real individuals have to confront.
Whose music is performed, and whose excluded? How are broad-
casting schedules and playlists determined? Which band gets the
recording contract? What sort of music is taught in schools? Sometimes these things 'just happen', but it would be naive (and sociologically incompetent) to ignore the activities of such big players as
major record companies and their marketing departments, or the
hidden (and not so hidden) agenda of arts funding bodies. Sometimes there is an identifiable cultural movement: Hughes and
Stradling's (2001) study of *The English Musical Renaissance*, for
example, is a fascinating account of the formation, and relative
success, of a powerful coalition of interests which in the 1890s and
subsequent decades aimed to replace German with English music in

British conservatoires, concert halls and radio schedules. Composers who were deemed to conform to the movement's programme were favoured; those who did not were marginalised. Little of this has to do with technical or artistic merit.

Other studies have examined socio-cultural factors influencing the development of particular ways of hearing, and their consequences for the reception of particular styles. For example DeNora has pointed to ways in which, in their efforts to maintain cultural distinction, Viennese aristocrats in the 1790s turned from a financial to an aesthetic strategy of social exclusion, in which Beethoven's new and unconventional music (and by extension his patrons) was associated with good taste, and in which there was 'a heightened emphasis on the appreciation of "greatness", from which derived the notion of master composers' (1995: 48). Ultimately, the process contributed not only to Beethoven's recognition as a 'master', but to the institutionalisation of a new discourse – involving an ideology of serious music and a reformulation of the concept of genius in which both his and others' works could be placed and evaluated (*ibid.*: 190). Before long, as Johnson shows in *Listening in Paris*, the elements of this discourse provided a context in which 'absolute' music could not only be rendered comprehensible but also heard as 'the divine language of sentiment and imagination' (1995: 272). Whereas Beethoven's First Symphony was 'rejected virtually universally' after its Paris premiere in 1807 (*ibid.*: 258), in 1828 his music achieved 'instant and sustained success (*ibid.*: 259), and in the 1830s and 1840s Haydn's work was 're-evaluated' in terms of its 'abstract meaning' rather than judged, as in his lifetime, by its programmatic elements (*ibid.*: 271).

Another example of a recent study which examines the effect of socio-cultural factors on the ways in which music is heard is provided by Scott DeVeaux's *The Birth of Bebop* (1997). DeVeaux rejects the two prevalent narratives of the development of modern jazz – one (particularly attractive to white critics) describing the more-or-less spontaneous evolution of the 'art', the other seeing the movement as black musicians' rejection of white society – on the grounds that *both* are retrospective constructions which decontextualise the music and its players. Instead, DeVeaux develops a nuanced interpretation of the evidence, emphasising the institutional and ideological constraints facing contemporary players. Thus the pioneering efforts of saxophonist Coleman Hawkins during the early 1930s led him into an institutionally anomalous situation, where his 'rhapsodic' solo style fitted in with neither the dance bands nor the pop songs of the day (DeVeaux, 1997: 85). At the time, there were virtually no locations in which Hawkins could be heard as a 'concert' performer, nor any institutional framework to support a black freelance virtuoso soloist, and indeed only a very limited acceptance of the idea that jazz could be a 'serious' music for listening to. As DeVeaux shows in detail, it was only as these and other conditions – such as the acceptance of small-group jazz – which we now take for granted, were realised over the next decade that Hawkins, but more particularly the emerging younger generation of 'bebop' players, could find acceptance as independent soloists. Drawing on Becker's analysis of 'art worlds' (*ibid.*: 45), DeVeaux thus shows how the conventions and constraints – notably economic and racial – confronting black musicians exerted a powerful influence both on the way in which the music developed and on the kind of music which could be publicly performed. This analytic perspective, emphasising the constraints and contingencies which affected real players as they tried to deal with the social and economic 'facticities' which confronted them, is also consistent with Peterson's view of the 'production of culture' as a process in which institutional factors constantly shape and constrain human activities, encouraging some things and inhibiting others (e.g. Peterson, 1990).

*Identities*
A further set of issues which may lead to a specifically sociological interest in music concerns the ways in which it is often an important factor in the assertion or imputation of identity, both for individuals and social groups. For Bourdieu, '. . . nothing more clearly affirms one's "class", nothing more infallibly classifies, than tastes in music' (1984: 18), and in Thornton's words: 'Tastes are fought over precisely because people define themselves and others through what they like and dislike. Taste in music, for youth in particular, is often seen as the key to one's distinct sense of self' (1995: 164). Thornton's study showed how recordings which were symbolic of 'underground' or oppositional values and identities were likely to lose their subcultural legitimacy as soon as they crossed over into the mass market. Conversely, being banned from airplay on the BBC's Radio One was celebrated as '. . . expert testimony to the music's violation of national sensibilities and as circumstantial evidence of

its transgression' (*ibid.*: 129). Many of the studies in which this theme was developed, such as those concerned with the idea of 'resistance through rituals' or the display of disaffection from the dominant culture, have been widely influential, though Middleton (1990: 147ff) has considered some of the problems raised by their assumption that there is a 'homology' between a group's fundamental values and the pattern of cultural symbols it adopts. So in the present context it may be useful simply to note a tendency to move away from the idea that music *expresses* the values of social groups, towards the view that in significant respects it should be seen as *producing* them (Frith, 1996b: 270). Frith's argument is that in this respect there is no difference between 'popular' and 'art' music, that what we term aesthetic appreciation is in the end not a matter of decoding meanings but of 'ethical agreement' on 'a way of being in the world, a way of making sense of it' (*ibid.*: 272) which inevitably involves being (or trying to be) a certain kind of person who belongs to certain sort of group. 'Music', writes Frith, 'constructs our sense of identity through the experiences it offers of the body, time, and sociability, experiences which enable us to place ourselves in imaginative cultural narratives' (*ibid.*: 275).

## Conclusion

In considering these concerns of the sociologist, the musicologist may object that little or nothing has been said about the music, and that sociological interest appears to focus on contextual and circumstantial factors which, in principle, are distinct from the music itself. The objection is understandable, yet not sustainable, I submit, as a criticism of the sociology of music. What I have suggested is that there are various ways in which sociologists may wish to approach music as an organised social practice, but which do not necessarily depend on an analysis of the music itself. Indeed, the aim may well be to examine the process by which the 'same' music is invested with quite different meaning and significance in different social contexts, in which case technical analysis, or decontextualised claims about how 'it' has its 'effects', will have little to contribute. If, as Edström remarks, it is an 'illusion' to imagine that there can be text without context (1997: 27): then it is important to recognise the ways in which social factors may be decisive in influencing the production of the 'texts' themselves. It is easy for anyone with a background in the

European tradition of 'serious' music to overlook this important point, since in it the role of the 'audience' at a performance is essentially passive. In other traditions, of course, interaction between performers and listeners is normal, as in the oral–aural traditions of African-American music (Jackson, 2003: 67); in the informal settings in which these styles developed, 'the audience . . . inevitably influences the performer's material' (Brown, 2003: 121). Moreover, it is also important to recognise the extent to which those who create music in *any* style, take cognizance of the conventions of the 'art world' (Becker, 1982) in which they are operating (Martin, 1995: 166).

So, as a final example, I will quote from Paul Berliner's *Thinking in Jazz* (1994), a magnificent ethnography of the process through which aspiring players learn to become recognisably capable jazz performers. Berliner is here describing an incident which occurred while the pianist Barry Harris was conducting one of his renowned workshops for young players:

> At a fifth student's performance . . . he shook his head and remarked 'No, you wouldn't do that in this music'. Stung by the rebuke, the student defended himself. 'But you said to follow the rule you gave us, and this phrase follows the rule'. 'Yes', Harris admitted, 'but you still wouldn't play a phrase like that'. 'But give me one good reason why you wouldn't', the student protested. 'The only reason I can give you', Harris replied, 'is that I have been listening to this music for over forty years now, and my ears tell me that the phrase would be wrong to play. You just wouldn't do it in this tradition. Art is not science, my son'. The student left the workshop early that evening, not to return for months. (*ibid.*: 249)

The episode nicely captures some points which are relevant here. Firstly, there is the evident authority of Harris, the acknowledged master performer and the students' mentor. Secondly, the fact that his authority is brought to bear on the fine details of the students' playing, and thirdly that it is not concerned simply with technical correctness but with matters of stylistic appropriateness which can only be decided on the basis of prolonged experience of the musical community and its expectations. It is clear that what is being communicated to these neophyte improvisers are detailed ways of shaping performance practices which are dictated not only by formal musical requirements, or the creative energies of individuals, but by the norms and values of an established 'interpretive community'

(Fish, 1980: 171). As in all interactions, the idiosyncracies and interests of individuals must somehow be reconciled with what Wittgenstein called a 'form of life'; this theme will be pursued, specifically in relation to jazz improvisation, in Part III below.

I have suggested that the perceived need to incorporate a 'social' dimension into musicological studies may not be met successfully by developing the idea that music somehow expresses or conveys 'social' messages of some kind, and that the sociological literature offers various alternative approaches, though these may not resonate particularly strongly with established musicological concerns. Musicological and sociological perspectives, then, are to be considered as emerging from, and grounded in, distinctly different academic discourses; as a consequence the way in which 'music' is constituted in each will be different. With a recognition of these differences, though, may come an awareness of, and a mutual respect for the complementary strengths of the different disciplinary perspectives.

# 3

# Over the rainbow? On the quest for 'the social' in musical analysis

## Introduction

In the previous chapter it was suggested that many of the challenges to the 'old' ways of musicology derive from the assertion that the study of music must recognise the inescapably social nature of the creation, performance and reception of music. While there may indeed be much to be gained in a technical sense by removing the creature – in this case the musical work – from its natural habitat and dissecting it in the laboratory, the essence of the critics' case is that this process inevitably obscures and ignores more than it reveals. Not only must the musical text be reconnected with its social context, they argue, but the 'text' itself has to be understood as constituted in and through social practices which have too often remained unexamined.

One of the responses of musicologists to these sorts of ideas has been a notable 'turn to the social' as far as the research agenda and its analytical purview are concerned, with the 'new' musicologists leading the charge. It goes without saying that this increasing engagement with the 'social' analysis of music is of considerable interest from a sociological point of view, and indeed has led to the welcome development of vigorous debates about themes which are quite congenial to the sociologist's mindset: for example, the idea that no music is independent of its time and place, the contention that all 'types' of music must be considered as part of the cultural matrix of a society, and the consequent refusal to presuppose the validity of the distinction between 'serious' and 'popular' forms. To sociologists, it should be added, such notions are not recent flashes of radical inspiration emerging from postmodern or deconstructive thought, but long-established premises that are entailed by sociology's concern with social practices and patterns of social organisa-

tion, which could in principle serve to guide the empirical investigation of all sorts of musical activities.

I say 'in principle' because, with a few outstanding exceptions, the
empirical sociology of music remains a relatively undeveloped field.
Despite the remarkable growth since the 1980s in both 'cultural
studies' generally and, more specifically, in the topic of culture
within academic sociology, the number of sociologists who have
produced substantial work on music remains quite small, in contrast
to the attention which has been paid to other areas of cultural production. I assume that this neglect does not stem from any lack of
interest in, or dislike of, music among sociologists; on the contrary,
experience of the professional community (and its students) suggests
quite high levels of involvement, certainly as far as the purchase of
recordings and attendance at musical events are concerned. The
sociologists' professional avoidance of the topic is more likely to be
a consequence, first, of the elusive and ephemeral nature of the
subject matter, making it difficult to define the musical 'text' for the
purposes of analysis, and, secondly, of the sociologists' own self-per-
ceptions of their technical inadequacies; most seem to have taken
the view that the study of musical activities is best left to those
specialists who can read scores, play instruments, take part in performances and so on. As a result, the 'social turn' in musical research
has been taken largely by musicologists (and others) venturing into
territories long ago staked out by sociologists. And while, in principle, interchange across disciplinary boundaries is to be welcomed, it
has to be said that the sociologists' respect for the professional competencies and concerns of musicians and musicologists has not
always been reciprocated. Indeed, as seen from the sociological side
of the fence, a good deal of recent work on the social analysis of
music, while usually interesting and often stimulating, is ultimately
disappointing owing to the authors' evident lack of familiarity with
the contours of contemporary sociological discourse and a consequent inability to engage with it.

In this respect, as in many others, a notable precedent was
established by Adorno, whose work still casts a long and dark
shadow. Like many of the social analysts of music who followed
him, Adorno's original and abiding commitments were to music
and to philosophy, and his main concern with the academic discourse of sociology was to dismiss it. The empiricist research agenda
he encountered in the USA was, to Adorno, simply one further

example of the cancerous positivism which was inexorably turning rational thought into ideology (Jay, 1973: 222; Wiggershaus, 1994: 236ff). To be fair, few sociologists would now defend the procedures that C. Wright Mills described as 'abstracted empiricism' (1959: 50ff), but that is precisely the point: there is a great deal more to sociology than the methodology of the mass communications research which Adorno found in the USA. What's more, another of Mills's targets was just the sort of 'grand theorizing' which Adorno seemed to assume was central to sociological analysis. For all his immense erudition and the sophistication of his theorising, Adorno's view of music in the modern West ultimately comes down to a fairly straightforward 'grand narrative' in which the emergence and decay of tonality is taken as a symbolic representation of the rise and fall of the ideology of bourgeois individualism. 'Because musical life registers inner-bourgeois structural changes so directly', wrote Adorno in 1932, 'analysis must necessarily consider the immanent differences and contradictions of the bourgeoisie' (Adorno, 1978: 151). So it is not surprising that despite Adorno's insistence on the centrality of his dialectical method, his perspective has been taken as little more than 'a sometimes crude sociological account of the reflection between music and social structure' (Berman and D'Amico, 1991: 71); in other words, just the sort of reductionist account to which many musicologists – with some justification – have objected.

Moreover, at the heart of Adorno's analyses is the procedure through which he seeks to decode or decipher the 'sedimented Geist' (1949: 38) which he takes to be immanent in musical works, for, as Paddison puts it, Adorno 'insists that society is . . . "inscribed" within art works' (Paddison, 1993: 262). This is because 'artistic objectification enables art to express a latent social content and thereby to supersede merely individual subjects' (Zuidervaart, 1991: 119). For Adorno, then, and those who have taken up his approach, the sociology of music was conceived as primarily concerned with demonstrating ways in which apparently autonomous works, produced by free individuals, none the less contained 'social' messages or meanings; in elucidating these through analysis, the hidden links between 'music' and 'society' could be exposed. It is, moreover, a conception of sociology which in one form or another has been influential in the humanities; for some, as we shall see, a beacon lighting the analytical way forward, for others (quite understand-

ably) a dismal effacing of artistic creativity which reduces the composer to a puppet manipulated by social forces.

In the present context, the point to be emphasised is that, as Mills
also pointed out, this tradition of 'grand theorizing' in which 'music'
and 'society', conceived as entities, are related to each other, does
not exhaust the possibilities of sociological analysis. In fact such a
conception not only misrepresents sociology, but is firmly rejected
by many practitioners. As I suggested in the previous chapter, just as
there are now said to be 'old' and 'new' musicological perspectives,
so there is something akin to the distinction between 'old' and 'new'
approaches in sociology, with the latter in the ascendant since at
least the 1960s. As Becker has put it, the 'old' version of sociology,
'has much in common with aesthetics' and is concerned with
'"decoding" art works, in finding the works' secret meanings as
reflections of society'. In contrast, an empirically orientated (as
opposed to an empiricist) sociology will have little interest in the
deciphering of texts, but a primary concern with, for example,
'occupational organisation, the development and maintenance of
traditions, the training of practitioners, mechanisms of distribution,
and audiences and their tastes' (Becker, 1989: 281–282). From this
perspective, all forms of cultural production are viewed as instances
of collaborative social organisation, so the focus of the 'new' sociology of music will be on various kinds of mediation: the social
processes which may be said not only to intervene between ideas and
motivations on the one hand, and texts or art objects on the other,
but – crucially in the present context – also to determine the forms
of the latter (e.g. Hennion, 1990, 1989).

The idea of the 'social' analysis of music, then, may generate a
quite different research agenda for the contemporary sociologist of
music from that which is derived from Adorno's aesthetic preoccupations, which have been characterised as 'speculative rather than
empirical' and philosophical rather than sociological in orientation
(Paddison, 1993: 184). The focus moves away from a concern with
establishing the 'meaning' of music and settles on its production and
use in social contexts; the discourse of 'art' is replaced by that of
'work', both in Becker's sense of people acting together to produce
'works', and in the sense of meanings as created in and through the
interpretive 'work' of individuals in interaction with each other
(DeNora, 1986). Such a perspective, it should be emphasised, does
not deny or avoid the idea that music can have powerful meanings

and effects. On the contrary, what is explicitly denied is that such meanings are 'inscribed' in texts, or that their effects are given off automatically. What is asserted by the sociologist is that both the achievement of intersubjective meanings and the generation and experience of effects are complex processes which (although normally taken for granted in everyday life) must be topics for analysis in their own right. The example of Adorno's own writings may serve to make the point in a less abstract way, simply by pointing out how contentious his arguments are. The way he interprets Bach, his hearing of Beethoven's late works, his championing of Schoenberg, his (qualified) dismissal of Wagner and denigration of Stravinsky, and so on, all proceed from an aesthetic position which was derived from philosophical speculation rather than scientific enquiry (Martin, 1995: 118–119). Adorno may claim authority for his conclusions, but then so do those who espouse contrary views. In short, the effect of his work is rhetorical: he provides a 'way of hearing', just as a good critic or lawyer would make a case in the context of a discourse in which many other persuasive voices are to be heard. The image which suggests itself is one of an arena in which there are many claims and counter-claims about the 'meaning' or value of a work. For the sociologist, 'meanings' cannot be disclosed through the dissection of (decontextualised) works, since they are in a perpetual state of assertion, negotiation, and challenge and contestation. The sociological analyst does not seek to take sides or adjudicate, but is concerned to examine the process and its outcomes, however fleeting these may be, and to investigate – for want of a better phrase – the 'politics of meaning' (see above, pp. 26–28).

I develop these arguments by discussing three books with widely divergent topics, and which resist assimilation to a single theme: Adlington (2000) is concerned with Birtwistle's compositions, Neal (1999) with popular music and black communities in the USA, largely from the 1940s to the 1990s, and McClary (2000) with the ideological foundations of musical styles. All, however, are concerned with matters to do with how we can and should hear the music, and may be approached – by a sociologist, I should emphasise – with the above considerations in mind.

## Birtwistle's provocations

Robert Adlington's discussion of Harrison Birtwistle's music has two purposes: to provide a comprehensive account of the works themselves – more than 90 pieces – and to consider them in relation to certain general issues 'of significance to Birtwistle's music, and to contemporary classical music in general' (Adlington, 2000: 1). It is therefore no surprise that questions of meaning and interpretation are confronted immediately; the strategy of Adlington's exposition is also intended, he tells us, 'to emphasise the music's multifarious ways of meaning – the ways in which it establishes a handle on things outside itself, negotiating a position for itself in a wider culture' (*ibid.*). Thus each chapter should be read as an essay in what Cook has called 'hermeneutic criticism', developing 'illuminating metaphors . . . that lead you to experience the music differently' (Cook, 1998: 78). Indeed, on this basis Adlington's study of Birtwistle not only has the merit of cataloguing each of the pieces, but of providing various 'ways of hearing' them (should you wish to – I will return to this point).

That this approach is particularly appropriate to a consideration of Birtwistle becomes clear early on, as Adlington demonstrates that making sense of this music is not a matter of breaking its code or uncovering its underlying representational scheme. Given the extent of Birtwistle's involvement in the theatre, he has faced in an acute form a dilemma of the self-conscious modernist; while the drama requires an established representational code, the abstraction of the music resists it (Adlington, 2000: 6–7). Birtwistle's response, however, has been an enduring preoccupation with processes of representation in themselves. In various ways, and in different contexts, these have been made explicit, challenged and subverted, to the point where, on occasion, any possibility of comprehensibility has been foreclosed. For example an early concern was with exposing the artificiality of theatrical representation by destroying any illusion of reality; other notions that have animated his work are the inseparability of the story from the way it is told, and the impossibility of grasping any entity in its totality.

Moreover, just as Birtwistle has problematised the role of music in drama, so he has exposed and explored the drama inherent in musical performance, examining from various angles the relationships between instruments (or particular players), refusing to grant secure

identities to individuals, enacting inclusion and exclusion, and giving musicians stage directions to provide a visual representation of
their musical relationships. Overall, again, the abiding concern is not
so much with the roles played by instruments or musicians but with
what is involved in taking and enacting a role in itself, and with challenging established conventions. For example, Birtwistle seeks to
resist the subordination of music to the text in songs (*ibid.*: 73–74),
or alternatively through repetition to privilege aspects of songs (the
words, the act of singing) which are central in pop music but marginalised in 'strophic classical song' (*ibid.*: 128). Birtwistle's investigation of established conventions has extended from the stage to
performance practices more generally, as when he sought to explicate the ritual of the concert itself, drawing attention to aspects such
as the performance space, the initiation of the event, its separation
of performance and intervals, the applause, and so on. 'This', says
Adlington, 'represented a move away from the assumption that the
classical concert format constitutes a "neutral" space for the presentation of music' (*ibid.*: 34). In general, as is well known, the outcome
of all this experimentation can be music of forbidding complexity,
which is so information-rich that it defies assimilation in real time,
and is suffused with deliberate ambiguity and contradiction.

So how are we to make sense of it? As I have already suggested,
Adlington's account indicates that this matter is not likely to be
resolved through detailed analysis of the 'texts' themselves. Take the
case of *Carmen Arcadiae Mechanicae Perpetuum* (1977), the 'inter-
leaved structure' of which 'is likely to remain obscure for most listeners' (Adlington, 2000: 141). Birtwistle's explanation is that the
work is built around 'six mechanisms which are juxtaposed many
times' (*ibid.*: 140); yet Adlington has to report that 'the three writers who have analysed the piece in detail have arrived at different
conclusions as to the identity and location of each mechanism'
(*ibid.*: 141), and his own view is that this piece 'does appear to flirt
with the idea of moment form' (*ibid.*: 142). Whether or not such
passages tell us much about the music, they do bring into clear focus
the sorts of sociological issues raised earlier. First of all, it is evident
that to reach an 'understanding' of this piece, or to attach a 'meaning' to it, requires interpretive 'work' of some kind or another.
Secondly, such meanings are provisional and contestable, and
involve individuals or groups making claims about the qualities or
characteristics of the art-work itself. Such claims, thirdly, have to be

made in the context of an established discourse or 'art world' which is organised on the basis of certain fundamental values or aesthetic commitments (Becker, 1982). In the present case, for example, while participants in the struggle over how the music is to be heard may differ in their views, they are none the less united in the belief that Birwistle's music is important, and that making sense of it is a serious matter. (Why else would academic analysts dissect it, or Cambridge University Press publish Adlington's book?) These beliefs, in turn, may be seen to be derived from a more general ideology of artistic modernism which legitimates this work and the activities of figures such as Birtwistle.

From a sociological perspective, it is this discourse, this framework of legitimation, and the claims and activities it licenses, which are of primary analytical interest, rather than 'the music' itself. Cases such as that of Birtwistle's music, where questions of meaning and interpretation are constantly foregrounded, are of interest precisely because they tend to make explicit what is often concealed or taken for granted, namely the underlying aesthetic values of the 'art world' and the conventions which derive from them. In speaking of conventions, though, we are led back to Birtwistle's relentless problematisation of familiar practices, and to Adlington's claim that his music should be heard as an expression of this. Hence Adlington's 'hermeneutic criticism' – perhaps intendedly – is ultimately rhetorical in its effect: he gives us a 'way of hearing' Birtwistle, offering all sorts of possible and plausible interpretations of what the pieces, or parts of them, might be about. This will be undoubtedly stimulating, and most helpful – but mainly, it should be said, to those who have already accepted the tenets of artistic modernism and who are thus predisposed to approach their encounters with Birtwistle as a serious undertaking from which some benefit will be derived. Others, however, could take a less positive view and become faintly irritated by the regular appearance in Adlington's text of evasive circumlocutions which suggest a possible meaning for a passage or a piece, only to withhold a clear assertion: for example, 'it is not totally impossible to reconcile' (Adlington, 2000: 60), or 'it is arguably "about"' (*ibid.*: 61), or 'has the capacity to convey the impression of' (*ibid.*: 115), or 'almost inevitably means' (*ibid.*: 163). There are many more of these, which to the sociologically minded reader appear less like descriptions of music than contributions to the discourse in which both the music itself, and the experience of it, are constituted.

It is only fair, though, to recognise that the expression of these evasions and ambiguities is entirely consistent with Adlington's general view of Birtwistle's artistic commitments. As I have said, Birtwistle persistently resists conventions, is intent on the 'exploration' – whatever that means – of their arbitrariness (*ibid.*: 25), and, when faced in recent times with a growing measure of public acceptance, reacted by producing *Panic* (for the Last Night of the Proms in 1991), which Adlington calls 'the most unremittingly ferocious eighteen minutes of music in his entire output . . . devised as an act of deliberate, snubbing provocation' (*ibid.*: 191). The disputes and debates over *Panic* provide an unusually explicit example of the politics of interpretation, and highlight the contestability not only of the meanings which may be attached to the music, but of the discourse in which it is framed. But in the end, not unexpectedly, Adlington comes to Birtwistle's defence, suggesting that the very incomprehensibility of the music is in itself 'a vivid and formidable stimulant' (*ibid.*: 197).

### Black music and black dysfunction

While Adlington's discussion of Birtwistle inevitably echoes Adorno's commitment to high modernism and art-music as a challenge to established conventions, Mark Anthony Neal's concern in *What the Music Said* (1999) is with the sort of music for which Adorno had little time or sympathy – black popular styles in the USA and their development through the twentieth century. Yet there is a link, in that both authors are concerned to understand music as an expression of the social and historical circumstances of its production; for Adorno this approach meant elucidating the process through which compositions were expressions of 'sedimented Geist', while Neal considers the ways in which the oral traditions of black music were codified and institutionalised in the context of the development of black communities in American cities, following the great northern migrations. Neal's focus is thus on both the formal and the informal aspects of black public culture as it emerged in the cities, on the ways in which popular music styles were important as expressions of the idea and the ideals of black culture and community, and on the importance of community contexts in shaping the music itself.

Above all, black culture in general, and its musical traditions in particular, must be understood as evolving in the context of, and as

a resistance to, institutionalised segregation and discrimination in
all their forms. However recognition of this view, as Neal shows
repeatedly, has the somewhat paradoxical consequence of rendering
problematic the idea of a homogeneous black culture. The early
black urban communities, he emphasises, were populated by people
'removed by force and ultimately choice from the mainstream public' (*ibid.*: 4), and thus differentiated economically and ideologically
while at the same time being treated as a homogeneous category by
'mainstream' white society. The churches, for example, largely
reflected the sensibilities of the 'liberal bourgeois' and integrationist
aspirations, whereas the informal public spaces provided by the
'jook joints', on the other hand, provided both a 'transgressive'
antithesis to church values and crucial sites for the development of
specifically African-American styles of music and dance. Simultaneously, the growth of consumer culture and the technologies of the
mass media provided the demand and the opportunity for the commercial exploitation of these styles, initiating a lengthy tradition of
the 'commodification of black dysfunction' in which 'African Americans are forced to be complicit in their own demonisation by producing commercially viable caricatures of themselves' (*ibid.*: 10).
The process is just as apparent in the nostalgic myths of the 'old
South' invented in the 1890s as it is in the 'gangsta rap' imagery of
a century later. For Neal, then, the various manifestations of
black music styles must be understood as forged in the context of
geographic dispersion and urban relocation, class and ideological
divisions, and a growing demand for suitably packaged music for the
mass market.

What emerges from Neal's account of the first half of the twentieth century is an emphasis, first, on the extent of social differentiation within black urban communities: the enforced concentration of
African Americans in such areas, epitomised by Harlem, did at least
ensure the development of a public sphere and of formal and informal organisations, and a kind of democratic dialogue among the
residents. Secondly, Neal points to the importance of musical traditions in such communities, and to the closeness of the links between
performers and their audiences. Again, Harlem's Apollo Theatre –
'a public space for communal critique of black cultural production'
(*ibid.*: 30) – is a prime example, although the tight, unmediated relationship between performers and listeners in a host of small, informal venues probably had a greater influence in shaping the musical

and performance conventions of black styles; such places were
where performers had to achieve the approval of audiences and
where, as a result, the community could quite informally exercise
control over the music as it developed. Thus the rhythm 'n' blues
and hard bop bands which worked the 'chittlin' circuit' in the 1950s
established and developed the musical conventions which best
expressed black urban America at the time. It was on the basis of this
musical language that 'soul' subsequently 'resonates among the total
diversity of an increasingly stratified black community' (*ibid.*: 31).
'Soul', drawing on elements of both sacred and secular black music
traditions and (as personified in Ray Charles) was ultimately a
'bricolage' which represented the 'hypercommunity' of the Civil
Rights era (*ibid.*: 40), and much of Neal's book is an account of the
vicissitudes of this stylistic movement – the ways in which it was
shaped by economic and political currents, taking on softer and
harder aspects, and expressing integrationist and separatist ideals.

In many respects, Neal's account is consistent with Ward's (1998)
examination of the links between the stages in the development of
political consciousness and the emergence of black music styles from
the 1950s to the 1970s, but Neal is concerned to take the story
forward into the 1990s. In fact, he sees the decade of the 1970s as
pivotal, beginning with the 'blatant state repression of black political expression' (Neal, 1999: 55) which broke apart the fragile soul-
based solidarity of the Civil Rights era, thereby fragmenting black
politics, and continuing with the 'urban renewal' programmes which
in many places destroyed the existing institutions of the black 'public sphere'. It was in this period, too, that the effects of economic
transformation – towards a 'service-based, post-industrial economy'
(*ibid.*: 66) – began to be felt, with the consequent inner-city decay,
the flight of the black middle class, the loss of jobs for men and the
development of an 'underclass'. Neal is concerned to highlight two
fundamental aspects of these processes – the increasingly corrosive
effect of the mass mediation of black music, and the catastrophic
collapse of black communities.

The wave of 'live' concert recordings during the 1970s by black
artists in a variety of styles is seen by Neal as a mass-mediated
response to the erosion of real communities, an attempt to create an
'aural community of resistance' which would 'reconstruct the
organic site of black popular music production' (*ibid.*: 80). Yet
despite the brilliance of some artists (such as Cannonball Adderley,

Marvin Gaye and Stevie Wonder) and the music through which they attempted to tackle such issues, their efforts were doomed ultimately by the growing fragmentation, both geographically and socially, of the black population and by the relentless exploitation of black music for commercial purposes. Berry Gordy's Motown record company, aiming at the mass market from the start, showed what could be achieved (for example, in the successful promotion of Diana Ross and Michael Jackson as global superstars), and Motown's relocation from Detroit to Los Angeles in the late 1960s is seen by Neal, not unreasonably, as 'an ironic and prophetic symbol of black middle class development' (*ibid.*: 88). Increasingly, with the corporate annexation of black popular music, 'soul', now divorced from its community origins, became a 'malleable market resource merchandised to black and white consumers alike' (*ibid.*: 94). The inevitable outcome, eventually, was the commercial success of one-dimensional, bland 'disco' music and the simultaneous association (once again) of black culture with drugs and escapism. Increasingly since the 1980s, then, the activities of music-industry 'ghetto merchants', and the 'late twentieth century sharecropping system' (*ibid.*: 116, 124) that they operate, have ensured the honing of new black talent for the mass market and an adulteration of the music. Indeed, the corporate orientation of black artists to the mass market has led to the abandoning of the separate black-music divisions which were formerly a feature of major record companies. In this respect as in others, says Neal, the process of integration has had the effect of weakening specifically black institutions and culture (*ibid.*: 117).

Inevitably, every stage in the corporate commodification of black music has produced a reaction, usually in the form of a separatist, oppositional movement, and by the 1990s the fragmentation of black values and lifestyles had found expression in hip-hop. Often derided and despised for their musical simplicity, political naivety, misogyny, arrogance and much more besides, hip-hop and rap styles none the less are of considerable significance in Neal's account. While soft soul music, suffused with a 'postindustrial nostalgia' for the vanished communities, is still sold to the black middle class, the uncompromising message of young black men in the inner cities was spelt out by hip-hop performers. They, says Neal, 'may represent the last black popular form to be wholly derived from the experiences and texts of the black urban landscape' (*ibid.*: 126). It was precisely the major recording companies' lack of interest in the style which allowed it to develop autonomously in its early stages; the outcome was a powerful 'counterhegemonic art' inevitably reflecting the unvarnished realities of the only public space left available to young black men – the street. While it is true that hip-hop and rap do draw on central elements of black music traditions – for example in the use of rhythmic repetition-with-a-difference and word games – its departures from that tradition are, if anything, of even greater significance. In their unconcealed celebration of materialism and violence, and in their sexism, these styles constituted the expression of an inner-city rage unrestrained by the close dialogue between performers and audiences which was a fundamental cultural element of the old urban communities. The communal critique of 'problematic narratives' (*ibid.*: 151) is a thing of the past, and the disintegration of the black public sphere is virtually complete. Furthermore, the styles and symbols of rap have themselves been subjected to the inexorable process of commodification, now formulated and marketed as an oppositional discourse which has proved to have considerable appeal to young white men, and a consequent source of profit for recording companies.

Like several other books on American popular music (e.g. Bayles, 1994; Clarke, 1995; Hyland, 1995), Neal's account is in the end a narrative of decline and fall. Whereas by the 1920s the industrial cities of the North had become mythologised as the 'promised land' for Southern blacks (Lemann, 1991), Stevie Wonder's 'Living for the City' (1974) is a tale in which the migrant rapidly becomes 'one of the walking dead that often inhabit the public spaces of the postindustrial city'. Indeed, it is a story, says Neal, which accurately 'foretells the emergence of an urban underclass' (*ibid.*: 112). So, inevitably, the book as a whole is at least as much about the effects of economic and political processes on communities as it is about music (*ibid.*: x), and in this respect may be of more interest to the sociologist than the musicologist. Yet it may serve as a powerful reminder to the latter that music in such communities is not primarily created or intended as an artistic object of contemplation (or, as in the case of Birtwistle, of analysis). Rather it is music whose meaning is defined by its use: for dancing to, as a means of escape or fantasy, as the cultural vehicle through which a sense of identity or solidarity may be engendered, or as a discourse of dissent. Moreover, in accounts such as Neal's we have the elements of a sociological explanation of the 'decline and fall' of American popular music: the reasons why 'they don't write 'em like that any more' have much to do with the sort of urban community disintegration that Neal is concerned with, and the more general processes that have produced it. The 'jook joints' and the 'chittlin' circuit' are, for the most part, things of the past, but so are, in the cultural mainstream, the night clubs, movie houses, ballrooms, theatres, roadhouses and bars which were the institutional sites for the performance of 'live' popular music, and which created the demand for specific forms of it. Neal is right to talk in general terms about the effects of post-industrialisation and urban decay, but more specific causes of the transformation of American popular music may be found by examining the social consequences of the proliferation of automobiles and the rise of mass television in the second half of the twentieth century.

Neal's account also directs our attention to the importance of processes of mediation, but in a way which may lead us to question the idea that institutions, like record companies or radio stations, provide an intermediate link between cultural 'producers' and 'consumers'. Market demand is not 'out there', but, as Hennion has argued, is formed and channelled in a reciprocal relationship between producers and consumers (e.g. Hennion, 1989). The local institutions of the black urban community, as Neal argues, were a consequence of the particular configuration of political and economic constraints imposed on their populations and the cultural resources which were available to them. To view the 'jook joints', the 'chittlin' circuit', the neighbourhood theatres and their associated businesses simply as intermediaries linking musicians and their audiences completely fails to capture the way in which such institutions were the hubs of community networks in which all sorts of activities were related, and the ways in which musical styles were forged in the interaction between the possibilities and constraints of the venues, on the one hand, and the aesthetic sensibilities of their clientele, on the other. There is always a risk, therefore, that by examining such styles, and the work of performers, from a specifically musicological perspective the object of analysis becomes decontextualised, so that the ways in which the music 'worked' in the culture, and resonated in particular times and places, is lost. Such a decontextualisation may then lead to futile attempts to specify what the music is 'about', what it 'tells us', independently of the actual circumstances of its

production and reception. Moreover, the fact that to some musicologists – and certainly to Sir Harrison Birtwistle – many of the songs
and recordings referred to in Neal's account are absurdly simple
does not in any way diminish their social importance or sociological
interest. It is unlikely that a technical analysis of, for example, James
Brown's 'Say it Loud, I'm Black and I'm Proud' will reveal the ways
in which, for Neal, it was in its time and place an anthem of contradictory significance, proclaiming black pride yet simultaneously
'emblematic of the limits of black political discourse' (*ibid.*: 61).
Attention to processes of mediation, moreover, also subverts futile
efforts to pin down 'meanings', by highlighting the fluid, dynamic
nature of interpretive processes. Indeed, one of the ironies of the
process which Neal describes is the way in which some of the songs
of defiance from the Civil Rights era and after are now routinely
used as marketing tools by mega-corporations which have, once
again, managed to commodify the sounds of black resistance. It is
obvious (though often overlooked in attempts to decipher musical
meanings) that the same music may mean very different things to
different people in different times and places. However, if we wish
to understand how this variation comes about we must examine not
just the sounds themselves, but the processes through which they are
mediated.

## McClary's conventions

For Susan McClary, it is precisely the distinctive features of African-
American music – its orientation to performances 'as the means
whereby the community enacts consolidation' (McClary, 2000: 23)
rather than the production of 'works', and its burgeoning influence
in the twentieth century – that call into question many of the traditional procedures and assumptions of musicology. The fundamental
aim of her work, she suggests, has always been to explore the cultural premises which underlie all music, and on which its effects
depend. In this respect she implies that the controversies aroused
by her feminist readings of well-known pieces have been something
of a distraction from her real business of examining the ways in
which apparently formal musical procedures are imbued with culturally specific values and premises (*ibid.*: ix), and it is this idea with
which she is concerned in *Conventional Wisdom: The Content of
Musical Form.* Thus the conventions of African-American music

'carry sedimented within them a worldview. . . . But no less does European music inscribe a world through its conventions and foundational assumptions' (*ibid.*: 28–29). It follows that the form–content distinction can no longer be sustained; as the book's subtitle suggests, the idea is that as taken-for-granted norms of procedure, 'forms' are in fact 'intensely ideological formations' in which 'genuine social knowledge is articulated and transmitted' (*ibid.*: 5). The notion that the development of particular styles or the elaboration of formal procedures are 'purely musical' matters is firmly rejected, along with the idea that music can develop independently of its social context. Instead, McClary's contention is that 'a great deal of wisdom resides in conventions: nothing less than the premises of an age, the cultural arrangements that enable communication, co-existence, and self-awareness' (*ibid.*: 5–6).

In much of the book, McClary is concerned to develop the theme that the formal procedures which, over time, have come to be accepted as natural or inevitable are none the less cultural constructions which – in a literal sense – resonate with the *Zeitgeist* in which they were created; they are to be understood as 'ways societies have devised for articulating their most basic beliefs through the medium of sound' (*ibid.*: 31). Her initial illustrations are Stradella's development of techniques for representing female subjectivity in the seventeenth century, and the Swan Silvertones' recording in 1959 of 'Jesus, Keep Me Near the Cross', both of which, she argues, draw on and express in their formal procedures the values and beliefs of their historical contexts, and incidently demonstrate that Baroque and African-American 'musical priorities' have more in common with each other than with more recent European art music (*ibid.*: 29). But McClary's two major examples are the conventions underlying the blues, and those of tonality itself. The former provides a good example of her approach. While our attention as listeners is usually drawn to the work of blues singers or instrumentalists, it is the underlying harmonic sequence framed by the recurring 12-bar structure, this 'facilitating pattern', which is 'the most important signifier of the lot: it acknowledges a social history, a lineage descending from a host of tributaries'. And with each verse, each performance, it reinscribes a 'particular model of social interaction. . . . the pattern guarantees coherence and the survival of collective memory' (*ibid.*: 41). However, this underlying pattern is itself appropriated and adapted in particular times and places: by Bessie Smith and the women of the 'classic' era who gave voice to black urban life, by the later rural bluesmen (retrospectively defined as 'authentic' by male musicians) such as Robert Johnson, and by the English art students of the 1960s whose activities generated the 'progressive' rock scene. Indeed, McClary makes some interesting comments about the way in which the British players brought to the music certain specifically European characteristics – the additive pattern became a goal-orientated 'narrative trajectory'; the enactment of community gave way to individualistic displays of (male) virtuosity and a Romantic concept of the 'artist'; the mind–body split reappeared. (Musicologists may wish to debate McClary's judgement that this fusion of European and African-American aesthetic elements 'permitted the first truly international wave of English musical creativity since perhaps Elizabethan times'; *ibid.*: 60.)

McClary's outline of the rise (and fall) of tonality emphasises those specifically European cultural movements that, in her view, shaped the conventions of tonal music in fundamental ways. These movements were not an inevitable development, but rather represent a selection from among the options available in seventeenth-century music, a 'package of conventions' (*ibid.*: 68) which constructed 'musical analogs to such emergent ideals as rationality, individualism, progress and centred subjectivity' (*ibid.*: 65). Moreover, the emergent musical package not only expressed these ideals, but had the effect of teaching listeners 'how to live within such a world: how to project forward in time, how to wait patiently but confidently for the pay-off' (*ibid.*: 67). Indeed, tonality – a musical procedure which has come to seem natural and inevitable – operates 'to affirm the ascent of reason in its ability finally to contain (but also to construct) human emotions . . . to inscribe [*sic*] admiring listeners into specifically eighteenth-century habits of rationality' (*ibid.*: 73). The theme of rationality is significant here, for what follows is an account of the rise and decline of tonal music which echoes Adorno's familiar narrative. For example, Vivaldi was so influential because in his work there are musical reconciliations of the individual and the collectivity, innovation and stability, digression and underlying progress. Similarly, Bach takes us 'from the static rigidity of the *ancien régime* to the impulsive desire for self-generation that stood as the ideal of the German intelligentsia' (*ibid.*: 101), while in Mozart we can find the assertion of a dynamic self anchored to a solid, immutable core (*ibid.*: 107).

Like Adorno, McClary hears dissent and disintegration in the nineteenth century with the emergence of Romanticism and the reassertion of heroic individualism. Whereas Bach and Mozart 'opted for negotiated settlements with social norms in their bids for closure . . . in the nineteenth century, appeals to community exerted less and less influence on artists or on the ideal listeners who learned to cheer stylistic transgressions from the sidelines. Norms became the enemy' (*ibid.*: 116–117). The new tensions, as Adorno argued, are above all evident in Beethoven's late works. In her discussion McClary seeks to reconcile 'Kerman's humanist interpretation and Agawu's formal analysis' (*ibid.*: 119), hearing 'an image of shattered subjectivity' in the opening of the Quartet in A minor, Opus 132, and suggesting that in the events of the piece we can 'recognise the signs of anguish' (*ibid.*: 122). Inexorably, the crisis of subjectivity deepens as time passes, through the stage when Schoenberg and others 'drew on images of madness' (*ibid.*: 135) to the point where finally, in Cage, we confront the possibility that 'beneath the discontinuous surface there lurks . . . nothing at all' (*ibid.*: 136). Readers of Adorno will know the story well.

By way of conclusion, McClary surveys the fragmented, *Angst*-ridden situation of music at the start of the twenty-first century, a literally post-modern terrain where all sorts of people – like Philip Glass, John Zorn, k. d. lang and Prince – are involved in 'active negotiation with the cultural past' (*ibid.*: 168) in all sorts of playful, transgressive, ironic and deconstructive ways. And McClary wishes to celebrate this multi-spouted fountain of creativity: now that we are liberated from the constraints of the old conventions, a variety of experiments, innovations, fusions and multi-cultural mixes becomes possible. To ignore rap because it 'sounds unpleasant', she contends, is to ignore 'some of the most important and innovative music of our time' (*ibid.*: 161). (Again, musicologists may wish to debate this; as a sociologist I have no view.) Overall, McClary is impressed by the vitality of the contemporary scene in all its diversity, which leads her to conclude that 'the problem is not so much that a dependable linear main stream has collapsed as that there never was such a thing, except in fictions constructed after the fact – and always for particular ideological purposes' (*ibid.*: 169).

It has to be said that, as ever, it is hugely enjoyable and immensely stimulating to read McClary. If her aim was to engage in 'hermeneutic criticism', she has succeeded. Once you have absorbed her 'take' on individual pieces, indeed whole styles, you will hear them differently. But the issue here is the extent to which she has developed a 'social' analysis of the music, and in this respect some critical questions arise. In one sense, of course, *Conventional Wisdom* is quite explicitly an argument for a 'social' understanding of music as bearing in its fundamental organising principles – its taken-for-granted conventions – the 'dominant cultural tropes' (*ibid.*: 66) of the social groups or societies which produce it. It is equally explicitly an argument against the view of Western music as developing autonomously, driven forward only by the amazing creativity of inspired (male) individuals and their composition of 'pure music'. In this respect, McClary's arguments are congenial to those with a sociological turn of mind. For the latter, though, certain difficulties remain; I will consider some of these, rather arbitrarily, in four groups.

First, McClary's contention that music somehow expresses the 'dominant cultural tropes', or the *Zeitgeist*, of a group or society, risks ascribing to these collectivities a coherence that they do not in fact possess. She is concerned, she says, with the 'countless ways societies have devised for articulating their most basic beliefs through the medium of sound' (*ibid.*: 31). This formulation, however, immediately raises the question of how this 'devising' occurs, and runs the risk of ascribing to an abstraction – society – an agency which it cannot possess. Moreover, since at least the time of Max Weber (who died in 1920), thoughtful sociologists have viewed social organisation not as an entity displaying characteristic properties such as 'basic beliefs', but as a process of interpersonal interaction in which diverse and incompatible interests, values and ideas are in perpetual competition (Hughes, Sharrock and Martin, 2003: 137–138). Thus the very notions of the 'core' values of a group or society, or indeed a *Zeitgeist*, are inherently problematic. In McClary's defence, it could be argued that her view of the eighteenth century fits with the accepted historical picture, since processes of rationalisation and the control of subjectivity do indeed seem to have been 'dominant'. Yet whether her narrative of the decline of tonality fits the pattern of the nineteenth century is more problematic. Sure enough, Romantics may have agonised over the fate of the individual, but (as Adorno himself emphasised) this was hardly the dominant ideological current in capitalist society at the time. And did tonality really decline? In McClary's own words, 'atonal projects themselves derive their meaning from tonality' (McClary, 2000: 140), and from a more sociological point of view – surveying all the music of Western industrial societies, rather than the marginal if sincere contributions of Schoenberg, Cage, Glass, Birtwistle and other self-conscious modernists – tonality looks pretty well entrenched at the start of the twenty-first century. Such issues are far beyond the scope of this discussion: all I wish to suggest is that in asserting a link between music and 'dominant cultural tropes' we must be careful to specify *which* music and *whose* cultural values. Moreover, as I suggested above, the idea that what the sociologist of music should be doing is 'decoding' the 'social' messages of musical 'texts' has been effectively demolished by Becker (1989).

Secondly, the postulation of a congruence between musical conventions and social value-systems raises the question of how the latter come to influence the former. Musicologists have – quite rightly – rejected the simplistic 'sociological' notion that composers are simply puppets whose strings are pulled by larger social forces, so that their music somehow 'reflects' society. So does McClary. Considering Beethoven's Opus 132, she writes that 'the crisis that Beethoven here traces with such force and internal integrity resonates with a much larger ideological crisis. To say this is not to reduce the details of this quartet to sociology or to imply some kind of determinism' (*ibid.*: 128). But does she then succeed in steering between the pitfalls of reductionism and determinism? What follows is not encouraging. Attali, says McClary, has 'argued that music prophesies', and Adorno has 'demonstrated how serious composers push up and wage war against . . . social contradictions' (*ibid.*). Now it is quite true that Attali (1985) has argued in this sort of way, but that hardly counts as a refutation of reductionism or determinism; all that Attali has done is to produce some bold assertions and sweeping generalisations. Nor is it clear, as I have argued elsewhere, that Adorno has 'demonstrated' how 'serious' composers convey social messages in their works; he did indeed assert such a connection, but ultimately failed to explain satisfactorily just how the process works (Martin, 1995: 114–116; see also Zuidervaart, 1991: 97–99). In this context it may be worth recalling Subotnik's conclusion that Adorno's view of the connection between 'artistic structure' and 'objective reality' is 'indirect, complex, unconscious, undocumented, and rather mysterious' (Subotnik, 1991: 271). In short, despite its centrality to her whole enterprise, McClary

produces no persuasive evidence to support the notion that social
content is 'inscribed' in musical works.

Thirdly, it is not entirely clear, at least to me, how the music
McClary discusses is supposed to have the effects she ascribes to it.
Does every performance of a 12-bar blues implicitly signify 'a social
history, a lineage descending from a host of tributaries' (McClary,
2000: 41)? Of course it may do, but again this effect has to be
demonstrated rather than asserted. Similarly, when considering
claims such as 'eighteenth century tonality works to produce a
particular construction of the self' (*ibid.*: 70) we might, rather prosaically, ask for the evidence of it actually working on some identifiable people. Are people affected by music in this sort of way simply
by being immersed in the symbolic discourse it generates? Or are we
to presuppose the 'ideal listener' (*ibid.*: 117) who listens passively,
knowledgeably and attentively to the 'work', when we know that
(*pace* Adorno) even in the nineteenth century such people were a
minority of those who attended concerts, let alone the rest of the
population? Of course, as McClary rightly notes, people had to be
encouraged and instructed by the 'reception industry' (*ibid.*: 114),
thereby implying that the meaning and significance of the musical
'texts' themselves is in fact indeterminate, and that people had to be
taught 'how' to hear them. Consequently, given the variety of 'ways
of hearing' which have been advocated by critics, composers and
other 'experts', we may be led to wonder about the status of
McClary's own account, especially given the particular kind of
phraseology which recurs in her discussion. For example, 'the
"Prague" [Symphony] relies on tonality's harmonic flexibility to persuade us that we are hearing individualist expression' (*ibid.*: 105), or
'Op. 132 so clearly enacts the tension between . . . ' (*ibid.*: 119),
or 'I hear this sequence as representing . . . ' (*ibid.*: 129). What is
being claimed here, and in many similar passages? Is she telling us
that some kind of meaning is 'in' the music, or is she teaching us
'how' to hear it?

With these questions in mind, it is worth recalling, fourthly,
McClary's discussion of Beethoven's Opus 132 in relation to the
alternative treatments of it offered in 'Kerman's humanist interpretation and Agawu's formal analysis' (*ibid.*: 119). Her aim is to offer
'a kind of reconciliation' between these. What is of interest here,
however, is the coexistence of a number of possible versions of
what the piece is about, or how it works. For the sociologist, it is the

production and reception of such alternative versions, and the discourse to which they contribute, that are of primary interest, rather
than their 'truth content', so to speak. For it is in the social processes
of this discourse that the meaning and significance of music are constituted. Seen from this perspective, then, McClary's analyses are in
the end rhetorical, in the sense discussed above (p. 36). Just as
Adlington's discussion of Birtwistle is an exercise in 'hermeneutic
criticism', McClary offers us a new or different way of hearing
things, and she wishes to persuade us to hear them this way rather
than that. In referring to alternative analyses, she is implicitly
acknowledging the parameters of an existing critical discourse, and
the 'politics of meaning' with which participants are concerned. Politics? Indeed so. At the very end of her book, as we have seen, she
suggests that the orthodox version of Western musical development
– the idea of 'the linear main stream' – is a retrospective fiction, a
narrative based on notions of progress and development, and further that such 'fictions' are always constructed 'for particular ideological purposes'. But surely McClary's own interpretations are also
derived from the presuppositions of a particular narrative, one
which owes much to Adorno, and which I have tried to outline
above. Is her narrative in any way less 'ideological' in its purposes
than the orthodox one?

## Conclusion

Three rather different books, then, but each in its way displaying a
certain aspect of the 'turn to the social' in the discourse of musicology. In certain respects, it is Neal's account of black popular music
which most immediately engages the sociologist of music. It provides powerful evidence of the ways in which musical styles and
conventions are shaped by particular historical and institutional
configurations, emphasising the growth and subsequent fragmentation of black 'public space', the evolution and disintegration of
urban communities, and processes of mediation. Moreover, Neal
provides excellent illustrations of the way in which, from a sociological perspective, the meaning and significance of music are not
assumed to be transcendental, but on the contrary are always and
inevitably realised through the activities and interactions of real
people in real situations. One aspect of such activities – and an
important one – is the political struggle over meanings which

energises many in the musical (and particularly the musicological) community, and it is in this context that the rhetorical basis of both Adlington's and McClary's works may be appreciated, as they offer us selected 'ways of hearing'.

In McClary's case, her preferred versions of styles and individual pieces derive from the presupposition of a specific narrative concerning the modernisation of Western music and its post-modern consequences. In this respect, the interested sociologist (or at least this one) is left with the strong suspicion that the 'new' musicology, of which McClary has become such a prominent representative, does not appear to be very much different from the 'old'. As I have said, the story that McClary wants us to accept owes a great deal to ideas that Adorno published in the 1930s. Moreover, her procedure is to use this narrative as the basis for uncovering the 'ideological basis of music's operations' (*ibid.*: 7), or making explicit the 'world-view' that musical conventions 'carry sedimented within them' (*ibid.*: 28). I have to reiterate the point that this emphasis on decoding or deciphering the hidden 'meaning' of a work looks very much like the sort of thing that some musicologists have always tried to do, albeit in various ways. What's more, while such deciphering was clearly central to what the 'old' sociologists of art (like Adorno) were trying to do, this kind of analysis is simply not on the agenda for contemporary sociologists (one of the reasons being the evidently 'ideological' nature of the 'old' narratives, which McClary has rightly noted).

In so far as it adopts a 'rhetorical' approach, then, and also concentrates on the deciphering of 'works', this 'new' musicology looks to the sociologist very much like the 'old'. There are other ways, which can only be noted here, in which that impression is reinforced. For example, despite her evident concern to deconstruct the canon and dissolve the art music/popular music distinction, a very considerable proportion of McClary's book is nevertheless concerned with the analysis of canonic works. Further, even in our post-modern times she is particularly concerned with serious, innovative, self-conscious artists like Glass, Zorn, Prince and k. d. lang, and with the 'stunning' (*ibid.*: 163) contribution of the rappers. Is this really an escape from the ideology of artistic modernism (especially as McClary appears to accept Adorno's criteria for the identification of 'serious' composers; *ibid.*: 128)? The issue cannot be pursued here, but what it does suggest is the wide gulf between the 'new' musicologists and the concerns of contemporary sociologists, who are increasingly interested in the uses which people make of ordinary music in their everyday lives (e.g. DeNora, 2000) rather than the decontextualised 'meaning' of serious, innovative 'works'.

Again, the programme of the contemporary sociology of music is beyond the scope of the present discussion. Yet, to conclude with a complaint I referred to at the start, there are few signs here that sociologists' respect for the musicologists' discourse is reciprocated. As we have seen, McClary's focus in *Conventional Wisdom* – note the title – is on the taken-for-granted conventions which serve to organise musical procedures. As it happens, the concept of 'convention' is developed in a sociologically specific and theoretically important way in Howard Becker's widely influential analysis of *Art Worlds* (1982). Yet it is surprising, disappointing and enormously discouraging to find not a single reference to Becker's work in McClary's book. If musicologists, whether 'new' or 'old', are serious about producing a social analysis of music, they had better start reading some sociology.

# 4

# Music and manipulation

Adorno's theory of contemporary society begins with the claim of a system integration which has become total; thus he can regard the entire media of the culture industry only as a means of domination and must rate popular forms of art as phenomena of psychical regression. (Honneth, 1995: 81)

## Introduction

The idea that people may be subject to manipulation by music is a familiar one, yet efforts to develop it sociologically soon run into difficulties. For one thing, the 'manipulation' in question always seems to involve *other* people; it seems that no one, however much of a 'music lover', likes admitting to being taken over by the sounds and controlled by them. Indeed, there is a hint here of the elitism which some have detected in the pronouncements of the Critical Theorists on the degradation of consciousness brought about by mass culture; a fate which only they (and connoisseurs of authentic art like Adorno) are able to resist. More seriously, the idea of manipulation by music runs the risk of descending rapidly towards a simplistic stimulus-response model of human motivation in which music produces 'effects' in people. Elsewhere, I have suggested some of the inadequacies of this way of thinking (e.g. Martin, 1995: 156–158); what I am concerned with here is the way in which such assumptions about music's 'effects', while theoretically inadequate and empirically dubious, are nevertheless presupposed in many influential discussions of popular culture, including – as the quotation above suggests – those of Adorno and the Critical Theorists.

Of course, there is a wide variety of ways in which authors have tried to pin down the 'effects' than music can have on people. For some, emphasis is placed on properties of the sounds themselves, as when McClary suggests that ' . . . most listeners have little rational control over the way [music] influences them' (1991: 151); for others, it is the words of popular songs which convey their 'message' (Hirsch, 1971: 376). However, as Hirsch also pointed out many years ago, the assumptions on which these sorts of claims are based are mostly unexamined (*ibid.*: 377). In fact, there is still relatively little empirical evidence concerning the place of music, and the uses which people make of it, in their daily lives, or more generally on the issue of the extent to which their thoughts, emotions and actions are influenced by music. Inevitably this raises various matters concerning the social contexts in which music is heard, and – once again – an interesting divergence between musicological and socio-logical concerns becomes apparent. The idea that I want to develop here is that, at least from a sociological point of view, music in everyday situations must be understood as *embedded* in patterns of social activities, and thus may be only a part – an important, even crucial, part – but a part nevertheless of a larger complex of activi-ties. In comparison with the number of analyses of individual pieces of music, abstracted from any actual performance context, or of musical perception under 'experimental' conditions, there are rela-tively few studies of 'real life' music use, but what they do suggest is the operation of a kind of circle of interpretation – some would call it hermeneutic – through which social activities receive their meaning from the music, and *vice versa*.

As I have suggested, the widespread assumption of music as a form of communication in which a 'message' is passed from a 'sender' to a 'receiver' does not provide a satisfactory model for the under-standing of musical effects, whatever they may be. As Blumer, for example, argued many years ago, mass media messages and their effects cannot reasonably be isolated from the dynamic social contexts of their production and appropriation. The 'message' model seems to imply, for example, that both active 'sender' and passive 'receiver' are individuals, isolated from any actual social context of music use, and to assume that the 'message' is both unam-biguous and effective in producing an appropriate reaction in the 'receiver'. Above all: 'Account must be taken of a collective process of definition which in different ways shapes the manner in which individuals composing the "audience" interpret and respond to the presentations given through the mass media' (Blumer, 1969: 188).

In the present context, Blumer's insistence on the fundamental importance of this collaborative process of interpretation is highly significant; what I will suggest is that studies of music use in 'real life' contexts serve to emphasise the serious limitations of the 'message' model, and that such studies, if pursued more vigorously, would lead to a greater understanding of the ways in which music and its effects are inevitably implicated in wider patterns of social activity.

In order to avoid any misunderstandings, I should make it clear that I have no wish to deny the value of, say, musicological analyses of particular musical 'texts', or of systematic psychological studies of responses to music. Such studies derive from certain specific – and quite different – academic discourses, and we have much to learn from them. In considering the actual use of music in everyday situations, however, we are led into the sociological domain, and thus to see music-making and hearing as sets of social practices in which people are collaboratively involved. From this perspective, the problem with many discussions of the 'reception' of music, and of popular music in particular, is that – to use a phrase of Honneth's to which I will return – they exhibit a specifically 'sociological deficit' (Honneth, 1993: 187) in the sense that they ignore the real situations of 'everyday social action' (*ibid.*: 210) in which people hear, use and interpret music.

In what follows, therefore, I will draw on some studies of actual music use – most of them relating to popular music – to consider some of the sociological issues which have emerged from them, with a particular emphasis on the relationship between music and personal identity. Participation in sets of activities organised around music can create or reinforce a sense of being a particular kind of person, of belonging to a particular group, and by extension may lead to the designation, definition and possible denigration of 'others'. But if music can thus be seen to affect the development of individuals' sense of self and others, is it not therefore a prime example of manipulation, in Foucault's use of the term? Could music not constitute a 'dividing practice', through which 'the subject is objectified by a process of division either within himself or from others' (Rabinow, 1984: 8). Inevitably, as I shall suggest, things are not so straightforward. Finally, in conclusion, I will consider some implications of the discussion for our understanding of the concepts of manipulation and social control.

## Popular music in use

For Adorno and the critical theorists, the nature and effects of the 'culture industry' were of fundamental importance in their search for an answer to the question of why the exploited proletariat generated by modern capitalism had failed to develop the kind of oppositional class consciousness envisaged by Marxist theorists. Thus in the *Dialectic of Enlightenment* the 'culture industry' – that is, the production and distribution of culture in the form of standardised, mass commodities – was famously viewed as producing 'mass deception' (Adorno and Horkheimer, 1979 [1944]: 120ff). Adorno's view was uncompromising; indeed the tone of his remarks makes the term 'manipulation' seem quite mild:

> In contrast to the Kantian, the categorical imperative of the culture industry no longer has anything in common with freedom. It proclaims: you shall conform, without instruction as to what; conform to what exists anyway, and to that which anyone thinks anyway as a reflex of its power and omnipresence. The power of the culture industry's ideology is such that conformity has replaced consciousness. (Adorno, 1991: 90)

From this point of view, and particularly for Adorno, popular music could be nothing more than a commodity produced by the 'culture industry', inescapably trivial and aesthetically degraded, producing and reproducing that 'regression of listening' which characterised mass audiences (Adorno 1991: 40–41). 'There is actually a neurotic mechanism of stupidity in listening, too', says Adorno, 'the arrogantly ignorant rejection of everything unfamiliar is its sure sign' (1991: 44–45). The synthetic products of the music business have now swept away all traces of the authentic voice of working people. Once, in an earlier era, the 'power of the street ballad, the catchy tune and all the swarming forms of the banal' were used to attack 'the cultural privilege of the ruling class'. Now, however, the masses are deluded into a preference for the very music that degrades them:

> The illusion of a social preference for light music as against serious is based on that passivity of the masses which makes the consumption of light music contradict the objective interests of those who consume it. (*ibid.*, 1991: 30)

Even in its details, popular music represents and reinforces that annihilation of the autonomous individual whom the critical theorists took to be fundamental in the totalitarian society of capitalist industrialism. 'The concepts of order which [the culture industry] hammers into human beings', writes Adorno, 'are always those of the status quo' – as when, for example, syncopated effects, and other 'rhythmic problems', are 'instantly resolved by the triumph of the basic beat' (*ibid.*: 90). It is hardly surprisng, therefore, to find that in the view of one commentator 'Adorno identified popular music as part of the effort of late capitalism to transform man into an insect' (Brunkhorst, 1999: 143). The principal function of popular music, then, was to 'affirm' the values and normative patterns of mass society and thus to reconcile the 'humming millions' to their existence as workers and, increasingly, consumers; in filling people's heads with simple tunes and escapist fantasies it inculcated an ideological acceptance of, and an unquestioning obedience to, the *status quo*, while concealing the exploitation and mystification on which it was based.

There could hardly be a stronger statement of the idea of music as manipulation, and on a massive scale. Interestingly, much American writing of the 1950s on the 'mass society' thesis adopted a similar position with regard to popular music, assuming that its endless succession of ephemeral love songs and 'Moon in June' lyrics effectively reflected and reinforced conventional morality (Hirsch, 1971: 373). In contrast to Adorno's despair, however, American commentators of the 1950s took some consolation from this situation: they agreed that the music itself might well be 'standardised trivia' (*ibid.*), but at least it had the merit of encouraging social stability and celebrating the American way of life; in the language of 1950s sociology, it could be seen as contributing significantly to the 'functional imperatives' of both socialisation and social control. All this was to change, of course with the volcanic eruption of rock 'n' roll in the mid-1950s and the emergence of 'oppositional' youth cultures in which music was a major component, culminating in the overt challenges to conventional morality and established institutions in the 'counter-cultural' music of the late 1960s.

Almost as soon as it appeared, rock 'n' roll was condemned as a force which would corrupt youth, undermine the family, and destabilise American society. Much of this moral panic, as Ward has shown, was orchestrated by Southern white supremacist politicians, whose main agenda was set by their resistance to integrationist policies which presented a challenge to their customary way of life

(1998: 95). In the present context, what is significant about this movement is the set of assumptions which it made – and which critics of styles such as rap and hip-hop still tend to make – about the music and its effects. Much of the evidence which was used to characterise pop music styles as *either* affirming conventional morality, *or* presenting a threat to it, was based on 'content analysis' studies of song lyrics. Methodologically, the limitations of this procedure are clear enough, and similar to the issues raised by the 'message' model of musical communication: the words of a song are treated as a 'text' independently of the music (which is then ignored), and both are decontextualised. It is further assumed that this 'text' has an unambiguous 'meaning', and that this meaning is effectively and unproblematically communicated to those who listen to the song (Hirsch, 1971: 376). It was against this background that Hirsch took the simple – but at the time quite novel – step of examining the actual use of pop music by real high-school teenagers. The results, which have been echoed in various subsequent studies, were instructive, and quite damaging to the conventional wisdom – whether of conservatives or critical theorists – about popular music and its effects. Not only did it emerge that there was a variety of interpretations of song lyrics, but even in the case of big-selling 'protest' songs 'the vast majority of teenage listeners are unaware of what the lyrics . . . are about' (Robinson and Hirsch, 1972: 231). Moreover, any analysis which neglects the actual *sound* of a record is unlikely to capture the essence of what it does for people: the rhythm, the 'feel', or what jazz musicians call the 'groove' of a record may give it its attraction, irrespective of the 'content' of its lyrics. More generally, as Denzin put it: 'There may be little correspondence between the intended and the imputed meanings' of such cultural objects, so that 'an art object, because it may not invoke the intended response in the audience, cannot be taken as an *a priori* valid indicator of a group's perspective' (Denzin, 1969: 1036). This is an important point, since it concisely but directly challenges all those interpretations of musical styles which take them to be in some way 'reflections', or 'representations', or 'articulations', of the central values of social groups, whether these be whole societies, dominant classes, or oppositional subcultures (Martin, 1995: 160ff; DeNora, 2000: 3).

It is also significant that empirical demonstrations of the inadequacy of the critical theorists' model of 'mass society' have been complemented by theoretical analyses which cast doubt on the validity of their assumptions about the culture industry and its manipulative effects. As I suggested above, Honneth has argued that there is a specifically 'sociological deficit' (1993: 187) in Horkheimer's programmatic formulation of critical theory: his preoccupation with large-scale economic forces, on the one hand, and psychoanalytic theories, on the other, led not only to an impoverished concept of culture – which simply serves to 'reflect the behavioural constraints of the economic system back upon the individual psyche' (*ibid.*: 208) – but also, crucially, to an almost total neglect of the actions and interactions of real individuals and groups. In Honneth's view, Horkheimer's perspective 'screens the whole spectrum of everyday social action out of the object domain of interdisciplinary social science' (*ibid.*: 210). In other words, the critical theorists' preoccupations with political economy and psychoanalysis led them to ignore precisely those phenomena which are the object of sociology as an 'autonomous science' (*ibid.*: 211). Horkheimer sees modern society only as a mass of atomised and passive individuals, with a consequent disregard both for the particular cultural and institutional configurations which constitute the social environment of real people, and for the specifically sociological process through which such configurations are enacted.

The sociological implication is that the meaning and effects of music cannot be assumed *a priori* but must be understood though an examination of the situations in which it is used. Whereas Adorno took his task to be the 'ideological-critical deciphering of the social content of the work of art' (*ibid.*), a sociological approach to music will be primarily concerned to examine the ways in which it is used and interpreted by real people, rather than to impute 'meaning' to it. Indeed, studies of the actual use of popular music emphasise the extent to which it is bound up in complex ways with people's participation in wider configurations of activity. It should not be simply assumed that they actively 'listen' to it with the close attention of the symphony concert-goer (although they may do); what may be far more important, for example, is that the experience of the music helps them to define both themselves and others as certain sorts of people. Indeed, another important implication of studies of popular music use is the extent to which musical meanings are derived from non-musical sources: 'significant others' such as friends or colleagues, or authoritative opinion leaders like DJs, journalists, celebrities or critics. Indeed, as in the worlds of jazz, folk or classical music, there is an array of journals and magazines which do much to constitute the discourse which provides possible ways of hearing specific sounds, songs, styles, bands, singers and so on. So from a sociological point of view, the use of music in everyday situations is not effectively conceptualised as the communication of messages from senders to individual receivers, but is to be understood as a collaborative process involving a network of relationships in which the music derives its meaning from the pattern of social activities in which it is embedded, and *vice versa*. In other words, musical meaning is not to be found 'in' the text, nor does it have autonomous effects; rather, it may be more productive to think in terms of a reciprocity of effects linking music and the configuration of social activities in which it is inescapably embedded. Such a conclusion not only reveals the distinctive perspective of the 'sociological gaze' as it is applied to music (see Chapter 2 above), but indicates some of the ways in which it differs from other approaches, such as those of the musicological analyst or the cultural critic. Indeed, DeNora has characterised recent sociological work in this sphere as marking ' . . . a shift in focus from aesthetic objects and their content . . . to the cultural practices in and through which aesthetic materials were appropriated and used . . . to produce social life' (2000: 6).

## Music and identity

A similar perspective has been developed in some of Simon Frith's work:

> the issue is not how a particular piece of music reflects the people, but how it produces them, how it creates and constructs an experience – a musical experience, an aesthetic experience – that we can only make sense of by *taking on* both a subjective and a collective identity (Frith, 1996a: 109)

As this quotation indicates, Frith's position emerged in criticism of 'reflection' theories which seek to demonstrate a correspondence or 'homology' between social groups and the styles of music they produce, whether affirmative or oppositional (see also Middleton, 1990: 147ff). But what does it mean to say, as Frith does, that music can 'produce' people? What this definitely does *not* mean is that there is some sort of Foucauldian 'discourse' which manipulates people in the sense that 'it' constitutes their subjectivities. What I think it does lead us to appreciate is the often neglected social dimension of musical experience, namely the ways in which having a musical experience inevitably involves us in relationships with others, whether they are present or not. In listening to, or performing, music we must, as Schütz (1964) argued, 'tune in' our subjectivity to that of others as we follow the succession of sounds in 'real time', thereby constituting the intersubjective 'we' which is the foundation of all social experience (see Chapter 10). For present purposes, one important implication is that rather than viewing collectivities – societies, groups, subcultures – as existing prior to the music or other cultural phenomena, which then express 'their' values, it is more productive to examine the ways in which a sense of participating in a distinct collectivity is *produced* through such collaborative activities and experiences (Frith, 1996a: 111). All such experiences are 'obdurately social' (Frith, 1996b: 277) in the sense that they involve the establishment of a relationship between 'inner' subjectivity and the 'outer' world of collaborative cultural practices. In a 'mass' industrial society music can thus provide a strong source of meaning and belonging. In short it affords ' . . . .a way of being in the world' and is a highly salient aspect of the process through which aspects of identity – such as gender, age, ethnicity, class, and religion – are established, maintained and changed (Frith, 1996a: 114).

It seems too that music, as a specific form of cultural practice, is particularly effective in contributing to the process of identity-formation. As Shepherd (1991) has argued, music, as a sonic medium, has an immediacy which purely visual media may lack, affording the sensation that significant sounds are – in a quite literal sense – resonating within us. Indeed, in considering the implications of the recent revival of sociological interest in the aesthetic (as opposed to the cognitive) dimensions of cultural practice, DeNora has emphasised the particular power of music to act as a constitutive, rather than simply reflective, medium: 'Its temporal dimension, the fact that it is a non-verbal, non-depictive medium, and that fact that it is a physical presence whose vibrations can be felt, all enhance its ability to work at non-cognitive or subconscious levels' (DeNora, 2000: 159). To anyone interested in the 'effects' of music, the point is unlikely to be contentious.

In any case, what is empirically undeniable is the persistence and strength of the attachment which people in modern industrial societies have to music, both as 'consumers' and performers. It is this attachment which sustains the recording industry, and also ensures that, for example, in every town and city in the developed world – and many outside it – there are dozens, sometimes hundreds or thousands, of aspiring musicians in a wide variety of styles (see Finnegan, 1989). For the sociologist this phenomenon has a particular fascination. Why should music matter so much in contemporary culture? I have suggested that this may well have something to do with the effectiveness of music, not in stupefying the masses (as Adorno thought) not in either representing or challenging conventional morality (though it can contribute to these things), but quite simply in its ability to give people a sense of secure identity – whatever they wish that to be – and a sense of belonging at a time when the accelerating pace of economic and technological change is making it increasingly difficult to achieve continuity and stability in social life (Sennett, 1998). Some remarks by Bernard Sumner, a musician who achieved success in the late 1980s with the Manchester bands Joy Division and, later, New Order, may serve to illustrate the point. Sumner described the effects of the dispersion and physical destruction of the community in which he spent his childhood thus:

> By the age of twenty-two, I'd had quite a lot of loss in my life. The place where I used to live, where I had my happiest memories, all that had gone. All that was left was a chemical factory. I realised then that I could never go back to that happiness. So there's this void. For me Joy Division was about the death of my community and my childhood. (quoted in Haslam, 1999: xxiv)

From this perspective music appears not as the manipulator of passive victims, but as a means through which individuals can actively construct a sense of self and proclaim a distinct identity. Indeed, one of the most promising areas of recent research in this field has been the concern to link the evident fragmentation of musical styles to the active process of identity construction which, it has been argued, is increasingly typical of late-modern, mass consumption societies, particularly in view of the declining salience of such 'traditional' factors as class, occupation, locality and gender (Bennett, 1999: 606). It may be added that such a view of the fragmentary and constructed nature of the self is neither new or distinctively post-modern: in his classic essay on the 'Metropolis and Mental Life' (first published in 1903), Georg Simmel suggested that while the modern city exposes the individual to intense psychological pressures, it also affords liberation from traditional community roles and thus an unprecedented degree of personal freedom (Simmel, 1997: 180). Simmel goes on to anticipate a strong theme in post-modern thought by remarking on the ways in which, through their choice of conduct and consumption patterns, people may seek both to assert their identities and secure social distinction (*ibid.*: 183). In the context of the present discussion, the significant point is the extent to which, a century after Simmel was writing, music – and especially popular music – has become an important means by which people seek to achieve these ends. Why else does Elvis Presley remain 'The King' to those whose teenage rebellion took place more than forty years ago? Why else do the fans of Heavy Metal stay attached to their guitar heroes three decades after they first appeared?

Moreover, despite the continuing trend towards global concentration in the music business, with four international corporations now selling around 80% of all recorded popular music (Martin, forthcoming) an unprecedented range and diversity of music styles is now available on the market (see Lopes, 1992). Technological developments, too, can have the effect of empowering individuals in ways which give them the potential to resist the 'culture industry'. Since the 1970s the increasing availability of low-cost recording equipment has meant that aspiring musicians are no longer dependent on orthodox companies in order to record their own music; moreover, the extent of small-scale, independent production of 'dance' music discovered in one study led its authors to question the validity of the distinction between 'producers' and 'consumers' (Smith and Maughan, 1997: 48). By the end of the twentieth century, too, the Internet was becoming recognised as a potential threat to the recording companies' control of distribution networks. These are excellent examples of the way in which, as Marx put it, constant development of 'material productive forces' (or technology) inevitably undermines the 'existing [social] relations of production', and as such may be considered one of the inevitable contradictions of capitalism. Here, however, the essential point is that the availability of a wide diversity of music styles, and of access to recording and distribution, are important in that they give people increasing opportunities to select, construct and express through music a range of possible cultural identities. Indeed, one of the notable developments facilitated by new technologies for recording, producing and reproducing music has been the increasing involvement of young people as producers of their own sounds and aural environments (Willis, 1990: 82). I will return to this point below.

## Music in social context

The discussion so far has suggested that the 'message' model of communication which underlies much thinking about music, manipulation and mass culture is sociologically unsatisfactory, and that a concern with the examination of actual music use by real people requires consideration of the wider context of social activities in which music is always embedded. As noted above, several authors have highlighted the significance of music as a medium through which individuals and groups seek to sustain and assert a sense of identity, often in the context of institutional changes and cultural instability which threaten the continuity of their experience. To amplify the above remarks, even if briefly, it seems appropriate to provide some examples of recent studies in which music may be seen to play a role in the establishment of social relationships and the formation of personal identities.

Andy Bennett (1997; 1999; 2000) has provided instructive accounts of ways in which musical involvements can provide individuals with a sense of secure identity, and how such involvements are bound up with wider complexes of activity. For example, ethnographic examination of the 'pub rock scene' – as opposed to generalised assumptions about the 'effects' of popular music – led Bennett to reject the notion that the 'consumers' of popular music were being manipulated by the 'culture industry':

> while the popular cultural industries may provide social actors with a common stock of cultural resources, the way such resources are subsequently re-worked as collective sensibilities will in every instance depend upon the conditions of locality, that is, upon the particular social discourses and practices which inform the daily lives of individuals in the places where they live. (Bennett, 1997: 98)

Similar themes are pursued in Bennett's account of the ways in which popular music styles are used by young people in the process of establishing and sustaining their own sense of identity. Bennett emphasises the sociological importance of the links between popular music and personal identity. Moreover, the use of music by young people is both rooted in their local social environment and is essentially *active*. Thus Bennett is critical of theories of globalisation (and, by implication, 'mass culture' theories) which diagnose not only the homogenisation of cultural experience but the reduction of individuals to passive consumers, and here his argument is entirely consistent with Honneth's view of the 'sociological deficit' inherent in the mass culture thesis. Although Bennett accepts that young people do make use of ' . . . musical and stylistic resources appropriated from the global culture industries . . . ', in practice it is in the contexts provided by 'local' networks of association that actions and identities are formulated (Bennett, 2000: 197).

This emphasis on the active constitution of a sense of identity in the context of local cultural environments has been an important element in the influential work of Paul Willis, and he too has placed considerable emphasis on the significance of music in this process. Given the erosion of traditional institutions and the continuing degradation of work, it is increasingly only in their so-called 'leisure' time that young people have the chance to establish a sense of identity and exercise their 'creative symbolic activities' (1990: 15). While it is true that the clothes, the videos, the computer games, the magazines, the radio and TV shows – and the music – which form such a large part of 'common culture' are the mass-produced commodities of the culture industry, Willis is concerned with the 'grounded aesthetics' through which the meanings of such items are 'selected, reselected, highlighted, and recomposed' (*ibid.*: 21) by young people so as to create their symbolic worlds, rather than simply being 'received' by passive consumers. Indeed, for Willis: 'Consumerism now has to be understood as an active, not a passive process. Its play includes work' (*ibid.*: 18). As far as popular music is concerned:

> The cultural meaning of Bros or Morrissey, house or hip hop, Tiffany or Tracey Chapman, isn't simply the result of record company sales campaigns, it depends too on consumer abilities to make value judgements, to talk knowledgeably and passionately about their genre tastes, to place music in their lives, to use commodities and symbols for their own imaginative purposes and to generate their own particular grounded aesthetics. These processes involves the exercise of critical, discriminating choices and uses which disrupt taste categories and "ideal" modes of consumption promoted by the leisure industry and break up its superimposed definitions of musical meaning. (*ibid.*: 60)

Given the strong claims that Willis makes, it is worth noting that his conclusions are based on many years of ethnographic work among young people, in marked contrast to the theoretical presuppositions and speculations of the critics of 'mass culture' in general and the music business in particular. Indeed, just as Hirsch's studies demonstrated back in the 1960s, detailed empirical investigations of real people in real situations tend to reveal a rather different picture from that painted by the 'grand theorists' of mass culture.

## Conclusion

I have suggested that general theoretical accounts which regard music in general and popular music in particular as a means by which people may be manipulated or controlled have tended to oversimplify a set of relationships which is far more complex – and far more interesting from a sociological point of view – than the theorists have allowed. Often such accounts rest on various *assumptions* about how music 'works', or how it has the effects it is supposed to have, which are not well supported by the (relatively few) empirical studies of actual music use. Such studies, however, do lead us to an understanding of music as inevitably implicated in wider configurations of social action in which there may be a reciprocal determination of meanings between the music and the activities. Such a perspective suggests the inadequacies of simple models of musical 'effects' which presuppose the communication of a message from sender to receiver. In contrast, it also suggests the sociological importance of examining the actual situations in which people collaboratively generate the symbolic worlds in which meanings and interpretations can be sustained. As Hennion and Meadel have put it: 'Culture is not the content of a message which follows a linear path through production and consumption; it does not force entry into people's lives, but is a material constructed by a constant process of iteration between all the actors' (1986: 284).

So in opposition to the notion that music somehow 'acts on' a more-or-less passive listener, I have emphasised some of the ways in which people may actively use music in the process of establishing and maintaining a distinct sense of self, an identity which, though constantly evolving, provides both psychological security and a feeling of belonging to a wider community. Just as Foucault realised the limitations of his early work on manipulation and various 'techniques of domination', and turned to the investigation of 'techniques of the self' (McNay, 1994: 134), so we are now, I suggest, in a position to move beyond the straightforward idea of social control as either external or internal coercion (or some mixture of the two), and to examine the ways in which the 'effects' of music are generated in and through the activities of real people in specific social situations. Moreover, some recent studies have begun to explore the *active* process of identity-formation associated with modern patterns of popular music use in relation to lifestyle choices and selective commodity consumption.

However, as I suggested earlier, this does not mean that individuals have the ability to define meanings or construct selves entirely as they please: on the contrary, it is precisely in the engagement between individual subjectivities and the 'objective facticities' (Berger and Luckmann, 1991: 78) of the social world that the process of self-formation is carried out. Moreover, while I would wish to emphasise the active aspect of this process, and the relative autonomy of individuals as they seek to 'identify' themselves, it must be recognised that all these activities are pursued, and 'ways of being' are achieved, in an engagement with the cultural and institutional parameters which constitute the 'objective facticities' of global capitalism. Willis is surely right to emphasise the active and creative ways in which young people use music (among other cultural resources) as an important means through which they 'make sense of the social world and their place within it' (1990: 82), claiming and proclaiming particular identities, asserting differences, and experiencing a sense of belonging in a world of increasing insecurities. However, as Willis also notes, the activities which sustain such 'grounded aesthetics' may be primarily defensive, in that above all they ' . . . enable survival: contesting or expressing feelings of boredom, fear, powerlessness and frustration. They can be used as affective strategies to cope with, manage, and make bearable the experiences of everyday life' (*ibid.*: 64). Described in this way, they appear as coping strategies, rather than resistant or even radical ones. I suspect, therefore, that for Critical Theorists the 'symbolic creativity' which Willis identifies might simply be regarded as a more sophisticated form of 'mass deception' in which, for example, the achievement of a sense of distinct identity is little more than a consequence of what Adorno called 'pseudo-individualisation' (Adorno, 2002 [1941]: 445). 'The peculiarity of the self is a monopoly commodity determined by society; it is falsely represented as natural' (Adorno and Horkheimer, 1979: 154). For the Critical Theorist, it matters little whether we buy CDs of rap or heavy metal, girl bands or grunge, acid jazz or disco, as long as we keep buying *something*, first because in doing so we sustain the culture industry's profitable production of commodities, and second because any of these musical 'styles' can form the basis of a symbolic discourse which, far from illuminating the fundamental economic and political relations of society, in fact obscures and mystifies them.

For some, therefore, there may be a temptation to conclude that Adorno and the Critical Theorists were right all along, not only in talking of the manipulation of consumers by the 'culture industry', but in pointing to ways in which we actively collude in our own subordination. Indeed, Marcuse's concept of 'repressive desublimation' was intended to describe the process in which people ' . . . buy into their own control by consuming ever larger quantities of goods on the promise that such consumption equals liberty' (How, 2003: 85). From this perspective, studies of popular music use, such as those mentioned above, might be criticised on the grounds that – however actively people are shown to be appropriating and redefining music for their own purposes – the 'symbolic worlds' and 'identities' which emerge in the end represent opportunities to escape from the conflicts and constraints of the real world. Oppositional youth subcultures, for example, may represent coping strategies rather than genuine efforts to subvert the *status quo* (Willis, 1990: 64). Similarly the creation of 'identities' through lifestyle choices implies that the price of escape from the former constraints of class cultures is an acceptance of the ideology of consumerism (see Bennett, 1999: 607–608).

Yet, however tempting, the Critical Theorists' conclusion remains sociologically unsatisfactory. As the remarks above have suggested, their diagnosis of the culture of modernity rests on the notion that we now live in what Marcuse called a 'one-dimensional' world, a world in which appearances are taken to be the realities that, in fact, they obscure and a world in which genuinely oppositional thinking is almost impossible. In this respect, Critical Theory echoes Marx's concern with the alienation of humanity entailed by modern capitalism, taking it to be an economic system created by people, but which now controls them, and which they regard as immutable. Yet, as Simmel argued nearly a century ago, *all* cultural production has this coercive aspect:

The 'fetishistic character' which Marx attributed to economic objects in the epoch of commodity production is *only a particularly modified instance of this general fate of the contents of our culture*. These contents are subject to the paradox – and increasingly so as culture develops – that they are indeed created by human subjects and are meant for human subjects, but follow an immanent developmental logic in the intermediate form of objectivity . . . and thereby become alienated from both their origin and their purpose. (Simmel, 1997 [1911]: 70; emphasis added).

In other words, all human beings, whether they live in a capitalist society or any other, confront a world of 'objective facticities', whether institutional, ideological or linguistic. Even the language we use, says Simmel, can be experienced as ' . . . an alien natural force, which distorts and curtails not only our utterances but also our innermost intentions' (*ibid.*: 67). That is, the particular form of language we have to use, while created by humans, has, through the process of its objectification, become a constraint on the way we think, limiting us to certain concepts, ideas and modes of expression while denying alternative possibilities. In such ways, Simmel suggests, the objective forms of culture enter into the constitution of subjectivity in every society.

The problem is that positing a 'one-dimensional' culture and the general condition of alienation presupposes some sort of non-alienated human condition or a pre-social, essential subjectivity which could be recovered. Simmel's point is that the process of objectification (or alienation) is an inevitable consequence of *all* cultural production. Developing this theme, Collins argues that there has never been a society in which people lived in an 'idyllically unexploited situation' (1986: 252). Indeed, for him the very idea is a Romantic myth (*ibid.*: 259), and Collins, like several more recent authors, regards the array of commodities available to modern consumers as presenting opportunities which were simply not available in earlier times:

> People who carry around cassette recorders or radios blaring out popular music are literally wrapping themselves in a cocoon of self-chosen meaning almost every moment of the day; in a pre-modern society they were subject to authoritarian scheduling of religious ceremonial, at which attendance was not free but enforced. (Collins, 1986: 254)

Far from being manipulated by the forces of the culture industry, then, the consumers of popular music are seen as having an unprecedented degree of control over their own 'means of ritual production' (*ibid.*) What's more, Collins suggests that the significance of this control is overlooked by intellectuals who are dismissive of 'popular culture' and committed to the bourgeois concept of 'the so-called high arts'. Clearly, there are echoes here of the argument between Adorno and Benjamin (see Leppert, 2002: 240–249) over the potential for technologically based mass culture to be regressive or progressive. Although the continuing ramifications of this debate cannot be pursued in this chapter, I hope it is now evident why sociologists should be suspicious of the assumption that people are manipulated by music, and why they have been increasingly interested in the various ways in which individuals and groups actively appropriate the musical products of the culture industry for their own purposes.

Part II

# The sound of social stratification: the din of inequity

# 5

# Class, culture and concerts

## Introduction

For Pierre Bourdieu, musical taste was a highly significant indicator of a person's position in the socio-economic order. Near the beginning of *Distinction*, he reports the outcome of a large-scale French survey which led to the identification of three 'zones' of musical taste, which 'roughly correspond to educational levels and social classes'. 'Legitimate' taste (for example the works of 'serious' composers) was found to increase markedly with level of education and thus 'was highest in those fractions of the dominant class that are richest in educational capital'. 'Middle-brow' tastes (such as for *Rhapsody in Blue* or the singers of chansons) was most prevalent within the middle class, while 'popular' taste (that is, 'songs totally devoid of artistic ambition or pretension') was 'most frequent among the working classes and varies in inverse ratio to educational capital' (Bourdieu, 1984: 16). On this evidence, Bourdieu finds confirmation of his general thesis linking socio-economic position and a person's 'habitus', and asserts boldly that ' . . . nothing more clearly affirms one's class, nothing more infallibly classifies, than tastes in music' (*ibid.*: 18).

Bourdieu's presentation of a close correspondence between levels of educational and cultural capital, on the one hand, and a hierarchy of musical styles and genres, on the other, is problematic in a number of respects, and in this chapter I will pursue some of the issues which arise. Nevertheless, there can be no doubt that his view of an identifiable association between general patterns of social stratification and musical tastes – as a significant element in the fabrication of lifestyles – is widely accepted. The consumption of 'classical' or 'serious' art-music in various ways – such as concerts, discs and radio – has been regarded as an activity characteristic of members of upper- and middle-class groups, while the very term 'popular' (often used as a pejorative opposite) conveys the sense of music made for, and often by, the masses. Empirical evidence, such as Bourdieu's, as well as established patterns of concert-going and the purchase of recordings, appear to confirm the relationship between social class and musical taste in general terms (see below, pp. 88–89). In what follows, however, I am less concerned to consider the details of this relationship than to examine some attempts to explain it, in particular the view that it is a consequence of the ways in which certain kinds of music express or articulate the values, or 'world-view', of distinct social groups. Specifically, the discussion will focus on the idea, elaborated in the work of some influential theorists, that there is a correspondence between the formal qualities of 'serious' music and the culture of dominant social classes.

Indeed, Bourdieu himself suggests that in the important matter of securing and displaying social distinction, 'legitimate' forms of music are highly salient for those occupying advantageous positions in the socio-economic order: 'as the objective distance from necessity grows, lifestyles increasingly become the product of what Weber calls a "stylisation of life", a systematic commitment which orients and organises the most diverse practices' (Bourdieu, 1984: 55–56). In effect, the exercise of taste, in the form of the 'aesthetic disposition', is 'a distinctive expression of a privileged position in social space', which is far more sociologically important, and much less innocent, than it may appear, since the incompatibilities and frictions between contrasting lifestyles amount to ' . . . one of the strongest barriers between the classes; class endogamy is evidence of this' (*ibid.*: 56). From this perspective, the nature of 'legitimate' music as a sonic, non-representational medium is crucial; it symbolises a spirituality which proclaims distance from the 'materialist coarseness' of mundane matters and, being a 'pure' art form, is unconstrained by the need to express 'social' messages. Thus music 'represents the most radical and the most absolute form of the negation of the world, and especially of the social world, which the bourgeois ethos tends to demand of all forms of art' (*ibid.*: 19).

The above remarks may convey something of the way in which Bourdieu sought to explain the persistence of the association between patterns of social stratification and the hierarchy of musical styles, and why he regards 'legitimate' music as so important in the processes through which the higher social strata attempt to display social distinction. There is, he claims, a deep affinity between the perceived 'spiritual' nature of Western art music and the 'bourgeois ethos' which demands the renunciation of the material world; in this sense, 'all concerts are sacred' (*ibid.*) Others have developed this theme in a somewhat Durkheimian way, arguing, for example, that the conventional symphony concert is to be understood as a ritual in which the dominant class is worshipping itself. For Small, the symphony concert is 'a celebration, undertaken not fully awares, of the shared mythology and values of a certain group within our deeply fragmented society' (1987: 6). And Small is in no doubt about the identity of this 'certain group':

> The whole event that is a symphony concert as it takes place today might have been designed and indeed was designed, even if not necessarily consciously, as an instrument for the reassurance of the industrial upper and middle classes, for the presentation to themselves of their values and their sense of ideal relationships, and for persuading those who take part that their values, their concepts of relationship, are true and will last. (Small, 1998: 193)

In Small's analysis, it is the whole event, rather than the works performed in it, which constitutes the essential ritual (*ibid.*: 185). Yet the music itself conforms to a very specific pattern: chosen from a very limited 'canon' of great works, repeated often, and – in the case of the symphony – organised around a narrative which tells of the overcoming of challenges to established order by the forces of 'logic, clarity, rationality'. In this way, for Small, the symphony is a sonic representation, and celebration, of Enlightenment values, patriarchal authority, and the power of the bourgeoisie (*ibid.*: 188).

Thus Small develops the theme that the public concert of 'serious' music should be understood as a significant ritual in which dominant social groups reaffirm their shared values and sense of order. The analysis, moreover, echoes Durkheim in another fundamental way, in that the details of particular cultural elements – in this case institutionalised musical conventions – are interpreted as manifestations of general underlying value patterns: for Small, indeed, the canon of symphonic music 'partakes of the nature of the great metanarrative' which 'appeals so strongly to members of the Western industrial bourgeoisie' (*ibid.*: 187–188). This is an idea which has been elaborated in the work of other theorists; both Shepherd (1991) and McClary (2000 and 1991) have sought to understand the connections between social class and musical tastes in terms of specific resonances between group cultural values and identifiable qualities of the music itself. Like Small, Shepherd hears the established conventions of functional tonality, on which the Western art-music tradition is based, as encoding the 'industrial world-sense' which is the dominant ideology of modern capitalist societies (1991: 122). For McClary, such conventions are in no way 'purely musical' procedures; on the contrary, they are 'intensely ideological formations' (2000: 5). In her view, Western tonality

> constructed musical analogs to such emerging ideals as rationality, individualism, progress, and centred subjectivity. Far from merely reflecting their times, these musical procedures participated actively in shaping habits of thought on which the modern era depended'. (*ibid.*: 65)

In linking the rise and development of tonality to the historical trajectory of the bourgeoisie, of course, these authors invoke the 'grand narrative' (Lyotard, 1984), which is implicit in Adorno's understanding of the course of Western musical history (Williams, 2001: 12–14), and his belief that, if correctly deciphered, a piece of music – like all artworks – can be revealed as a ' . . . monad whose internal tensions express the larger sociohistorical process' (Zuidervaart, 1991: 71). Running through these accounts, then, is the idea that the values and cultural commitments of dominant groups are in some way represented, articulated or encrypted in the music itself, or, to use Adorno's preferred term, that they are 'immanent' in it. Thus the congruence between the pattern of social stratification and the hierarchy of musical styles has been explained in terms of the way in which musical styles are heard as sonic representations of cultural values.

The remainder of this chapter is concerned with some of the implications of these arguments, which will be considered further, as will some of the empirical evidence which has been used to support the idea of a continuing link between class position and musical taste. It will be suggested, however, that the empirical data reveal a rather more complicated situation than the theorists have presented, and that the connection between social stratification and musical styles is looser, and in many ways more interesting, than would appear from accounts such as Bourdieu's.

## Theoretical perspectives

As I suggested above, the idea that specific cultural patterns represent the core values of groups or whole societies owes much to Durkheim. More recent theorists, however, have developed the idea in a neo-Marxian way, suggesting that established discursive patterns may ultimately be traced back to the material or political interests of dominant groups. In Marx and Engels' famous formulation, the 'ideas of the ruling class are in every epoch the ruling ideas' since the class that controls the material means of production also controls the means of intellectual production (1974: 64). Building on this, much work in cultural studies has been influenced by Gramsci's concept of hegemony and by Foucault's concern with the practices (like functional tonality in music, which also flourished in the 'classical age') that produced 'subjected and practised bodies' (Foucault, 1991: 138). In such perspectives, domination is maintained only ultimately, and occasionally, by coercion; for most of the time it rests on consent, since power is ' . . . invisible, disseminated through the texture of social life and thus "naturalised" as custom, habit, spontaneous practice' (Eagleton, 1991: 116). This sort of idea is evident in several influential contributions to the 'social' analysis of music in Western societies: the now-taken-for-granted system of tonal music (which sounds 'natural' to Western ears) is heard neither as the sonic form of natural forces, nor as the culmination of human progress in music-making, but rather as a particular set of conventions – 'intensely ideological formations', in McClary's words – which represent the dominant forces in the culture, established in the eighteenth century and increasingly challenged since the twentieth (McClary, 2000: 5).

There are unmistakeable echoes of Adorno here. Despite his fierce opposition to the notion, evident in some contemporary Marxist analyses, that artworks reflect or convey the ideology of social classes (particularly the dominant class), and to the widespread assumption that history could be grasped as a unified process, there *is* clearly a 'grand narrative' which governs Adorno's view of the relationship between music and society. Many of his musical analyses focus on the works of successive European composers as representations of various stages in the transition from liberal democracy to the 'crisis of individuation' and the rise of totalitarianism (Witkin, 1998: 157; Martin, 1995: 103ff). The point may be illustrated by

Adorno's treatment of crucial figures along the way. At the dawn of modernity, the works of J. S. Bach show the composer emancipating himself from the demands of tradition or authority (Adorno, 1967), with the process culminating in Beethoven. Beethoven was a figure of immense significance for Adorno, his life coinciding with the 'classical' period of Western art music and the high tide of bourgeois humanism. From Adorno's perspective, it is not surprising that at the beginning of the twenty-first century Beethoven's symphonies remain firmly established as fundamental items in the classical 'canon', since in their formal properties they represent 'the dream of all bourgeois individualism':

> Adorno claims that the popularity of Beethoven's second-period com-
> positions with audiences in his own day was probably due to the extent
> to which they embodied, in music, the structural dynamics of . . . an
> identity between individual and society – to the extent, that is, that
> they inscribed bourgeois ideology. (Witkin, 1998: 62–63)

Yet this happy reconciliation was doomed by the inexorable progress of the 'dialectic of enlightenment', and Adorno hears the abrupt stylistic changes in Beethoven's last pieces as prefiguring the individual's loss of autonomy (Subotnik, 1991). From then on, works representing the free individual or the harmonious social totality are to be regarded as ideological mystifications; since Beethoven's time such works have come to function as affirmative ideology rather than authentic – that is, critical – art (Horkheimer and Adorno, 1973: 109–110).

Just as the ideals of bourgeois individualism were contradicted by what Adorno saw as the objective tendency towards totalitarianism, so the system of tonal music which Bach had done so music to establish was in crisis, and in Mahler (1860–1911) Adorno found ' . . . a metaphor of the unattainability of a harmonious, reconciled totality . . . '. Like many others he heard a profound pessimism in Mahler's works, and he is unusually explicit about its implications:

> In Mahler's music the incipient impotence of the individual becomes
> conscious of itself. Aware of the imbalance between himself and the
> superior might of society, he awakens to a sense of his own utter unim-
> portance. (Adorno, 1992: 97)

It was in Schoenberg, though, that the crisis was most dramatically expressed, since he, above all, confronted the breakdown of tonality and in his own works produced, for Adorno, both a dialectical critique of conventional compositional principles (and thus of bourgeois ideology) and an expression of the *Angst* which accompanied the eclipse of the 'sovereign subject' (Jay, 1984: 150). In fact it was Schoenberg's critical, radical response to the musical 'crisis of tonality' which provided Adorno with a model of the tasks of critical social theory and in particular the importance of the critique of ideology (Buck-Morss, 1977: 15).

Adorno's view of the connections between tonal music and bourgeois ideology are sociologically problematic in a number of respects which cannot be pursued here (see Martin, 1995: 111ff). In the present context, however, the essential point is his assertion of a close correspondence between the elements of bourgeois ideology and the basic characteristics and procedures of tonal music, a correspondence most clearly evident in Beeethoven's middle-period works. For Adorno, Beethoven had produced the

> quintessential realisation in music of an apparent reconciliation between the collective force of society, which [Adorno] identified with 'form' in music, and the spontaneous movement of free individuals – represented in music by the sensuous particulars or elements, the motives and materials which the composer forms into musical works. (Witkin, 1998: 63)

As suggested above, this idea of a correspondence between bourgeois ideology and formal musical procedures has found expression in some more recent theoretical contributions, which aim to specify precisely the ways in which these procedures in themselves represent basic elements of bourgeois ideology. Indeed, for McClary all kinds of music, seen as particular bundles of conventions, express in their formal procedures the values and ideals of the groups which create them:

> African American music relies heavily on conventions – conventions that carry sedimented within them a worldview that has proved to be both durable and flexible . . . But no less does European music inscribe a world through its conventions and foundational assumptions. (McClary, 2000: 28–29)

For McClary it is largely through these presuppositions and taken-for-granted, normal procedures that music has its effects; they are the 'seemingly automatic dimensions' (*ibid.*: 6) which resonate with particular cultural values, and which therefore affirm and reinforce such values:

The power of music – both for dominant cultures and for those who
would promote alternatives – resides in its ability to shape the ways we
experience our bodies, emotions, subjectivities, desires, and social relations. And to study such effects demands that we recognize the ideological basis of music's operations – its cultural constructedness.
(McClary, 2000: 6–7)

As I have argued elsewhere (e.g. Martin, 1995: 156) there is in this
sort of formulation a distinct risk that a theoretical approach which
initially emphasises 'cultural constructedness' will relapse into a simple behaviourism in granting to music an 'ability to shape the way
we experience our bodies'. My main concern here, however, is to
establish that, like Adorno, McClary hears music not as 'pure' or
'absolute' but as inherently ideological, and that its ideological
'work' is carried out through its fundamental conventions and normal procedures. In this way, then, these theorists have sought to
explain the persistence of the links between the 'classical' art-music
tradition and class-based centres of power and control in Western
societies. This is taken to be more than a matter of prestigious patterns of cultural consumption, though that is important – as I shall
suggest below. What is being asserted is that symbolic elements of
the dominant ideology are inherent *in the music itself*. Moreover,
for all the theoretical sophistication displayed by these authors, it
will be evident by now that their accounts rest ultimately on a fairly
straightforward view of the evolution of Western art music as a consequence of capitalist industrialisation. Adorno's implicit narrative
of the rise and fall of bourgeois individualism is – rather paradoxically, given the intricacy of his formulations – a clear expression of
this view. However, and this is the theme which will be developed in
the remainder of this chapter, there is now an accumulation of historical and sociological evidence which suggests that the relationship
between music and social class, both during the initial period of
industrialisation and since, was rather more complex than these theoretical accounts allow (Elias, 1993: 24). It is therefore appropriate
to reconsider the notions that music bears some sort of ideological
message, that there is an identifiable 'structural homology' between
forms of music and forms of social organisation (Shepherd, 1991:
89), and that 'nothing more infallibly classifies, than tastes in music'
(Bourdieu, 1984: 18).

## The middle class and musical activity

Studies of musical life in various phases of the eighteenth and nineteenth centuries throw much light on the relationship between music and class in a crucial period of social transformation (see, among others, Broyles, 1992 and 1991; Burchell, 1996; DeNora, 1995 and 1991; DiMaggio, 1982; Johnson, 1995; Levine, 1988; McVeigh, 1993; Tawa, 1989; W. Weber, 2001, 1994, 1992, 1977, 1975). Inevitably, several of these are much concerned with the challenge which the emerging bourgeoisie posed to the increasingly insecure European aristocracy, though none suggests that there was a straightforward transfer of power from the old order to the new. On the basis of his examination of concert life in London, Paris and Vienna during the 1830s and 1840s William Weber concluded – as have other historians – that there was not so much a conflict between the classes as a gradual accommodation which resulted in the ' . . . merger of the aristocracy and the upper-middle class into a single upper class' (1975: 118). 'Indeed', writes Weber, 'it is astounding how smoothly the upper classes have either guided the transformation or prevented themselves from being hurt by it' (*ibid.*: 115), and when the details of the process are examined, it becomes very difficult to identify specific classes or class groupings with particular kinds of music. As Weber suggests when referring to an earlier period in London's musical history, the pattern of class stratification and the hierarchy of musical styles may vary independently (1992: 1). This topic will be considered further below. At the moment, the essential point is the finding of such studies that the 'middle class' cannot be considered a homogeneous 'taste public' (Weber, 1975: 10). Moreover, they cast considerable doubt on the assumption that members of the bourgeoisie responded positively to the representation of their ideology which was 'inscribed' in the great works of 'heroic' figures such as Beethoven.

In fact, studies of the reception of Beethoven's music, during his lifetime and after, offer very little support to the notion that his works resonated with the cultural values of the emerging bourgeoisie. As noted above, for Adorno (and others) Beethoven was the composer who above all embodied, in his life and his work, the ideology of the new middle class. Yet, as Subotnik put it, 'Adorno does not examine empirically the actual response to Beethoven in the latter's own lifetime' (1991: 305). However, DeNora (1995) did investigate the circumstances of Beethoven's rise, during his early years in Vienna, from an unknown outsider to a 'great' composer of 'serious' music, and the results of her research are in various ways difficult to reconcile with Adorno's view. De Nora's basic thesis is that:

> a serious-music ideology, which took as its exemplars Beethoven and reconstituted, more explicitly "learned" and grandiose conceptions of Mozart and Haydn, emerged during the 1790s in Vienna, and that this ideology was primarily subscribed to by the old aristocrats, not the middle class. (DeNora, 1995: 35)

Why did the 'old aristocrats' adopt this new ideology, and embrace the challenging music of the young Beethoven? DeNora's answer centres on the aristocrats' efforts to maintain their elite status in the face of the growth of the prosperous new middle class; to do so they switched from a 'quantitative' strategy of social exclusion (maintaining their own orchestras at considerable expense, with diminishing returns in terms of the social distinction thus conferred), to a 'qualitative' one (*ibid.*: 48). Increasingly, this involved the adoption of an ideology of 'serious music' which involved, among other things, 'an appreciation of musical complexity' and a rejection of the more 'inclusive aesthetic' which accepted such lesser forms as Italian opera, and shorter, simple-textured pieces (DeNora, 1991: 324, 314). In doing so, the Viennese aristocrats unwittingly gave a powerful boost to the development of the ideology of 'serious' music which was to have such pervasive effects in the years to come. Indeed, as Johnson has shown, the few early performances of Beethoven in Paris were not well received, and his success there had to wait until a more widespread acceptance of 'absolute' music had occurred (Johnson, 1995: 258, 276).

But this acceptance came a generation later. The implication of Johnson's and DeNora's studies are that in his early years Beethoven was not acclaimed as the quintessential composer of the bourgeoisie, but, on the contrary, was recognised as possessing a talent which was configured and promoted by the *aristocrats* of the old order, for the purpose of sustaining their social distinction. It was they, not the 'new' middle classes, who were his patrons and who constructed the notion of his 'genius':

> Praising Beethoven was simultaneously, albeit implicitly, praising his aristocratic patrons. Through the pursuit of the greatest composers

(whose status depended on recognition by aristocratic powerful patrons), Vienna's social aristocrats could themselves be identified as aristocrats of taste. (DeNora, 1995: 48)

Moreover, the 'ideology of serious music', and the idea of the 'great' composer – now taken-for-granted elements of the Western art-music tradition – were only just taking shape, and 'independently of Beethoven' (*ibid.*: 58). Within this emerging discourse his 'genius' was configured by his aristocratic patrons.

Further, an examination of the response to Beethoven in his early years also calls into question the assumption that it was primarily the middle class who appreciated his music. Flamboyant performers and light operetta were what really filled the halls, and DeNora suggests that the 'serious' works of Beethoven (and the 'reconstituted' Haydn and Mozart) would have been 'beyond the horizons of most middle-class musical experience' at the time (1991: 342). Setting aside his modern reputation, it is important to recognise how different, and difficult, Beethoven sounded to contemporaries, both as a pianist (DeNora, 1995: 118) and as a composer, with one critic complaining (in 1799) that his work displayed 'a striving for strange modulations, an objection to customary associations, a heaping up of difficulties until one loses all patience and enjoyment' (*ibid.*: 181). What is certain is that the great majority of Beethoven's concerts in his early career were organised by the 'old aristocrats' (*ibid.*: 30). Although 'the most distinctly middle class of Vienna's concert locations at this time was the Leopoldstadt theater', there is no record of Beethoven's music ever being performed there (*ibid.*: 31). At one of the other 'socially mixed' concert venues, Jahn's Restaurant, Beethoven's name appears on only three programmes (in 1797, 1798 and 1806) and he was clearly 'not part of the staple repertory' (*ibid.*: 33).

In short, the evidence suggests that Beethoven's early acceptance in Vienna owed much to aristocratic patronage and the development of the 'ideology of serious music', rather than any perceived resonance between the music and the world-view of the new bourgeoisie. In examining correspondences between patterns of social stratification and the hierarchy of musical taste, therefore, it may be more useful to examine the ways in which music is defined and used by particular groups – that is, with the mode of its appropriation – than to assume that there is a 'homology' between musical and social structures. This point will be considered further below.

## Social class and musical tastes

I have dwelt on the initial reception of Beethoven, and some of the issues it raises, since he occupies such a central position in Adorno's (and others') influential narrative of Western art music (see Williams, 2001: 43–44). In later years, it is incontestable that Beethoven and the other 'great' composers of the classical period did indeed become defined as expressing in their art the spirit of Enlightenment humanism, and widely celebrated for it. Moreover, as more recent studies have shown, there can be no doubt that the connection between the dominant social groups and 'classical' music has endured. In fact one such study has become something of a bench-mark for enquiries into the links between individuals' musical tastes and their socio-economic positions: the re-analysis of data from the 1982 Survey of Public Participation in the Arts in the USA by Peterson and Simkus (1992), which considers 'How musical tastes mark occupational status groups'. At first sight, these findings do indeed appear to support Bourdieu's idea of a close correspondence between class position and musical taste: 28.9% of people in the 'higher cultural' occupational groups, for example, said that classi-cal music was the style they liked best, while the figure for 'laborers' and 'farm laborers' was 0.0%. Moreover, with a few deviations, this percentage fell quite consistently from the 'higher' to the 'lower' occupational groups. By contrast, while only 8.9% of the 'higher cultural' groups liked country music best, 42.6% of 'farm laborers' did so, with the percentage choosing this style *rising* fairly consis-tently from the 'lower' to the 'higher' groups (*ibid.*: 158). Yet, as Peterson and Simkus are quick to point out, ' . . . even among the highest-status groups, only a minority participate in the elite arts' (*ibid.*: 152). What these figures show is that classical music was 'liked best' by well under a third of the 'higher cultural' groups, while in the 'higher managerial' category – presumably one in which bourgeois economic values are firmly established – the correspond-ing figure was less than one in ten (*ibid.*: 158). Given the cultural prestige of 'classical' music, its privileged position in educational curricula, and its extensive coverage in the 'serious' media, this could be regarded as a remarkably *low* level of support, and one which clearly does not accord with Bourdieu's notion of a close cor-respondence between cultural tastes and class position. Indeed, putting the matter another way, it might be said that while Bourdieu was right to claim that the majority of concert-goers (or museum attenders) are middle class, it does not follow that the majority of the middle class are concert-goers. I will return to this point.

In general, the US data examined by Peterson and Simkus indicate that while it is possible to identify the 'distinctive patterns of aesthetic preferences and rates of arts participation' of different occupational groups, a great deal is left unexplained, and the authors draw particular attention to 'two unexpected findings' (*ibid.*: 168). First, while there was general agreement that 'classical music' was the 'most prestigious' style, there was far less consensus on how other types of music should be ranked in the prestige hierarchy, with people's preferences clearly influenced by race, gender and age factors. This finding led Peterson and Simkus to propose that the 'taste hierarchy' should be visualised not so much as a 'slim column' representing a generally agreed rank order of styles, as ' . . . a pyramid with one elite taste at the top and more and more alternative forms at about the same level as one moves . . . toward its base' (*ibid.*). Moreover, these 'alternative forms' serve to distinguish groups 'defined by age, gender, race, religion, life-style, etc.', not in terms of vertical status *levels* but in terms of horizontal social *boundaries*. Secondly, Peterson and Simkus argue that the relatively high levels of appreciation of prestigious art forms found among high-status groups has to be understood in the context of the tendency for these groups to participate in a relatively wide range of cultural and leisure activities. Whereas in the past members of high-status groups were mostly 'univores', confining their attention to the 'high' arts, disdaining other forms and thereby claiming social distinction, a 'profound change' has taken place: such groups now claim social prestige by demonstrating their appreciation of a broad range of cultural activities and a consequent aesthetic pluralism. They are now 'omnivores' (*ibid.*: 169). Combining this idea with the notion of the taste 'pyramid' mentioned above, Peterson and Simkus summarise their results: 'The omnivore, we suggest, commands status by displaying any of a range of tastes as the situation may require, while the univore uses a particular taste to assert differences from others at approximately the same level holding a different group affiliation (*ibid.*: 170). In subsequent work, Peterson has developed the theme of the movement from 'snob' to 'omnivore' (Peterson and Kern, 1996: 900), and further statistical support for this trend was found in data collected ten years later. To some extent this is due to 'cohort replacement' (younger people with broader tastes moving into high-status social groups), but mostly it is because ' . . . in 1992 highbrows, on average, reported liking significantly more kinds of nonelite music of all genres than did highbrows a decade earlier and also that in 1992 highbrows are more omnivorous than non-highbrows'. For Peterson, this evidence 'may suggest the formulation of new rules governing symbolic boundaries' (*ibid.*: 904). Various social changes have contributed to this through the twentieth century, including generally higher levels of education and upward social mobility, urbanisation and increasing tolerance of others' cultural traditions, greater accessibility of art forms through the media, and the weakening of the boundary between 'high' art and other aesthetic traditions. Peterson concludes that the new 'omnivorous' pattern of cultural consumption is itself an effective strategy for the status group which is now in the ascendant:

> While snobbish exclusion was an effective marker of status in a relatively homogeneous and WASP-ish world that could enforce its dominance by force if necessary, omnivorous inclusion seems better adapted to an increasingly global world managed by those who make their way, in part, by showing respect for the cultural expressions of others. (*ibid.*: 906)

In general, Peterson views this 'change in the empirical criteria of status honor' (Peterson, 1997b: 76) as the most recent stage of the historical process in which dominant groups have attempted to establish and legitimate the bases of their cultural supremacy and social distinction in American society. While 'highbrow' exclusivity was once an effective strategy, the trend in the twentieth century (and particularly in its latter stages) was for those in high-status occupations to display more inclusive, tolerant and cosmopolitan attitudes. As far as music is concerned, one implication is that attachment to the 'great composers' of the Western art-music tradition and the 'canon' of their works has not so much been replaced as *supplemented* by an increasing openness to other genres and traditions. Jazz, blues and other once-marginalised styles deriving from African-American music, for example, are now accorded respect and even a measure of academic legitimacy, as are the musical traditions of other cultures (especially when marketed as 'World Music'), while rock and pop musicians are featured extensively in 'serious' newspapers. The idea is that eclectic, more open-minded attitudes are replacing the former exclusive attachment to Western classical music and as a consequence deep knowledge or devotion to it yield less prestige among high-status groups than (what Peterson has called) a 'passing knowledge' of a wide range of styles, which ' . . . may work as a social lubricant in a world where the ideal of democracy increasingly implies the principal equality of many cultural forms' (van Eijck, 2000: 219).

In one sense, the idea of the shift from 'snobbish' to 'omnivorous' patterns of cultural consumption seems to raise even more doubts about Bourdieu's notion of a close correspondence between the cultural and social 'fields' (van Eijck, 2001: 1163–1164) since attachment to 'high' culture is no longer seen as an effective means of securing social distinction. However, this shift may not seem a major difficulty if we recall, firstly, Peterson's emphasis on the ways in which the *criteria* of status honour have changed over time, and secondly his contention that these changing criteria do reflect real changes in the occupational sphere, from an era when the 'entrepreneurial upper-middle class' was dominant, to the ascendancy of 'today's new business-administrative class' (Peterson and Kern, 1996: 906). In other words, what is being suggested is consistent with Bourdieu's underlying theme that the correspondence between socio-economic groups and their cultural tastes and preferences persists, although these preferences have themselves changed as a result of broader social changes. Following Peterson's lead, other studies have developed this idea in relation to the idea of the emergence of a 'new' middle class, managerial rather than entrepreneurial in ideology. Its members are:

> younger, well-educated, often upwardly mobile persons whose lifestyles might be characterised as postmodern because their consumption patterns encompass leisure activities and preferences that seem incompatible from a traditionalist point of view, such as visiting amusement parks *and* museums or listening to classical *and* pop music. (van Eijck, 2001: 1167)

On the basis of his analysis of data from a large sample of the Dutch population, van Eijck identified two distinct clusters of tastes, one a 'highbrow' group with 'a liking for classical legitimate genres' which, using Bourdieu's terms, was concentrated in 'the dominant fraction of the dominant class', the other an 'ominvore' group with broader tastes, to be found largely within the 'dominated fraction of the dominant class or the new middle class' (*ibid.*: 1179). This latter group, with a 'broad cultural repertoire', was significantly younger, leading van Eijck to conclude that these results are 'not (just) an age effect, but rather indicative of a trend', and the emergence of 'a generation for whom the difference between elite culture and pop culture has little meaning' (*ibid.*: 1181).

A more detailed study, conducted in Manchester in the late 1990s, examined the attitudes and lifestyles of some members of this 'new middle class' who were mostly young, well-educated, and who had chosen to live in new apartments built as part of the city's regeneration programme (Wynne and O'Connor, 1998). Given the direction of the discussion above, it is not surprising to find that in general these people were 'enthusiastic' users of the city's cultural facilities, although their attendance at classical music concerts was 'limited' in comparison with their participation in other art forms, such as theatres, galleries and films. Moreover, and consistent with Peterson's notion of 'passing knowledge', most respondents had similarly limited knowledge of classical music – only 19 out of 148 interviewees could name more than six composers (*ibid.*: 847) – while it was also evident that 'pop music has ceased to signify "low" culture amongst the educated middle class' (*ibid.*: 857). Once again, then, there is little evidence of a general resonance between the values of this group and the qualities of 'classical' music. However, as I have suggested, findings such as these *could* be explained by treating them as an instance of the shift from 'snobs' to 'omnivores' which is ultimately rooted in the occupational culture of the new middle class. But it would be hard to reconcile such results with Bourdieu's notion of a close correspondence between pattern of social stratification and a single hierarchy of musical taste. It was suggested above that from a historical perspective the idea of a 'homology' between classical music and bourgeois values was always problematic; more recent empirical studies are consistent with this conclusion, showing, firstly, that while there is still *some* sort of association between social class position and musical taste, the relationship is neither particularly strong nor easy to specify with any degree of precision and, secondly, that the trend towards cultural 'omnivorousness' is likely to weaken it still further.

Moreover, Wynne and O'Connor's findings also call into question Bourdieu's idea that these respondents were in fact seeking to display social distinction through the strategy of accumulating 'cultural capital'. In each area of 'artistic' activity (music, theatre, films, etc.) there was a minority of 'serious enthusiasts' and around a quarter of the sample who had little or no involvement in cultural activities. This leaves a 'relatively large middle grouping experiencing a variety of cultural pursuits – a "sampling culture" constructed by individuals – in which established practices and competencies are rejected or, at least, no longer adhered to' (*ibid*.: 853). The respondents did 'exhibit high degrees of reflexivity and a concern with image and presentation of the self' and enjoyed the urban centre as a 'stage' for their lifestyle (*ibid*.: 855), yet this concern with what for Foucault were 'techniques or practices of the self' (McNay, 1994: 134) clearly did not involve the accumulation of traditional cultural capital as a strategy of displaying social distinction. As Wynne and O'Connor put it, 'the autodidact has turned flaneur' (1998: 857). For these 'postmodern' city-dwellers, identity is formed through lifestyle choices, not rooted in class relations (*ibid*.: 858), and their choices range across a broad range of cultural options, rather than exhibiting an orientation to a single aesthetic hierarchy.

These and other empirical findings (e.g. Kolb, 2001) not only cast doubt on Bourdieu's claim that social distinction is achieved by the appreciation of 'legitimate' high culture; but also seriously undermine his basic assumption that individuals are motivated primarily by the aim of securing and displaying social distinction, and that participation in high cultural activities is an effective strategy for doing this. Although, as I have suggested, Bourdieu does claim an affinity between bourgeois musical taste and the 'negation' of the material world (1984: 19), most of his work is concerned with the ways in which cultural practices have to be understood primarily as *means* of achieving social distinction. Thus the association between dominant social groups and art music (insofar as it can be demonstrated) is explained not in terms of the intrinsic qualities of the music, or a deep appreciation of it, but in strategic terms: by participating in high culture they are making a claim – consciously or not – to superior social status, and to a basis on which they can distinguish themselves from those who do not. In fact, Bourdieu's persistent concern to understand social practices in terms of people's desire to accumulate symbolic capital has provoked criticism of his general approach: 'symbolic capital is circularly defined so that whatever one acquires by one's social behaviour can be tautologically reencoded in terms of symbolic capital . . . . Everything from acquiring monetary capital to praise for being burned at the stake automatically counts as symbolic capital' (Dreyfus and Rabinow, 1993: 42). In the present context, Bourdieu's perspective leads to an explanation of the links between social class and musical taste which could be described as sociologistic, in the sense that it treats the conscious feelings, emotions and motivations of individuals in everyday situations – such as the actual experience of music – as only the consequence of underlying class-based processes which (it is supposed) generate the 'habitus' which ultimately ensures the reproduction of patterns of social stratification. (See also Dreyfus and Rabinow, 1993: 41).

Consequently, despite his initial intention to overcome the opposition between social 'structures' and the 'agency' of individuals, Bourdieu's approach fails to escape from its structuralist origins (e.g. Jenkins, 1992: 61; Cicourel, 1993), and emphasises continuity and the reproduction of the social order at the expense of its dynamic elements (Calhoun, 1993: 72). Building on this criticism, others have questioned the close 'fit' which Bourdieu posits between individuals' social class position, and their aesthetic tastes and consumer practices. In attempting to explain the latter in terms of the former, write Longhurst and Savage, Bourdieu's methodology is ultimately – again, despite his denials – positivist, in the sense that he takes these as independent and dependent variables (1996: 285). Having created an imposing theoretical framework, Bourdieu's research was driven by the need to find evidence to support it (Cicourel, 1993: 95). Yet what other empirical studies reveal is the difficulty of assigning people unambiguously to social class positions, the complexity and varying significance of their consumption practices, and the problematic nature of the assumption that these practices are driven by the underlying motivation to secure social 'distinction'. The people studied by Wynne and O'Connor, for example, 'did not seem terribly concerned with "performing" cultural distinction in any clear way' (Longhurst and Savage, 1996: 284). Above all, it may be suggested that, as Longhurst and Savage put it, 'habituses do not do not simply establish differences between people, but . . . construct identity and solidarity' (*ibid.*). Bourdieu's fundamental view of human motivation as based on the 'maximising of material or symbolic profit' (Bourdieu, 1977: 183) is revealed as sociologically deficient, because it rests ultimately on a (conscious or unconscious) calculation of individual self-interest, just as in utilitarian or rational-choice theories.

Bourdieu's approach, then, leads him to focus on the differences among individuals and groups at the expense of these powerful aspects of social relations which bind them together, and Longhurst and Savage use Bourdieu's analysis of musical taste to make the point. There is a demonstrable relationship between social class position and the chances of a person expressing a taste for a particular style of music. But as we have seen, it tends to obscure the fact that such probabilities are not very strong. While high-status music is much more popular among 'higher education teachers' than among 'clerical and commercial employees', Bourdieu fails to consider why ' . . . this music is generally unpopular, even amongst the most culturally privileged groups' (Longhurst and Savage, 1996: 287). And as Longhurst shows elsewhere, while it is true that members of higher social class groups buy more 'classical' recordings than do those in other groups, more than half their purchases are of 'rock and pop' albums. (Longhurst, 1995: 208). Once again, the implication is clear: although there is evidently some sort of relationship between social class position and musical taste, neither Shepherd's idea of a 'structural homology' between them nor Bourdieu's postulation of a class-based 'habitus' is particularly successful in elucidating it.

## Music in social life

How then is the general connection between class and musical preference, and in particular the link between Western art music and dominant social class groups, to be explained? To pursue this theme, it may be useful to review the explanations considered so far. As we have seen, for those who take their theoretical orientation from Adorno, the class–music conjunction could be understood in terms of the intrinsic qualities of the music itself, and in particular the ways in which the conventions of 'classical' music are a symbolic representation of bourgeois ideology. It is of some significance that this line has been taken by some prominent musicologists, thus displaying their disciplinary commitment to analysing and interpreting musical 'texts'. Although, as I have suggested, there are a number of problems with this approach, in the present context the main difficulty is that empirical research, whether historical or more recent studies of lifestyle patterns, has failed to demonstrate the close correspondence between class position and musical taste which the theory requires.

On the other hand, it is equally evident that most of those who have approached this issue from a sociological perspective have said almost nothing about the music itself, concerning themselves above all with the ways in which it is held to operate above all as a 'status marker' (Peterson and Simkus, 1992). Clearly, this work has been important in demonstrating the extent to which aesthetic tastes of all kinds are socially distributed, and not simply a matter of individual preference. However, there is a risk here that the everyday experience of real people in real situations is rendered invalid, or at least treated as secondary to more fundamental social processes. As noted above, one important criticism of Bourdieu's work is his tendency to treat the inherent qualities of cultural objects or processes as more or less irrelevant to the underlying struggle for social distinction; it follows that his analysis of any given 'field' 'necessarily denies the validity of the manifold significance of the practices to the practitioners' (Dreyfus and Rabinow, 1993: 41). Once again, the reasons for doubting whether Bourdieu really escaped the limitations of structuralism are apparent: his model of social life involves a distinction between everyday appearances, and a hidden or underlying reality in which 'fields' are structured and, as a consequence, the 'habitus' of each human agent is generated.

In the end, it is the ontological status of this underlying 'reality' that is at issue. We are (once again) confronted with two contrasting paradigms for sociological work: one which takes social structures, however defined, as the paramount reality (and which, despite his intentions, is represented by Bourdieu's work), the other which treats such structures as reifications, as concepts which arise out of the practical interests of real people (especially sociologists), but which do not denote entities independent of their everyday actions and interactions (King, 2004). It is thus of some significance that Longhurst and Savage, having considered the way in which Bourdieu's approach attempts to explain consumption practices as the effects of underlying structural causes, conclude that such work is 'importantly deficient' in its 'inattention to the dynamics and complexities of everyday life' (1996: 296). Consumption practices cannot be explained simply in terms of one factor, such as the aim of securing distinction; they may be important, for example, in strengthening a person's subjective sense of self, rather than being 'other-directed', and they are likely to be shaped by the contingencies of the local situations in which people find themselves. Above all, Bourdieu's emphasis on the ways in which individuals seek to distinguish themselves neglects the ways in which consumption practices serve to sustain social solidarity, in other words those 'processes forming links and bonds with significant others'. To remedy this neglect it is necessary to go beyond the survey data used by Bourdieu (and most other recent researchers), which have the quite considerable methodological weakness of being derived from people's reports on their activities, rather than the investigation of what they actually do. For this reason Longhurst and Savage recommend 'a return to more ethnographically based studies of interaction within specific "localities"' (*ibid.*). Similar points have been made by Warde, in noting that the preoccupation with individuals' strategies of distinction has tended to obscure the 'collective aspects of consumption associated with social participation . . . . Being with others at a particular site or at a "live" performance, say a concert or a sports contest, is a source of satisfaction in itself' (1996: 305–306). Moreover, only ethnographic research *in situ* is likely to produce an understanding of the meanings and significance of practices and events for people in real situations, as opposed to the hypothetical ones on which survey data are based. Here Warde refers to the sociological importance of understanding 'the various "social worlds" which individuals inhabit' (*ibid.*: 308).

With these points in mind, it is now possible – at last – to reconnect the concerns of those who have understood the link between music and social position in terms of the assumed qualities of the music – the *meanings* which it articulates – and those for whom this affinity is primarily a result of individuals' *use* of music as a 'status marker'. There could be no better way of doing so than through a consideration of Ruth Finnegan's study of those she calls *The Hidden Musicians* (1989) in Milton Keynes. At first sight, Finnegan's research methodology seems straightforward – 'an empirically based ethnography of amateur music in one modern English town at a particular period' (*ibid.*: 5). Yet the huge extent of the music-making that her work revealed meant that this turned out to be an enormous research task, and her consequent report is a book rich in both data and insight. For present purposes, the importance of Finnegan's work is, first, that it focuses on musical activities as social practices in which large numbers of people are involved (and not, as in most studies, on 'professional' music) and, second, that it was exactly the sort of ethnographic study of local social 'worlds' which Warde (and

Longhurst and Savage) recommend as the most effective means of understanding the consumption practices of real people going about their everyday lives.

In this short discussion it is impossible to do justice to the breadth and depth of *The Hidden Musicians*, and inevitably it is highly selective. In fact, I will be concerned with only three general themes. First of all, in common with other empirical studies, Finnegan's work did *not* demonstrate the close correspondence between social class and musical taste which theorists have often assumed. On the contrary, while 'active music-making of any kind was a minority interest', those who were involved were remarkably heterogeneous in terms of their education and occupation (*ibid.*: 312). Moreover, the widely assumed associations between social class and particular musical worlds were not supported by the evidence; although the 'country and western' world was 'largely a working class one' (*ibid.*: 99) and that of 'folk music' was largely 'middle class' (*ibid.*: 68), these degrees of social homogeneity were unusual. Indeed, 'jazz and operatic activities were particularly heterogeneous' (*ibid.*: 314), and Finnegan explicitly rejects the assumption that involvement in classical music was primarily a middle-class pursuit. In this world, 'local musicians and participants in local musical activities varied enormously in terms of educational qualifications, specialist expertise, occupation, wealth and general ethos' (*ibid.*: 44). In place of the 'preoccupation of so many social scientists' (*ibid.*: 311) with social class, Finnegan emphasises the role of families in facilitating access to 'pathways' into the different musical worlds, of gender and age, and of particular opportunities and constraints in shaping patterns of participation (*ibid.*: 305ff). Of course, class-related processes did operate, although mediated by these kinship and friendship networks, and various local contingencies, resulting in a much looser connection between class and musical participation than theorists have often assumed. But this finding is quite consistent with the results of other empirical studies, which, as we have seen, reveal some sort of association between these factors, but not a strong one, and leave much unexplained. Through her ethnographic work Finnegan is able to identify the specific social processes through which some people, in certain circumstances, became involved in one or other of the musical worlds she identified. Such processes were not random or haphazard but ' . . . culturally established ways through which people structure their activities on habitual patterns that – however unnoticed by outsiders – are known to and shared with others' (*ibid.*: 323). It is through identifying and examining these, the patterns and practices which form the cultural realities of everyday life, that Finnegan can begin to explore the connections between music and other activities in the lives of real people. Enough has been said, I hope, to suggest that her findings raise serious doubts about approaches which reduce such connections to one-dimensional associations between social class position and musical taste.

A second theme emerging from *The Hidden Musicians* concerns Finnegan's use of the concept of musical 'worlds' as an effective means of organising her material and as a metaphor describing the realities of musical life as she observed it. Following Becker (1982), Finnegan is concerned to show how each of these worlds is organised around certain conventions and aesthetic values which are taken for granted by participants, although she strongly resists (as Becker did) the implication that such worlds are static or clearly bounded (Finnegan, 1989: 190). She is concerned to emphasise the *processes* through which individuals collaborate, and the particular *practices* that they engage in, particularly the interactional 'work' which is necessary for the realisation of even the most well-established convention (DeNora, 1986). While such mundane matters are normally taken for granted by participants, and (perhaps for this reason) overlooked by social scientists, it is by examining them that we can begin to understand both the distinctiveness of these worlds and the patterns of social organisation which sustain them. Indeed, one of the great strengths of Finnegan's work is that it enables us to put music back, so to speak, into the social contexts in which it is, inevitably, created and heard. Whereas a long tradition of musicological research – probably the vast majority of studies – deals with 'music' as 'works' which are analysed independently of the circumstances of their production and reception, Finnegan insists, time and again, on the importance of a sociological perspective from which musical activities must be understood as social practices carried out by real people and embedded in specific contexts. To an extent this re-contextualisation involves demystifying music and depriving it of its 'aura'; the gain, however, is the ability to appreciate the ways in which individuals' participation in musical activities – at any 'level' – involves them in networks of social relationships and experiences of sociability which are not specifically musical, and which require sociological rather than musicological analysis.

As Finnegan's data demonstrate, the activity of performing music not only involves individuals in relationships with other people – some of them players, others not – but can provide experiences of sociability that are valued in themselves and can be important in giving people a sense of identity and worth which, Finnegan notes, may be denied to them in other areas of social life (1989: 328). Moreover, a further advantage of using the concept of social worlds is its inclusiveness. Attention is not restricted (as in many discussions of 'music') to the performers. The sense of belonging, of having a secure place in a social world, may be a powerful attraction for members of audiences, and Finnegan gives many examples of people whose involvement in the worlds of, for example, folk, or jazz, or country and western music is a major part of their lives. Like the players, they have their individual likes and dislikes, but they are nonetheless bound together through a shared understanding of the appropriate conventions and their acceptance of an aesthetic ideology which gives meaning and value to musical practices. Indeed, far from denying or ignoring the importance of such an ideology (cf. Zangwill, 2002), the sort of sociological perspective being considered here gives it a central place in the analysis. While sociological analysis may deprive the music of its 'aura', it is important to keep in mind that for the *participants* in these worlds the music itself is indeed perceived as special, the source of heightened aesthetic experiences, and it is the pursuit of such experiences which motivates them. Moreover, this sense of musical 'greatness', sometimes described in terms of 'authenticity', appears characteristic of *all* musical worlds (Frith, 1996b), irrespective of whether the inspired icon is held to be J. S. Bach, John Coltrane, Bruce Springsteen or Kurt Cobain. Two points should be emphasised here. First, while the powerful aesthetic experiences which participants may have are felt, often deeply, as personal and subjective, they nonetheless are derived from their involvement in patterns of collective action, in which their acceptance of aesthetic ideologies, and participation in collaborative rituals are important elements. In this respect, the study of musical worlds may be related directly to the long tradition of empirical sociological research which has examined ways in which the identities of individuals, and the experiences they are able to have, must be understood as a consequence of their socialisation in particular institutional contexts, both formal and informal. Secondly, this sort of analysis can make explicit the social processes which are normally taken for granted by participants, but which are essential to the social organisation of musical worlds: the nature of their conventions, rituals, aesthetic ideologies, socialisation patterns and so on. In other words, it is possible to identify sociological features which are *common* to these worlds, rather than concentrating on the musical differences between, say, brass bands, folk singers, and heavy metal groups. This is not to deny the powerful effects of the music, but rather to emphasise that such effects are always realised and experienced in specific socially organised settings.

Relatedly, a third general theme arising from Finnegan's research is the idea that participation in musical worlds, of whatever style, gives individuals positions in networks of social relationships, thereby linking them to the wider society in various ways. Indeed, her use of the term 'pathways' nicely illustrates both an important aspect of the various music worlds which is common to all of them, and the ways in which such culturally established routes relate people 'both to each other and, through the series of personal networks, institutional links and social ordering of space and time necessarily implicated in each of these pathways, to other elements in social life' (Finnegan, 1989: 329). Such pathways not only provide accepted ways of doing things which ensure the effective collaboration of individuals, but 'routes' which provide them with narratives about the wider scheme of things and their own positions in it. Indeed, while involvement in music may be, statistically speaking, a minority activity (though not an insignificant one), it is this sort of configuration of activities – and all the other 'worlds' in which people are involved – which ultimately constitute the social order. While we may talk in 'macro' terms about institutions, social structure, class, society, and about cultural traditions or ways of life, in the end all such abstractions are derived from the specific actions and interactions, often 'apparently trivial', of real people in real situations (*ibid.*: 330). Moreover, although 'leisure' activities in general, and music in particular, have often been regarded as 'peripheral' aspects of the social structure, Finnegan is concerned to emphasise the important ways in which participation in all such activities can provide people with both a sense of their own identity and of their position in a wider community.

Conclusion

This chapter has been concerned with some aspects of the presumed relationship between class cultures and musical taste, and the main ways in which this has been explained. For Adorno, and some of the 'new' musicologists, this key to this relationship lies in the music itself, as they assert a correspondence between the conventions of Western art music and the ideological commitments of dominant social groups. Sociologists have placed less emphasis on the meaning of the music and more on its use, especially as a means of claiming or displaying social status, notably in Bourdieu's insistence on the closeness of the 'fit' between social class position and musical preferences.

However, as we have seen, the main difficulty with the proposed class–music conjunction is that the empirical evidence yielded by both historical analyses and more recent research offers little support for it. Certainly there is some sort of relationship between class cultures and musical tastes, but the studies leave much unexplained. What empirical researchers tend to find is that social groups have fairly heterogeneous musical tastes, and, moreover, that assigning individuals to 'classes' is highly problematic. The studies considered above, therefore, suggest that neither the idea of a homology between class cultures and musical styles nor the claim that people use music as part of a strategy for achieving social distinction is particularly helpful in elucidating the links between class and music. Both exaggerate the strength of these links, and the extent to which individuals' dispositions are shaped by their socio-economic circumstances – it is instructive, for example, to contrast Bourdieu's remarks, quoted on p. 77, with the finding that classical music is 'generally unpopular, even amongst the most culturally privileged groups' (Longhurst and Savage, 1996: 287).

However, the studies also point to some sort of relationship between class culture and musical taste – there are, that is, 'undeniable gradients by social location' (*ibid.*) which require a more sociologically satisfactory explanation than the perspectives considered above can supply. With this in mind it is significant that researchers in the more general field of consumption and lifestyles have recommended ethnographic, qualitative studies of real people carrying out 'everyday' activities, and – either explicitly or implicitly – have recognised the serious limitations of macro-sociological models which posit class–culture 'homologies' or underlying 'structural' processes. Such models reflect the long-established tendency for sociologists to reify collective concepts which ultimately turn out to be empirically unsustainable (Jenkins, 2002; Martin, 2004). By contrast, it is instructive to consider the implications of Finnegan's point that, in the last analysis, institutions, customs, indeed the whole way of life of a society must be understood as deriving from the local, mundane practices of people interacting with others (Finnegan, 1989: 330–331).

So what, finally, are we to make of the widely assumed connection between high social status and 'serious' art-music? It has been suggested above that this assumption rests on an oversimplification of various complex, and sociologically interesting, processes. As I have said, in response to Bourdieu, while it may be true that most concert-goers are middle class, it does not follow that most of the middle class are concert-goers. An examination of all the factors involved in the rise to cultural hegemony of 'classical' music is far beyond the scope of this chapter. By way of conclusion, however, it may be suggested that the achievement of what Bourdieu called cultural legitimacy by people in the world of 'classical' music (and indeed the appropriation of the term itself) may be better understood in terms of the dynamics of social movements, rather than as the reflection in culture of underlying class processes. As Crossley has argued, the use of the term 'social movement' need not imply moments of crisis or radical confrontation; indeed, to be effective, movements must inculcate 'a degree of stability and durability' in the thinking of their adherents; moreover, movements must be understood as 'constituted by way of social practices' (Crossley, 2002: 55, 61). Something of what is involved here is conveyed by the familiar use of the phrase 'the brass band movement' (Herbert, 1991), suggesting an organised collectivity with a particular aesthetic ideology, an accepted narrative of its own history, a sense of the inherent value of its activities, and a commitment to making 'progress' through the pursuit of its interests. Indeed, in relation to 'classical' music, historians have emphasised both the legitimating idea that it engenders morality and discipline (e.g. Russell, 1997: 23ff), and the extent to which it has been promoted by commercial interests (e.g. W. Weber, 1977).

The ways in which the idea of 'serious' music was established as a dominant cultural trope in industrial societies, and accepted in media, educational and political discourses, have thus been seen as a result of the activities of particular 'cultural entrepreneurs' (DiMaggio, 1982) and their followers, rather than as the inevitable outcome of underlying class processes. Discussing developments in the organisation of concerts, William Weber made the point graphically: 'We must not think that these changes were caused by dark, impersonal forces. The use of power and gain have been central to the process; some people have wanted new things, and many times they have gotten them' (1975: 115). In the next chapter I will consider this process in more detail.

# 6

# Musical life in the 'first industrial city'

With the Concert of Ancient Music [1776] began a peculiarly modern institution: upper class people displaying their social status and their musical sophistication while revering great music from the past. It is necessary to recognise that two quite distinct factors are involved here – social class and musical taste. While in some respects they reinforced each other, in other ways they bred contradictions. (William Weber, 1992: 1)

## Introduction

It was argued in the previous chapter that the relationship between people's social class position and their musical preferences is both more complex and more sociologically interesting than several influential theorists have allowed. In what follows I wish to pursue some of the implications of William Weber's contention that although they are related in some ways, social class and musical taste must be considered as 'quite distinct factors'. This theme will be developed through a consideration of some of the historical research into the growth of musical institutions in urban areas since the eighteenth century, with particular reference to the situation in Manchester, often considered to be the world's 'first industrial city' (Messinger, 1985: 5). Following from the position developed in the previous chapter, it will be argued that the results of this work cast doubt on the notion that music bears some sort of inherent ideological message, or the proposal that there is an identifiable 'structural homology' (Shepherd, 1991: 89) between musical forms and patterns of social organisation.

As noted above (p. 85) various studies have investigated the development of musical institutions through the period of industrialisation in Europe and North America. The outcome of this research is to render problematic the general notion of a straightforward correspondence between social class position and musical taste, and in particular the idea that the values of the social elite are somehow expressed in high-status art music. Indeed, as Weber puts it, 'the upper classes are not ones to miss out on the pleasures of popular culture, and many of them are quite unsophisticated in their tastes' (1992: 20). Indeed, it is worth remembering that in the 1880s, with the concept of 'classical' music well established and *maestros* like Charles Hallé at the height of their influence, the Prince of Wales, future King of England, was taking banjo lessons from James Bohee, a black American (Parsonage, 2005: 111–112).

Similarly, it is evident that the middle class, broadly defined, has been far from homogeneous as far as musical preferences were concerned. McVeigh noted 'a certain independence of taste even among the higher reaches of the middle classes' when writing of London's concert life at the end of the eighteenth century, and concluded that 'a simple model of musical progress supported by the elite and emulation by the broad middle classes cannot . . . be sustained' (1993: 13). As Citron (1993: 32) suggests, the new middle class was of great importance, especially in London, the largest and most dynamic economic centre in Europe by the middle of the eighteenth century (Brewer, 1997: 28–29). By the nineteenth century, this expanding business and professional group had not only stimulated the development of commercial (as opposed to subscription) concerts, but generated the demand for goods (such as instruments and sheet music) and services (particularly music teaching) which led to the growth of the music business in something like its modern form (Weber, 1977; Scott, 1989: 45ff; Chanan, 1994: 153–155). 'In addition to public performances by professionals', writes Mace, 'amateur musicians pursued their interests in musical societies and in their homes, creating a demand for printed music tailored to the average player. As a result, the print trade in music grew rapidly, making music a valuable market commodity' (Mace, 2004: 1). But here was another potent source of stylistic diversification within music. While composers were increasingly free from the constraints of church ritual or aristocratic patrons, the strict discipline of the market meant that it was risky to venture too far from prevailing public taste (Elias, 1993: 129), or from the demands of publishers who wanted music which could be played by amateurs. Such pieces are clearly to be distinguished from the masterworks of the great composers which have so often been considered the epitome of bourgeois music. In short, the demands of 'art' and 'commerce' were, perhaps inevitably, pulling in different directions, and the larger the musical public became, the less demanding the music to which it responded. As Scott puts it, 'in music the effects of bourgeois democratic ideas were seen in a deliberate popularisation and simplification of style' (1989: 3–4).

It is also clear that as the audience grew, appreciation of artistic nuances declined in favour of dramatic and virtuosic recitals (often given by charismatic pianists). Of course, the popularity of domestic music-making and flamboyant recitalists does not preclude a widespread appreciation of the works of the great masters. Nevertheless, the essential point is that it cannot be assumed *a priori* that members of the middle class constituted even a relatively homogeneous 'taste public', or that their ideological commitments – whatever these may have been – were somehow expressed in the music they played at home or heard in concerts. It follows that a theoretical explanation of the relationship between social class and musical styles in terms of a supposed correspondence between ideological values and musical conventions is problematic, and runs the risk of reifying both 'classes' and musical 'styles' (Martin, 1995: 147). Empirically, it is hard to reconcile this view with the sheer variety of the music produced in any particular era (e.g. Dahlhaus, 1989: 193), with the 'looseness' of the connections between music and social groups (e.g. Middleton, 1990: 159ff), and with the frequently observed heterogeneity of the elements which have been taken to constitute 'the' middle class (e.g. Savage *et al.*, 1992: 19ff).

## The development of musical institutions

Seen in historical perspective, the eighteenth century – especially prior to the 'great transition' brought about by the French and industrial revolutions – has often been portrayed as a period of stability 'when cultural hierarchies were respected and the rule of taste prevailed'. As Brewer argues, however, such a view is not how contemporary artists, critics, or the emerging 'public' experienced things:

> They saw flux and change where we, less well placed to understand them, see stability, unity and order. Of course in the eighteenth century

the audience for the arts was smaller and the variety of media was less. But the dynamism of those who produced, sold and enjoyed the arts ensured that the boundaries – between fine art and popular forms of expression, between the discerning and refined spectator and the cheerful punter, between the rich patron and the less affluent audience – were every bit as hard to draw. (Brewer, 1997: 664–665)

In concluding his magisterial survey of the development of English culture during the eighteenth century, Brewer specifically warns against viewing the transformation of the arts in this period as 'smooth, gradual, inevitable, almost "natural"' (*ibid.*: 663), pointing, for example, to the tensions between influential amateurs and the emerging professionals, to the commercialisation of cultural production and the suspicion of 'traders', and to the enduring criticism of ideas of 'politeness and sentiment'. These processes of collaboration, competition and conflict are not well comprehended by general and often teleological narratives of historical transformation, or macro-sociological theories of 'structural' change leading to institutional adaptation (Kidd and Nicholls, 1999: 2). Indeed, the whole idea of a 'great transition', although enormously influential, is problematic, since it proceeds from two assumptions: first, that societies may be conceptualised as totalities, and second that in this case one relatively stable 'type' of society (with pre-modern characteristics) has been transformed into another (modern) 'type' (Francis, 1987: 33). To conceptualise societies in this way is to understand them as entities, and to conceive of change as proceeding from the whole to the parts; for this reason Francis argues that ' . . . the methodological implications of the great transition debate go to the very heart of sociological theorising'. On the one hand are those 'who are committed to an holistic approach to social change and an historicist conception of history' and on the other 'those who reject such a commitment' (*ibid.*: 32–33). For the latter, the idea of a relatively rapid social transformation is not well supported by historical evidence; in their view social change is a gradual, uneven, but fairly constant process. Moreover, from a sociological perspective, this latter approach rejects the reification entailed in conceptualising societies as structured totalities, instead seeing both change and the regularities of social life as the *outcome* of the actions and interactions of real people. The direction of explanation is reversed, so to speak, with the constant process of interpersonal relations seen as producing and sustaining the orderly but dynamic patterns of social life, rather than being determined by them.

It will be apparent that the contrasting theoretical perspectives evident in the 'great transition' debate are, as Francis suggests, representative of a much wider bifurcation in sociological thought. Indeed, some have spoken in terms of 'two sociologies', of which one 'views action as the derivative of system, whilst the other views system as the derivative of action' (Dawe, 1970: 214). Clearly, the fundamental issues raised by this opposition cannot be pursued here, but it should be evident that Brewer's conclusion, and the historical evidence he discusses, is consistent with the latter view, which understands the social order and its development as the outcome of the 'flux and change' (1997: 664) of everyday life. Brewer's analysis offers a dynamic view of real people pursuing their interests and aspirations in the light of a variety of ideological commitments, of the resistance and constraints they encountered, of the technological changes which presented threats to some and opportunities to others, and of outcomes which were contingent and contested.

More specifically, one of the benefits of historical hindsight is to be able to move beyond oversimplified notions of a transition from pre-modern to modern societies, and to view the development of musical institutions in terms of change, conflict and innovation. For example, studies have shown that the opposition between 'serious' and 'popular' music – often taken for granted as an enduring part of the cultural matrix of modern societies – was in fact a specific ideological configuration, not institutionalised until quite late in the nineteenth century, always challenged and apparently dissolving quite rapidly by the end of the twentieth (Weber, 1975; DiMaggio, 1982; Levine, 1988; Kolb, 2001). Similarly, the music profession, in the sense of a group of people whose primary occupation was concerned with the performance or teaching of music, can be seen to have developed and declined in a series of stages which were shaped by both technological innovations and wider social changes (Ehrlich, 1985). To understand the development of musical institutions, then, it is far more productive to see them, not as the inevitable outcome of more fundamental changes in the 'structure' of societies (e.g. Shepherd, 1991: 96–97) but as the result of the collaborative activities of real people in specific historical contexts.

Perhaps the most general theme running through the European studies is the development of public concerts independent of royal or aristocratic control. As we have seen, this was a topic of considerable significance in DeNora's study of Vienna in the 1790s, especially in relation to the emergence of a 'serious music ideology' (1995: 4) among the aristocrats, as part of their strategy of distinguishing themselves from the new bourgeoisie. The implication, of course, is that the 'serious' music of Beethoven and his successors cannot simply be assumed to express or articulate the values of the new middle class. A similar theme is explored in Weber's study of the rise of 'musical classics' in England, as he discusses the 'cultural hegemony' exerted by the nobility in the latter part of the eighteenth century, and its successful integration into 'a new political structure – a kind of broad-based Establishment that masked its own internal divisions' (W. Weber, 1992: 14). For Weber, the late eighteenth-century creation of a 'canon' of great musical works and their regular performance in the 'Concert of Antient Music' was an important ritual which legitimated and consolidated the British state. By providing a 'model to counteract the low standard of music being sold at the time', it was also part of a reaction against the commercialisation and fashionable consumption which London's relative affluence had made possible (*ibid.*: 19).

Once again, such considerations suggest that it would be a mistake simply to identify 'classical' music with the bourgeoisie. Weber's studies lead him to emphasise how the established nobility and the higher ranks of the middle class in Britain gradually fused into a new dominant class, and also the extent to which elements of the nobility retained a 'tight control' of 'ancient music' well into the nineteenth century (*ibid.*: 247). Moreover,

> Nineteenth century classical music concerts also continued the moral ideology of taste that originated in the eighteenth century. Its themes were an antagonism toward commercialism, fashion-worship, and virtuosity; the sense of an elite of educated listeners; the demand that audiences be serious and quiet; and deference to the classics as the ultimate source of authority in musical taste. (W. Weber, 1992: 21)

Given the origins of this ideology in a period of aristocratic control of musical life, it is not surprising that such themes are scarcely consistent with those usually considered as fundamental to bourgeois values. Moreover, the continuing influence of the aristocrats ensured that the idea of 'classical' music 'took root in society: in the church, in provincial assembly rooms, and in London's elite concert halls' (*ibid.*).

In Paris, Johnson has traced the emergence in the last years of the Ancien Regime of a 'public sphere of judgement implicitly opposed to the authority of the crown' (1995: 92); this new 'musical public' was made up of individuals whose musical tastes were no longer determined by the need to follow the arbitrary judgements of aristocrats. What was at stake was 'the cultural authority of absolutism' (*ibid.*: 94) in this and other fields. In the decades that followed, two related developments contributed to the development of the 'musical public': the increasing acceptance of non-programmatic, 'absolute' music (which made possible the enthusiastic reevaluation of Beethoven in the 1830s) and an 'emergent code of silence during performances' (*ibid.*: 232) which contrasted markedly with the flamboyant inattention of audiences in earlier years (see also Sennett, 1992: 27).

Studies of the growth of musical institutions in the urban centres of the USA during the nineteenth century provide an instructive contrast to the European research. Here there was no tradition of aristocratic dominance, but the outcome was similar, namely the acceptance, by the late nineteenth century, of a 'canon' of great works, a distinction between 'cultivated' and 'vernacular' music, and, more generally, the 'emergence of cultural hierarchy' (Levine, 1988). Indeed, while some contemporaries had seen the institutionalisation of 'serious' symphonic music as evidence of higher levels of civilisation and the march of progress, others have regarded it with some dismay, pointing to the ways in which the hegemony of European music had the effect of stifling specifically American musical traditions, and fostering an elitism which was held to be incompatible with America's democratic values (Broyles, 1992: 9–10). This latter theme is explored by DiMaggio in examining the role of the 'cultural capitalists' (1982: 35) such as Henry Higginson, whose activities created (in 1881) an 'organisational base for high culture' in the form of the Boston Symphony Orchestra. For DiMaggio, the 'sacralisation of art' (*ibid.*) was an important part of the process through which members of Boston's 'Brahmin' elite achieved ideological dominance. While appearing (not least to themselves) to pursue 'communitarian goals' (*ibid.*: 39), their activities in fact established ' . . . institutions that could claim to serve the community, even as they defined the community to include only the elite and the upper middle classes' (*ibid.*: 38). Moreover, acceptance of this ideology spread through the middle class more generally: 'The growth of the middle class during this period – a class that was economically and socially closer to the working class and thus in greater need of differentiating itself from it culturally – provided a natural clientele for Boston's inchoate high culture' (*ibid.*: 40). Both this impulse towards cultural distinction, and the receptiveness to the mythology of 'high art' which it engendered, are important in understanding the emerging affinity between the new urban middle class and 'serious' music, in both American and Europe.

## Concert life in Manchester

It was suggested above that studies of musical life and institutions in European cities in the eighteenth and nineteenth centuries are much concerned to elucidate the tensions – or the processes of accommo-dation – between the royal courts and the aristocracy, on the one hand, and the rising middle class, on the other. Yet the progress of capitalist industrialisation also entailed the emergence of new cen-tres of power where there was no court or tradition of aristocratic dominance to hinder or circumscribe the activities of the flourishing bourgeoisie. Manchester provides a dramatic example, developing at a remarkable rate to become the world's 'first industrial city' (Messinger, 1985: 5). The population had increased steadily in the eighteenth century, but leapt from around 40,000 in the 1780s to 77,000 in 1801 and 316,000 by 1851. The great majority of this influx, of course, were manual workers, yet industrialisation and urbanisation on this scale also generated an increasingly substantial middle class, and there is evidence of public musical activity among this group quite early on, certainly in the 1740s, around the time of the second Jacobite rebellion (Kennedy, 1960: 3).

The Manchester 'Gentlemen's Concerts' were founded in 1777 by an existing group of 'amateur flautists and music enthusiasts' who bought a plot of land, built a concert room and organised an orches-tra which gave regular performances (Allis, 1995: 9); indeed, the series survived until 1920. In the context of other studies of cultural change in this period, notably Habermas's (1992) discussion of the emerging 'public sphere', musical activities in early modern Man-chester are of considerable interest, given that – in the absence of an established aristocratic presence – the development of the city's institutions gives some indication of the tastes and proclivities of the new middle class in something like its pure state. Indeed, the 'Man-chester Man' of the industrial revolution has long been regarded as prototypical of the new breed of capitalist entrepreneurs (e.g. Kidd,

1993: 63ff), and it is evident that many of them were subscribers to the Gentlemen's Concerts. The activities of this organisation, which pre-dates the better-known Manchester Literary and Philosophical Society by four years (Kargon, 1977: 5), are thus suggestive of what real members of the bourgeoisie actually did when they had a relatively free hand in such matters.

So did the Gentlemen's Concerts, founded and run by 'Manchester men' in the very moment of their ascendancy, reflect the ideology of 'serious music' which has been regarded as expressing the essence of the bourgeois world view? In general, they did not. On the contrary, concert programmes, from the earliest to the last, indicate that the preferred music ranged across a miscellaneous selection of light pieces, extracts from longer works, popular songs, operatic arias, and instrumental novelties. This range is perhaps not surprising in the early years, when distinctions among musical *genres* were less well defined than later, and when the notion of a 'canon' of great works was not well established (W. Weber, 2001). However, there is clear evidence from the programmes of the Gentlemen's Concerts that 'miscellaneous' concerts were presented *throughout* the nineteenth century and beyond; there are thus initial grounds for supposing that Manchester's leading citizens were not particularly responsive to the ideology of 'serious music'.

Equally significant is the attitude of concert-goers to the music, as revealed in the society's minutes. Time and again, throughout the history of the Gentlemen's Concerts, the directors were forced to issue warnings about loud conversations during performances, subscribers walking about the room, or entering and leaving while music was being played. It seems that such warnings had little effect (Allis, 1995: 177). Even when Chopin, then near the end of his life, played for the Gentlemen's Concerts on August 28th, 1848, Charles Hallé, who attended, was moved to note in his diary 'how appalled he was at the disrespectful reaction of the audience' (*ibid.*: 38). None of this suggests an audience deeply committed to music, or responding to its articulation of their deepest values.

As the name of Chopin suggests, the Gentlemen's Concerts did present some of Europe's most renowned musicians – 'every artist of renown who had visited England had been engaged', wrote Hallé (Kennedy 1972: 122) – and paid them generous fees (Allis, 1995). Liszt played twice in 1825, Paganini appeared in 1832, Mendelssohn conducted *Elijah* in 1847, and there were performances by several of the leading singers of the era (*ibid.*: 15). From the perspective of the modern concert-goer, the combination of substantial payments, top performers, and widespread disinterest on the part of the subscribers seems incomprehensible. But this reaction both presupposes the validity of the 'serious music' ideology discussed above and illustrates how pervasive it has now become. The behaviour of many of the subscribers of the Gentlemen's Concerts is better explained, I suggest, in the context of their concern with the display of social distinction, in Bourdieu's sense, rather than musical aesthetics, especially in an urban context where the degree of residential segregation was limited (Kidd, 1993: 39). It was important to them not only to belong to the select group of members – limited in numbers, carefully vetted, and paying substantial subscriptions (four guineas per year at the start) – but to be seen to belong.

It was also important that the society be seen to present the best performers, and be known for paying them high fees. In such ways the emerging industrial Manchester could be seen to be the equal of London or other European centres, and certainly superior to its rivals Liverpool or Leeds. As Veblen put it, in these circumstances the 'only practicable means of impressing one's pecuniary ability on . . . unsympathetic observers of one's everyday life is an unremitting demonstration of one's ability to pay' (1994: 54). Moreover, in a way which may be consistent with the ideology of the real 'Manchester men', just as it was important to engage the best performers, so it was necessary not to show a submissive or deferential attitude to them. In other words, many of the subscribers were adopting, consciously or not, the attitude of aristocratic patrons of the old order; musicians were engaged for their abilities, but remained essentially servants or hired hands, whose offerings might be attended to, or might not.

The generous fees paid to performers by the Gentlemen's Concerts raises further issues, since from the 1840s onwards the society was faced with increasingly severe financial difficulties. Consistent with the interpretation offered above, it is notable that top rates continued to be paid, thus exacerbating the problem (Allis, 1995: 172). Faced with a growing deficit, it would have been possible for the directors to make businesslike decisions – reducing the expenditure on artists, for example, or lowering the subscription rates (five guineas in the mid-nineteenth century) to attract a wider range of people. It is simply not credible to suppose that the directors allowed the situation to deteriorate through financial incompetence, since among their members were the bankers and merchants who were the very embodiment of the capitalist ethos, men whose fortunes had been made at the cutting edge of entrepreneurial activities on the world markets. What seems more likely is that they were far more willing to see the Gentlemen's go into debt, and survive on the basis on loans secured against the Concert Hall, than to allow them to become less socially exclusive. As Allis put it 'the society was to continue its policy of having a low annual subscription despite its mounting problems, and retaining its rigid policy of social exclusion' (1995: 100).

At the peak of its influence in the age of industrialisation, then, Manchester's leading citizens felt it important to subscribe to, and attend, the Gentlemen's Concerts. Yet it seems that many were motivated less by a concern to hear music than by the pressing need to display their social status within the city, and to this end it was essential that the Concerts remained exclusive. Of course, it is evident that this attitude was not universal, and that some of the subscribers did take the music very seriously, hence the managers' constant but generally ineffective pleas for what they described in 1803 as 'good order and decorum' (Allis, 1995: 44). In itself, though, this reaction is a further indication that the audience was far from homogeneous as far as musical taste is concerned.

Such evidence leads us to consider the *diversity* of 'middle class' musical taste, rather than assuming its uniformity. Certainly, some of the Manchester bourgeoisie – particularly members of the city's German community – were deeply influenced by the 'serious music ideology' and its implication that performances should be attended to in respectful silence. But contemporary accounts of the Gentlemen's Concerts give a clear indication of the divergence between the motivations of this group and others, and the consequent (largely unsuccessful) attempts to control the audience. As I have suggested, most of the preferred music was not 'serious' orchestral material; it is more likely that what a large section of the audience actually wanted from attending the Gentlemen's Concerts was an exclusive forum for the achievement and display of their social standing as persons of 'quality', a means of distinguishing themselves from the *hoi polloi*. It may be objected that this is too facile a judgement, and one made, moreover, with the benefit of hindsight. There is persuasive evidence, however, that this view was shared by observant

contemporaries. Commenting on the decline in the number of subscribers to the Gentlemen's Concerts, the *Manchester Guardian*
suggested on December 27th, 1883 that:

> It is probable that more general recognition of the fact that the Con-
> cert Hall is, or rather was, as much a social as a musical institution,
> would do much to restore its former prestige. There is no denying the
> fact that formerly, subscribers came as much to see and be seen as to
> listen to the music provided. The majority of the audience will never
> be quite so happy as in the good old days when general conversations
> went all along the line. (Quoted in Allis, 1995: 110)

As these remarks suggest, by the 1880s the Gentlemen's Concerts
were in decline. In part this was as a result of Charles Hallé's success
with his own orchestra, which would have attracted those with a
serious interest in the music itself, as well as those who were relatively well-to-do, but who would not have been permitted to
become subscribers to the Gentlemen's Concerts. But it is likely that
an increasingly important factor was the increasing physical segregation of the social classes. The construction of railways and the pro-
vision of public forms of transport had accelerated the departure of
the middle and upper classes from the central areas of the city
(Gunn, 1997: 209; Messinger, 1985: 119), and many of those with
sufficient means moved away altogether, commuting from such
healthier climates as rural Cheshire or the Fylde coast. Increasingly,
too, upper-class lifestyles were centred on elaborate houses, land
and gardens far from the mass of working people, so that social
exclusion could be achieved by physical separation. Just as the
Viennese aristocrats abandoned their *Hauskappellen* when they no
longer conferred prestige on their patrons, so the Manchester bourgeoisie drifted away from the Gentlemen's Concerts when they were
no longer necessary as a means of displaying social distinction.

The point is emphasised by events following the arrival of Charles
Hallé in Manchester in 1848. Hallé was attracted to the city, and initially supported in it, largely through the German community, active
in commerce and international trade and directly in touch with contemporary European cultural developments. (Among many notable
immigrants, Friedrich Engels was a regular attender at Hallé's concerts; Whitfield, 1988: 103). Through his participation in the
Parisian music world of the 1840s, Hallé was already thoroughly
imbued with the 'serious music' ideology fostered, as we have seen,

by aristocrats in both Vienna and London, but by then widely accepted (Johnson, 1995: 270ff). Hallé's subsequent career in Manchester was driven by this commitment. As a recent refugee from what he considered the centre of the musical world, his first experience of the Gentlemen's Concerts was a rude awakening:

> . . . the orchestra! oh, the orchestra! I was fresh from the 'Concerts du Conservatoire', from Hector Berlioz's orchestra, and I seriously thought of packing up and leaving Manchester so that I might not have to endure a second of these wretched performances. (Charles Hallé, quoted in Kennedy, 1972: 122–123)

The following year Hallé was offered the post of Conductor of the Gentlemen's Concerts, and ' . . . accepted it on the condition that the band should be dismissed and its reorganisation left entirely in my hands' (*ibid.*: 125). Hallé set about making improvements for the Gentlemen's Concerts, but only after 1856, when he was able to form his own orchestra, was he able to present the concerts of symphonic music which were consistent with his artistic values and commitments. Hallé's programmes with his own orchestra were devoted almost exclusively to the 'serious' music of the master composers, in contrast to the heterogeneous collections of 'light' pieces which continued to be the staple fare of the Gentlemen's Concerts.

What is also notable here is Hallé's energetic proselytising for 'serious' music and his explicit commitment to making it accessible to as wide a public as possible. Hallé's concerts were moderately priced and, in principle at least, open to all, again in marked contrast to the exclusivity of the Gentlemen's Concerts. In fact, it seems that much of Hallé's success came as a result of being able to attract support from a wide range of the city's population. In his own words, his aim was to present 'high class orchestral music' and to bring it to ' . . . the ears and hearts, not only of the rich, but of the most humble' (1896: 132, 143). It would be naïve not to detect something of a self-serving tone in these and other remarks; nevertheless, there can be little doubt about Hallé's genuine delight that as a result of his efforts 'thousands and thousands of people from the northern counties' who visited the Art Treasures Exhibition held in Manchester in 1856 'there heard a symphony for the first time . . . ' (Hallé in Kennedy, 1972: 136). Moreover, it seems that many of Hallé's most enthusiastic and attentive audiences were drawn from 'ordinary people' rather than the self-conscious elite of the city (e.g. Hallé,

1896: 180–181), and the point is supported by evidence of the 'unexpected propriety' of the large audiences at DeJong's 'Working Men's Concerts' in the early 1870s (Allis, 1995: 88).

The general picture that emerges of concert life in nineteenth-century Manchester, then, is one in which a high-status minority – without doubt the dominant fraction of the city's bourgeoisie – subscribed to the Gentlemen's Concert series. They were described by Hallé himself as 'an exclusive society' since it admitted subscribers only, declined to publish its programmes (until his appointment), and offered mostly 'light' miscellaneous programmes, to which the audience's response was often indifferent. From 1857, though, Hallé – explicitly objecting to 'conducting concerts of this clandestine sort' (Kennedy, 1972: 138) – attracted large audiences from a much wider range of the social spectrum, played 'high-class orchestral music' (Kennedy, 1972: 139), and was evidently gratified by his audiences' response. It should be clear that this picture is not consistent with the notion of a close correspondence between social and musical hierarchies; indeed, it could be argued that the situation in Manchester was its very *opposite*, since Hallé played 'high-class orchestral music' to a socially inclusive audience, while the exclusive Gentlemen's Concerts offered mainly light and heterogeneous programmes to the city's elite.

It would be wrong, however, to oversimplify the situation. While there is no reason to doubt Hallé's sincerity in wishing to bring 'high class orchestral music' to 'the most humble', and while his concerts did consistently offer low-priced tickets, it is evident that, as Gunn has shown, the great majority of people in his audiences were relatively prosperous, and that the proportion of low-priced tickets was 'steadily reduced' – down to about 15% by 1882–83 (1997: 213). The Hallé concerts 'rapidly became a social rite for the rich and fashionable' (*ibid.*: 210). At first sight it might seem that this evident affinity between the social elite and 'serious' art music could be explained in terms of the way the music articulated the values of the elite, but there are various reasons to suggest that this explanation would also be an oversimplification. Central to Gunn's discussion of these concerts is the idea of a 'social rite' in which, from a sociological point of view, the music itself appears as only one element in a complex configuration of activities.

## Hallé as cultural entrepreneur

By the 1830s, the new ideology of serious music was well established in Paris (Johnson, 1995), and it was in this atmosphere that from 1836 to 1848 Charles Hallé served his musical apprenticeship, in the process becoming imbued with a commitment to the ideals of 'serious' music which motivated him for the rest of his life. The events of the Revolution of 1848 precipitated his abrupt departure from Paris, his eventual arrival in Manchester, and his rapid realisation of the wide gulf between his musical ideals and the reality of bourgeois music-making in the 'first industrial city'. From the start, Hallé was an indefatigable 'cultural entrepreneur', but his greatest achievement was the concert series which began in the city in 1857, conducted by him and performed by his own orchestra – the first permanent professional symphony orchestra in Britain. As Gunn (1997) suggests, the substantial audiences for Hallé's concerts did not represent the whole social spectrum. Nonetheless these audiences were drawn from a much wider pool of the Manchester population than the Gentlemen's Concerts, and as I have suggested were in principle inclusive rather than socially exclusive. Nor is there any reason to doubt Hallé's sincerity in seeking to play his music to the widest possible cross-section of society, or his evident pleasure when it was well received by 'large audiences of working men'. 'It is impossible to believe', wrote Hallé's son, 'that the taste thus formed in one direction should not have had its effect in others, and possibly have coloured their whole lives' (C.E. Hallé, in Kennedy, 1972: 166). In these words, the younger Charles Hallé expresses concisely both the belief in the inherent value of serious music which animated his father, and the more general idea that exposure to this music would act as a civilising influence (Russell, 1997: 23ff).

So although 'the Hallé concerts rapidly became a social rite for the rich and fashionable' (Gunn, 1997: 210), it does not follow that this was because Hallé's symphonic music somehow expressed their fundamental values. On the contrary, Gunn speaks of Hallé's mission, and that of others like him, as a 'project' aimed at *creating* a public for 'classical' music (*ibid.*: 216), and involving the inculcation of a new 'neo-romantic musical aesthetic' (*ibid.*: 217). While ultimately successful in establishing the ideology of serious music, the task was not always easy. Hallé's performance of all nine Beethoven symphonies in 1870–71 raised concerns that he would lose a

considerable part of his audience, and prompted Edward DeJong –
up until then the principal flute – to leave the orchestra (along with
about a quarter of Hallé's players) and set up a rival series of popular promenade concerts. As Russell (2000: 247) has noted, this was
a significant challenge – not only to Hallé's musical leadership, but
to the musical aesthetic which he represented and championed.
Moreover, it is evident that, as with the Gentlemen's Concerts
earlier in the century, Hallé's performances were as much social
events as musical ones, surrounded by elaborate rituals and the public display of social distinction (Gunn, 1997: 214). For Gunn, such
rituals must be understood as *collective* performances in which
members of the middle class asserted their identity in the face of the
many threats and dangers presented by the very modernity of the
city (Gunn, 1999); the highly formalised etiquette of the concert,
and the silent attention paid to music perceived as 'art', were a
significant part of displaying the gentility and experiencing the 'sublime' which distinguished cultured people from the vulgar masses.

The acceptance of this new mode of musical appreciation, however, did not just happen, but came about through the efforts of
certain significant people. As noted above, Hallé himself did not
simply respond to the musical taste of the Manchester bourgeoisie,
but energetically sought to shape it and confront it when he thought
it necessary; indeed, the term 'cultural entrepreneur' seems to capture well his activities as ' . . . the impresario of a public sphere of
culture based on a mixture of commercial opportunism and didactic
highmindedness' (Gunn, 1997: 212). Hallé's concerts, too, did
much to stimulate the development of a critical discourse, in which
authoritative writing about 'serious' music provided people with
ways of hearing it, ' . . . defining a hierarchy of cultural value
together with appropriate categories of aesthetic and moral judgement' (*ibid.*: 219). And just as 'classical music' was thus positioned
ideologically as the essence of 'good taste', in opposition to the popular music of the music halls or the streets, so its audiences could
reassure themselves that their favoured positions in society were
deserved (in contrast to the masses who lacked such taste and refinement). Hallé's cultural entrepreneurship, then, did much to promote
the acceptance of 'classical music', just as critical writings 'framed' it
(DiMaggio, 1982: 35) in terms of a new discourse of aesthetic
appreciation. At the same time, as Weber has shown, various commercial energies were devoted to marketing this music on a large

scale; orchestral conductors like Hallé ' . . . made themselves into charismatic figures at the podium and devised grand programs which made the music of the masters seem awesome rather than esoteric' (W. Weber, 1977: 19). Publishers, too, realised that reproducing the works of dead 'masters' provided a relatively stable source of income and 'probably exerted some influence on the shift of programming' towards 'classical' as opposed to 'new' works (*ibid.*: 20). In this context, the development of Manchester's musical institutions in the nineteenth century may be seen as exemplifying 'the need of the new industrial society to manifest its potency through its own grand rites of secular religiosity' (*ibid.*: 21).

Charles Hallé may be considered an exceptional example of a 'cultural entrepreneur', in the sense that he successfully promoted a particular set of aesthetic values, in this case the ideology of 'serious music' which had captivated him during his Paris years, and managed to generate a broad audience for his concerts. One implication is that the rise to prominence of 'classical' music need not be considered as the inevitable expression of dominant class values, but as the successful outcome of a struggle for cultural legitimacy through which German symphonic music, previously regarded as difficult, forbidding (and foreign) was invested with aesthetic value. It would thus be appropriate to understand the rise and acceptance of 'classical' music not as the inevitable outcome of underlying 'structural' forces, but as a 'social movement', in this case a collective, multifaceted, and ideologically driven effort to define a certain style of music as 'art', with all its contemporary connotations of good taste, refinement, discipline and moral superiority. Hence the rise of 'serious music' in Manchester was not the inevitable expression of 'middle class' values but the outcome of the activities of groups of people who advanced the cause of the music while pursuing their particular interests. Some of these were 'connoisseurs', for whom the music itself was the primary fascination; for others – once described by Mozart as 'those less knowledgeable' (W. Weber, 1977: 16) – it was a means of displaying social distinction, for others again both commitments were combined. Moreover in Manchester, as elsewhere, the rise of 'serious music' depended on the collaborative activities of groups of people in securing the material resources (to build the halls, pay the orchestra, buy the tickets, and so on), in establishing a critical discourse which invested the music (and by extension its audiences) with cultural dominance, and in providing all the goods and services essential for the creation and maintenance of an 'art world' (Becker, 1982) of classical music. Finally, while attendance at Hallé's concerts was undoubtedly a major social ritual in late nine-teenth-century Manchester, and although further research may be necessary to document the point, it is important not to exaggerate the strength of the connection between music and the middle class. As I suggested in the previous chapter, while Bourdieu was certainly correct in claiming that most concert-goers were middle class, it does not follow that most of the middle class were concert-goers.

## Social class and the discourse of serious music

It should be evident that in general the results of the studies consid-ered above call into question the view that the rise to predominance of the 'classical' art-music tradition may be explained by the way in which the organising principles of this music are consonant with the fundamental values of the bourgeoisie, or that there is a 'struc-tural homology' between them. Moreover, as argued above (pp. 88–99), recent empirical evidence casts considerable doubt on Bourdieu's contention that musical taste and socio-economic posi-tion are as closely linked as is often supposed. However, if these approaches are inadequate, we still require a satisfactory explana-tion of the undeniable affinities between social groups and styles of music, and in particular of why art music has been such a valuable element in the 'cultural capital' of dominant social groups. In this context studies of specific institutions – such as the Manchester Gentlemen's Concerts or the Hallé Orchestra – or the activities of 'cultural entrepreneurs' – such as Hallé in Manchester or Higginson in Boston – may prove particularly fruitful. As DiMaggio has put it 'the notion of cultural capital presupposes the existence of institu-tions with the power to establish authoritatively the value of differ-ent forms of culture' (1992: 21), and it is the operation of these institutions which would seem to be fundamental to an understand-ing of the links between 'serious' music and the upper classes. For Frith, the 'art music discourse' has developed on the basis of its val-idation in academic institutions, which effectively legitimate partic-ular conceptions of musical talent, appropriate training and performance conventions, and which sustain the notion that certain music can provide a 'transcendent experience'. It is an experience, however, that is only open to the 'right' sort of people (1996b: 39).

Significantly, it was Charles Hallé's ambition, finally realised, to establish a Conservatory in Manchester.

Some important aspects of the art-music discourse, and the practices which it supports, have been considered above. The studies by DeNora and Johnson illuminate crucial moments during which, in Vienna and Paris respectively, a critical language was developed in which Beethoven's 'harsh' and 'overlearned' compositions (DeNora, 1995: 182), 'grating on the ears while freezing the soul' (Johnson, 1995: 258), could be heard and appreciated in a new and very positive way. Prior to the middle of the nineteenth century: 'For most bourgeois throughout Europe, Beethoven and Mozart were regarded as approachable only by esoteric minds' (W. Weber, 1977: 17). In a succession of studies, William Weber has considered the emergence from the eighteenth century of this 'new musical discourse', which 'focused on musical practice rather than philosophical or scientific theory':

> Musical empiricism – journalism, criticism, history, pedagogy, social commentary – was to be fundamental to musical learning and culture in the modern age. In England this literature was canonic from the start, for it vested the highest level of authority in the music of great composers from the past and in the idea of ancient music, which it began to call 'classical' music. Most important of all, these ideas emerged in close conjunction with performed repertories of old works, as was not true in other countries during the eighteenth century'. (W. Weber, 1994: 517)

The term 'discourse' seems particularly appropriate in the present context, since – despite the well-founded objections to the deterministic cast of Foucault's usage (e.g. Fox, 1998: 419) – the discourse of 'serious' classical music which is presented here in its embryonic form has come to exert the kind of power in Western societies which Foucault ascribed to discourses more generally. 'Music' is presumed to involve the 'performance' of the 'works' of 'composers' by 'musicians' in 'concerts' before 'audiences' who must 'listen' (and so on). Other musical practices and traditions – that is, most music in most societies – are devalued and marginalised. In addition, as Green has put it, the 'appearance of autonomy from social contexts is . . . possibly itself the very most prominent and prevalent aspect of the delineation of classical music' (1997: 9). Yet the institutionalisation of this discourse cannot be explained simply as a reflection in culture of the rise of the bourgeoisie to economic and political dominance; it is perhaps better understood as a consequence of a specifically artistic movement *within* what Bourdieu (1993) called 'the field of cultural production', in which a new way of hearing instrumental music – that is, as serious art – was promulgated by individual connoisseurs and groups of enthusiasts, with the essential support of musicians, critics, publishers, agents, instrument manufacturers and other participants in the 'art world'.

## Conclusion

The implications of the discussion in this chapter and the previous one are similar: that the development of concert life is best explained not in terms of 'structural homology' or a generalised will to 'distinction', but through the analysis of activities of real people in particular situations. That is, rather than treating the 'middle class' or the 'bourgeoisie' as reified entities, it is important to distinguish, for example, among musical enthusiasts, those for whom participation in musical life was part of the social ritual of middle class urban life, those who promoted serious music as one means of 'gentling the masses', as well as those who had little involvement with the musical world. In practice, of course, it is likely that these groups were fluid and overlapping; but the cumulative effect of their activities was to establish connections between 'serious' music and dominant social groups, to institutionalise a discourse of 'classical' music as an enduring aspect of the culture of Western societies, and so, in Bourdieu's terms, to valorise it as a source of 'cultural capital'. It is interesting to note that the elements of this discourse began to coalesce in exactly that period in which, according to Foucault, comparable transformations were occurring in other areas of the natural and human sciences (1974: xii).

Moreover, it should be emphasised that, as William Weber's work has shown, the retrospective identification of a canon of musical 'classics' and its legitimation as high art did not occur spontaneously but was vigorously encouraged by the activities of, among others, music publishers and printers, agents, concert promoters, instrument manufacturers, teachers and musicians themselves. In the 1850s and 1860s, however, the devotees (such as Hallé) of the German 'classical' composers ' . . . forged the concept of the Masters. In so doing they fashioned the values for seriousness and learning which were eventually to become the basic tenets of European concert life' (W. Weber, 1977: 17). Flashy displays by virtuoso performers now fell from favour among concert audiences, and the increasing availability of relatively cheap sheet music further established 'the difference between connoisseurs and the general public' (*ibid.*). 'Learned' music was increasingly separated from mere entertainment, and there emerged in urban centres a core of 'accomplished listeners' (*ibid.*: 19) who became dominant in amateur musical life, but who championed professional performance standards and practices. By around 1870, the now-familiar opposition between 'popular' and 'classical music was well established (*ibid.*: 20), and thus available for the burgeoning middle class as a potential basis on which social distinction could be claimed. It is in this sense, as Bourdieu has suggested, that there is an affinity between the ideology of serious music, with its implication of secular spirituality and the renunciation of the material world, and the ' . . . bourgeois world which conceives its relation to the populace in terms of the relationship of the soul to the body . . . ' (1984: 19). It is indisputable that the cultural effects of this mythology remain potent; however, historical studies have demonstrated the heterogeneity of the 'bourgeois world', and led to doubts concerning the general applicability of the will to distinction which Bourdieu posited (see above, p. 94; also Longhurst and Savage, 1996).

A clearer understanding of the attractions of 'serious' music to the bourgeoisie, finally, also requires an appreciation of the qualities of the medium itself. Although I have argued that that idea of a 'structural homology' is difficult to sustain, Shepherd's (1991) insistence on the significance of the specifically *sonic* qualities of music is valuable, and suggests promising directions for further research. 'Through its supposed capacity to touch the emotions', writes Russell, 'music was uniquely suited to the task of shaping . . . thoughts and actions' (1997: 24), and in the second half of the nineteenth century 'the bourgeoisie began to place increasing trust in the power of music to win the working class over to their values' (Scott, 1989: 194). Both the performance and appreciation of music, it was held, were likely to inculcate self-discipline and self-control, and thus to promote 'good order and decorum' in society generally. Foucault's discussions of the embodiment of discipline may provide a useful basis for the analysis of these particular disciplinary practices: 'The watchword of middle class values', writes William Weber, 'was discipline, and musical training helped instil it in young people. For girls especially, learning the piano was virtually a puberty rite, since it was conceived not as a hobby but as a social obligation integral to their upbringing' (1975: 30; see also Chanan, 1994: 141). A focus on music as the embodiment of self-discipline, then, is perhaps a more promising way of elucidating the links between 'serious' music and bourgeois culture than is an attempt to show how the latter is 'inscribed' in the former. Such a focus, moreover, helps to account for both the particular emphasis on the acquisition of musical skills by women in the dominant social groups, and the prohibition on their using these skills professionally. As Leppert has suggested: 'For women the male perception of music as a misuse of time was the very source of music's uselessness. It helped ensure that women's use of time would be non-productive . . . hence advantageous to men' (1988: 200). It may be in these ways that music was most closely implicated in the reproduction of patriarchy, rather than by having a patriarchal master-narrative (McClary, 1995: 55) inscribed in its formal organisation.

More generally – and here Shepherd's emphasis on the specifically sonic character of the medium is particularly valuable, as is Foucault's examination of the 'systems of micro-power' (1991: 222) which secure control in the modern era – music served as a metaphor for, and a demonstration of, the achievement of order and the imposition of control in a hostile, often intractable, environment. This theme is brilliantly captured and satirised in Hogarth's (1741) depiction of 'The Enraged Musician' who cannot escape the cacophony and disorder of London's streets in the eighteenth century. For Leppert this engraving represents ' . . . the ancient dialectical opposition between order and chaos; more important it is a statement about who has the power to define and regulate the components of order (1988: 214). A century after Hogarth's engraving, the inventor Charles Babbage was 'driven to distraction' by the 'vile and discordant music' of London street players, and with characteristic precision he calculated that 'one fourth part of my working power has been destroyed by the nuisance against which I have protested'. Others did, too, and in 1864 legislation was enacted to control the 'abominable nuisances'; the main outcome of his campaign, however, seems to have been to turn Babbage into a figure of fun in the popular imagination (Swade, 2000: 211–213).

The same dialectic was being played out on the streets of Manchester: in his account of popular music-making in the city, Eva contrasts the polyphonic 'uproar' of the streets and the 'free and easy' performances in public houses (1997: 94, 95) with the 'restraint' and 'refinement' which were considered to define good taste and acceptable conduct in the middle class. Recurring in the many condemnations of 'vulgar' music, Eva suggests, is a strong hostility to the *sound* of popular music, as pub or street singers, for example, are described as 'howling' or 'roaring'. In part, this may be accounted for by the simple physical problems of making themselves heard. Yet it is Eva's contention that the very 'coarseness' of performance styles, and the immediacy of the relationship between singers and their audiences, must be understood as elements of a distinct 'popular aesthetic' of music which valued 'surrender to the sensual pleasures of sound' for its own sake and the opportunity for 'unconstrained, "natural", and carefree release' (*ibid.*: 94–95). It was these kinds of surrender and release, and all their attendant dangers, that disciplined music had to confront and overcome if 'order and decorum' in social life were to prevail over the 'free and easy'.

# Part III

# Improvisation and interaction

# Spontaneity and organisation

## Introduction

'Improvisation', wrote Gunther Schuller in his ground-breaking study of *Early Jazz*, 'is the heart and soul of jazz' (1968: 58). Yet improvisation is only one of the distinctive elements of the music, and indeed Schuller immediately qualifies his assertion by pointing out that improvisation is also an essential ingredient of other folk and popular music traditions. Even more to the point, improvisation is not a major ingredient in many celebrated jazz recordings. Louis Armstrong's classic 'Cornet Chop Suey' of 1926 was copyrighted almost as recorded (and in the trumpeter's own hand) more than two years earlier (Gushee, 1998: 298–299). Duke Ellington's celebrated 'Concerto for Cootie' of 1940 was described as a 'masterpiece' by another pioneering analyst, André Hodeir (1956: 77), yet one of the characteristics of the piece is 'the elimination of improvisation' and, as the recorded evidence shows, other renowned soloists can be heard to repeat familiar solos in all essential respects, and over considerable periods of time (Berliner, 1994: 240). As Louis Armstrong himself put it: 'always, once you get a certain solo that fit in the tune, and that's it, you keep it. Only vary it two or three notes every time you play it' (quoted in Gushee, 1998: 313). Across the stylistic spectrum, too, performances have been praised mainly because they achieve the elusive quality of 'swing' (see Keil, 1995) or because the player's instrumental tone – as on 'Clifford Brown with Strings' (1955) – is judged to be particularly expressive. Only the pedantic, however, would disqualify these and many other pieces from acceptance as jazz on the grounds that they lack a substantially improvised component.

The presence or absence of such a component, then, will not do as a distinctive criterion in determining what is, or is not, jazz. On the other hand, as Schuller suggests, it will not do either to minimise the importance of improvisation. The iconic figures of the music, from Armstrong and Bechet to Parker, Ornette Coleman and John Coltrane, have been recognised above all for their abilities as improvisers, and even Ellington, whose reputation rests largely on his composing and arranging, was a distinctive piano soloist (with a direct influence on Thelonious Monk, among others). Moreover, whatever the particular mixture of musical elements in a jazz performance, it is in the *practice* of improvisation – not rhythm, nor melody, nor harmony – that jazz differs most clearly from established procedures in the tradition of Western art music. Indeed, some of the most interesting aspects of jazz as a music, as well as some of the most intractable difficulties affecting its reception, are highlighted in drawing this contrast, since we are inevitably led to consider not only the music in its technical aspects, but the distinctive character of the 'art world' (Becker, 1982) in which its players and their performances are embedded.

In this chapter, the concept of the art world will be used as a basic approach to understanding jazz improvisation as an organised, collaborative social practice occurring in the context of a specific artistic community. In approaching the subject in this way, it is possible to move beyond the remarkably tenacious, yet quite erroneous, view of the improviser as an inspired individual guided only by intuition, and in addition to supplement psychological studies of improvisation (see Pressing, 1988) by recontextualising the musicians and their performances. Moreover, even a cursory examination of the specific culture of the art worlds in which jazz players operate shows the fundamental importance of *performance practice* in the aesthetics of these groups, in marked contrast, for example, to the central position occupied by the *composition of works* in the European art-music tradition. With this in mind, it may be argued that while jazz musicians have made contributions to music in a wide variety of ways, their greatest achievements have been the restoration of improvisation to the mainstream of western musical culture (see Peretti, 1992: 112–113), and the creation of an art world in which the practice of improvisation is the musicians' fundamental commitment.

Irrespective of styles, unplanned self-expression is not, typically, what happens in jazz performances. As Albert Murray put it:

no matter how deeply moved a musician may be, whether by personal, social or even aesthetic circumstances, he must always play notes that fulfill the requirements of the context, a feat that presupposes far more skill and taste than raw emotion . . . . Indeed on close inspection what was assumed to have been unpremeditated art is likely to have been a matter of conditioned reflex, which is nothing other than the end product of discipline, or in a word training. (1978: 98)

Years earlier, Ralph Ellison had identified the essential paradox in speaking of 'true jazz' as 'an act of individual assertion within and against the group . . . because jazz finds its very life in improvisation upon traditional materials, the jazz man must lose his identity even as he finds it' (1967: 234). Or in the words of Wynton Marsalis: 'It's a very structured thing that comes down from a tradition and requires a lot of thought and study' (quoted in Berliner, 1994: 63). In the present context, it is the appearance of terms such as 'context', 'training', 'group' and 'tradition' which is of particular significance, suggesting the possibilities of a sociological, as opposed to a purely psychological, approach to the understanding of improvisational practices.

## Jazz as an art world

In developing the concept of the 'art world', Becker was concerned to illuminate the cultural practices and institutional constraints which become established in any field of creative activity (Becker, 1982 and 1974; Gilmore, 1990). But Becker's purpose is not simply to reveal the features of the 'social context' of any process of artistic production (though these may be important); rather, the point is to demonstrate the ways in which such patterns of social organisation must be recognised as themselves having an effect on what gets created – what gets made, written, painted or played, and the ways in which it is done. As in other areas of social life, people engaged in artistic activities are seen as orienting themselves to recognised 'conventions' concerning what it is proper and appropriate for them to do; without this, no effective collective action would be possible (See Martin, 1995: 172ff). As often as not, the conventions which are established in a particular art world are simply taken for granted as 'the way things are' by the participants and consequently regarded as trivial, or the common sense that 'everyone knows'. Yet in bringing them to light fundamental features of the art world are revealed,

since the orientations of individuals to such socially accepted conventions constitute the links between them and the wider artistic
community. This may be illustrated by considering the concept of
performance 'style' in jazz (or any other music). From an 'art world'
perspective, musical styles are to be understood as the inevitable
configurations of conventions which guide performance practice
(see Chapter 8, pp. 187–193). The point seems obvious, even trivial, yet it is quite fundamental in the present context, since it suggests some of the ways in which jazz musicians, operating within an
art world which values musical creativity and self-expression above
all else, are nevertheless guided and constrained in what they do by
the normative conventions of the musical community to which they
belong. We are dealing, in short, with the relationship between individual inspiration and the expectations of the collectivity in which it
must be expressed.

   As is well known, people involved in particular art worlds often
form a deep attachment to specific ways of doing things, and a
highly developed aesthetic sense which is related to them: the conventions of a particular musical style, for example, as well as habitual ways of playing it, and a highly developed sense of musical
rightness or wrongness, can become unconscious, embodied aspects
of a player's taken-for-granted reality. In fact, as is well known,
many supremely capable musicians become relatively inarticulate
when it comes to explaining why they do what they do – making
remarks about how 'it felt right' or 'it just didn't work' and so on.
For Becker, much of the explanation lies in the fact that 'editorial'
decisions about what to do during the creative process have become
'acts rather than choices', as conventionally sanctioned ways of
doing things are internalised: 'in those moments of simultaneous
feeling and thinking what is being thought consists of a continual
dialogue with the world relevant to the choices being made. The editorial and creative moment fuse in a dialogue with an art world'
(1982: 204).

   An important implication is that in order to become recognised as
a capable performer, the aspiring jazz player will find it necessary not
only to acquire the necessary high level of technical skills, but also
to become immersed in the culture of this particular art world. And
as Paul Berliner brilliantly shows in *Thinking in Jazz* (1994), this is
just how things work in the jazz community. This authoritative study
will be considered further below, but at this point it is worth simply

noting some of the ways in which its results are consistent with Becker's art world perspective: Berliner places particular emphasis on the ways in which jazz musicians acquire the culture of, and operate within, specific artistic communities with their own aesthetics and patterns of organisation, and the ways in which such communities may exert an influence on both individuals' musical performances, their sense of self, and their more general lifestyles. In contrast to many purely musicological analyses, Berliner is concerned to relate the details of performances to the social context in which they occur, and to emphasise the interactional, collaborative nature of jazz playing. Moreover, by re-placing performers in their social milieu, Berliner also goes beyond those studies which have approached improvisation from the perspective of cognitive psychology (e.g. Pressing, 1988). Cognitive investigations may ultimately reveal much about *how* music is played, but studies such as Berliner's, and more generally an art world perspective, may be more revealing about *what* gets played.

It is immediately apparent that the art worlds within which jazz musicians develop and practise their craft contrast in significant ways with those of classical (or rock) players. Whereas, for example, classical trumpet players are trained to produce a 'pure' tone (which would be indistinguishable from others in an orchestral setting), jazz players are encouraged to develop a recognisably individual sound, which, if achieved, may be regarded as evidence of originality and emotional depth. Further, while the classical player is rewarded for performances which are impersonal, in the sense that they act mainly as a medium for the realisation of a composer's intentions, jazz musicians (although nowadays expected to possess excellent reading and ensemble skills) strive above all to achieve an individual 'voice'; it is this attainment of a distinct, recognisable musical identity which is most highly valued in the jazz community. The process of acquiring the necessary skills, too, has been very different in the two musical worlds. Whereas almost all classical players are trained from an early age in colleges and universities, with highly formalised programmes of instruction and examination, most jazz musicians acquired their skills informally at least until the 1970s, through professional experience 'on the job', through studying privately with established performers, through immersion in a strong 'oral tradition' in which knowledge of the music is passed on, and in collaboration with other aspiring musicians. Since then, however, formal jazz courses have become an increasingly important aspect of music education (Marquis, 1999), with implications which will be considered further below. Moreover, despite its informal pattern of organisation, the jazz world is highly centralised; since the 1940s, New York City – 'the world's largest jazz community' (Berliner, 1994: 5) – has been recognised as the 'scene' where players must establish themselves if they are to be acknowledged as top performers. Whereas in the classical music world performance standards are maintained through formal training and examination, the development of jazz musicians – though no less rigorous – is subject to the scrutiny of established elders in the jazz community, and final recognition is only granted once a player has convinced these master performers of his or her capabilities. Here again it should be emphasised that the central figure in the jazz art world is not the composer of 'works' but the improvising soloist. This point is often not fully grasped by those who are schooled in the ways of other performance traditions, but it is of quite fundamental importance for an understanding of jazz as an art world, with far-reaching implications for its organisation, its aesthetic priorities, and the activities of its members. (Arts funding bodies, for example, still find it difficult to deal with musicians whose aim is *not* to produce 'new works' or 'innovative' compositions). To repeat, the primary aim of jazz musicians is not the production of 'works', but the creation of performances.

An understanding of the undoubted creativity and spontaneity of jazz playing thus requires that any particular instance is set in the context of the expectations of a particular 'interpretive community' (Fish: 1980) whose conventions serve to guide the improviser's artistic decisions. Yet to avoid one possible source of misunderstanding, it should be emphasised that the art world perspective does not entail an undue emphasis on conformity at the expense of innovation. Indeed, as Becker puts it:

> Every art work creates a world in some respects unique, a combination of vast amounts of conventional materials with some that are innovative. Without the first, it becomes unintelligible; without the second, it becomes boring and featureless. (1982: 63)

However, as Lester Young, Charlie Parker, John Coltrane and Ornette Coleman, among others, discovered, there may be a high price to pay in the pursuit of innovations which are perceived to threaten established conventions. Radical innovators – however

talented – are likely to be marginalised or condemned as incompetent, almost inevitably attracting the hostility of those whose sense
of security – musical, psychological and economic – is derived from
their acceptance of the aesthetic *status quo*. Though it would be
unwise to push the parallel too far, the succession of improvisatory
styles in jazz displays some of the characteristics of the development
of scientific thought as presented by Thomas Kuhn (1970; see also
DeVeaux, 1997: 42ff). In both science and jazz, a high value is
attached to creative thinking and the production of new ideas. Yet,
Kuhn argues, most scientists, for most of the time, work quite productively and creatively within the constraints of a particular 'paradigm', or general framework of assumptions and beliefs which holds
the scientific community together. Revolutionary transformations in
thinking – 'paradigm shifts' – take place relatively rarely and are
experienced as periods of conflict and disruption, with a small number of individuals becoming identified as inspiring large-scale movements of thought. Moreover, just as Kuhn spoke of 'normal science'
as characterising what most scientists do most of the time, so it
seems appropriate in the present context to speak of 'normal'
improvisatory practices, in the sense that most players, most of the
time, while motivated by the goals of self-expression and finding
their own 'voice', nevertheless operate within an accepted framework of stylistic conventions which both influences their artistic
choices and provides a foundation for what they do.

## The concept of improvisation

Improvisation now plays little or no part in the dominant art-music
tradition of Western societies, although this has only been the case
in relatively recent times. A full discussion of the demise of the
improviser is beyond the scope of this chapter; for present purposes,
however, the essential point is that since the mid-nineteenth century
the art world of 'serious' music has been organised around the composition of 'works' and their performance in formal concert settings,
and the identification of a 'canon' of 'masterworks' produced by the
great composers (e.g. W. Weber, 1992, 1977). One of the effects of
these processes has been the consequent devaluation and marginalisation of improvisation in much of the discourse of 'classical' music:
it has generally been regarded as a 'somewhat mystical art' (Tirro,
1974: 285) but not one which could or should be incorporated into

established performance conventions or aesthetic theories. Indeed, Derek Bailey suggested that the term 'improvisation' has acquired largely negative connotations among orthodox musicians – 'something without preparation and without consideration, a completely *ad hoc* activity, frivolous and inconsequential, lacking in design and method' (1980: 5). Since these words were written, there have been clear signs of reappraisal and a reawakening of interest in improvisation among music scholars, doubtless encouraged by their increasing interest in jazz more generally. Nevertheless, in introducing a recent collection of essays on the topic, Nettl still found it necessary to observe that ' . . . within the realm of art music, improvisation is on a low rung, just as musics outside the realm of art music are often associated with the inferior practice of improvisation' (1998: 9).

Where the practice of improvisation has been discussed, and often in consideration of the great jazz players of the twentieth century, it has tended to be seen as a gift bestowed on a few exceptional individuals. It has certainly not been regarded as part of the normal skill-set of 'trained' musicians, whereas reading (or better still, 'sight-reading') from notated music is an essential part of competence. Once again, it might appear as though this is simply a statement of the obvious: this kind of competence is what is taken for granted in the world of 'serious' music. Yet one of the most interesting aspects of this situation is how unusual it is, when seen from the perspective of music cultures more generally. Improvisation is an important aspect of the musical cultures of many societies (Nettl and Russell, 1998), and, of particular importance in the present context, improvised elements occur in all the styles of African-American music which have been increasingly influential in the Western world during the second half of the twentieth century. From a cross-cultural perspective, then, the ability to improvise is not usually regarded as the special gift of a particularly talented individual; on the contrary, it is this belief in the special gift that is exceptional.

In one sense, of course, there is an improvised element to all musical performance. Even the rank-and-file orchestral player confronted by a score must 'play' in the sense of making the sounds happen; even the most detailed score allows some scope for 'interpretation'. (Indeed, all social interactions, such as conversations, are improvised in the sense that we do not – other than on ritual occasions – speak from scripts. The routine encounters which constitute social life must be *enacted*). So what is at stake, then, is not the principle of improvisation, but the extent to which individuals have autonomy within the context of particular performance traditions (and, as we shall see, the conditions affecting such autonomy). Moreover, the specific skills required for musical improvisation may be regarded, not as exceptional, but as normal and achievable in appropriate cultural contexts. This does not imply that in such settings everyone will become a skilled improviser, any more than that, in Western societies, all children will become capable composers. The important point is that *in principle* a practical capacity for improvisation may be achieved, just as people of varying initial abilities usually manage, with practice, to ride bicycles and drive cars. What is crucial here is the extent to which individuals' expectations and aspirations are shaped by their cultural environment. As Berliner has put it: ' . . . children who grow up around improvisers regard improvisation as a skill within the realm of their own possible development. In the absence of this experience, many view improvisation as beyond their ability' (1994: 31). For example, children in black American communities, however disadvantaged in other respects, have often been immersed in a cultural milieu which values both linguistic and musical improvisation, and affords prolonged exposure to the ' . . . complex rhythmic juxtapositions, cadences, timbres, body movements and so on . . . ' which are characteristic of African-American music. It is this cultural factor, argues Kofsky, and not any alleged 'racial memory' or innate qualities, which can explain the pre-eminence of black musicians as jazz innovators (Kofsky, 1998: 137).

The widely held view of improvisational ability as a gift possessed by a few exceptional individuals is a myth, the prevalence of which is related to the marginalisation of improvisation in the Western art-music tradition. Indeed the fallacy of this premise is demonstrated by the number and variety of musical cultures in which improvisation is a normal element. At this point, however, it remains to dispose of another, related, myth, which Kernfield has expressed succinctly: 'Somehow the casual and romantic notion that jazz is generated in an entirely spontaneous manner has become deeply rooted in our society' (1995: 99). Indeed, insofar as they have considered it at all, music scholars have often assumed that improvisation involved 'unpremeditated, spur-of-the-moment decisions' made in the 'suddenness of the creative impulse' (Nettl, 1974: 3). Nettl goes on to argue, however, that this view is misconceived; the conventional distinction between composition and improvisation is not sustainable because improvisers in all musical cultures are oriented in their performances by a learned 'model' which serves as a guide to practical action. For Small, such a model is indispensible, since the spontaneity and creativity which are, rightly, taken to be characteristic of the accomplished improviser must nevertheless be set within the context of a musical culture with its own conventions and constraints. As he puts it: 'both improvised speaking and improvised musicking take place within a framework of rules. Neither is uncontrolled invention – indeed it is doubtful if the human mind is capable of such a thing – and both feed off a great deal of pre-existing material . . . musical responses will always be governed to a greater or lesser extent by the demands of the idiom' (Small, 1984: 3, 4). In the present context, what is significant about the remarks of both Nettl and Small is not so much their dismissal of the idea of improvisation as unpremeditated (a notion which even a moment's serious reflection would show to be absurd), but – once again – their use of terms such as 'model', 'culture', 'framework of rules', and 'idiom'. For it is in the use of such terms that the practice of improvisation is revealed as collaborative and collectively organised, a social as much as a psychological matter, in which the impulses and aspirations of individuals must somehow be reconciled with the configuration of normative conventions which confronts them. With this in mind, we may return to the art world of the jazz musician, and specifically to studies which have illuminated the model of performance practice to which the improvising player must attend.

### 'Thinking in jazz'

Although the literature on jazz and its players has grown enormously in recent years, relatively little of it is concerned with actual musical practices, so the appearence of Paul Berliner's *Thinking in Jazz – The Infinite Art of Improvisation* (1994) was something of a landmark. In this book Berliner reports the results of his meticulous ethnomusicological investigation of the jazz community in New York City. His account is structured to reflect the lengthy and rigorous process which players must go through if they are to acquire the necessary skills to perform at the highest level, and – of equal importance – if they are to achieve recognition from established performers. In contrast to the art world of the classical musician, most apprenticeships are organised through informal networks of players, including the processes through which bands and groups are formed and musicians recruited to them. In the present context, Berliner's title is particularly significant, since he demonstrates how the 'thinking' of improvising jazz musicians is shaped and influenced by the ethos of the jazz community in general and by the particular networks of players in which individuals are involved. Just as socio-linguistic studies have shown how the function and meaning of language are dependent on the activities – and normative authority – of 'speech communities', so Berliner demonstrates how jazz players are socialised into accepting the values and performance practices of the wider community of players. Creativity and self-expression are central values in this community, but – and this is the point which must be emphasised – in order for players' efforts to be considered as aesthetically valid, or even competent, they must orient their practices to a specific set of musical conventions which represents, and constitutes, the performance tradition. This orientation does not mean simply accepting such conventions; what is involved is a process of engagement with them, or as Berliner puts it: ' . . . from the outset an artist's ongoing personal performance history entwines with jazz's artistic tradition, allowing for a mutual absorption and exchange of ideas' (1994: 59).

This set of conventions, which Berliner terms 'the formal structures of jazz' (*ibid.*) constitutes the model, in Nettl's sense, with which improvisers work. In very general terms, improvised 'solos' must conform in acceptable ways to the harmonic progression and formal structure of the piece (indicated by using the widely accepted system of 'chord symbols'), which must normally retain a constant rhythmic pulse. There is, moreover, a standard repertoire of pieces in each jazz style that competent performers are expected to 'know' (in the sense of memorising both melody and harmonic 'changes'), and a number of pieces generally recognised as suitable tests of a player's capabilities (such 'standards' as 'Body and Soul', 'Cherokee' or John Coltrane's 'Giant Steps'). Though the principles of the model are simply enough explained, the acquisition of jazz performance skills is both musically and intellectually demanding, and Berliner documents the many ways in which aspiring players study, practice (alone and with others) and more generally immerse themselves in the ways of the jazz community. Typically, Berliner suggests, musicians will only achieve recognition as capable performers after 'seven to ten years of attention to the stringent routines . . . required for basic competency in jazz improvisation' (*ibid.*: 494).

Far from representing the free play of individual creativity, then, jazz players' musical statements are tightly constrained by the demands of the model. In fact, from the perspective of the elders of the community, the extent to which a player can develop an aesthetically satisfactory synthesis of established conventions and personal expression is itself the supreme measure of aesthetic merit. Iconic figures are those like Armstrong, Parker or Coltrane, whose musical imagination has been sufficiently powerful to transform the tradition from within; Berliner refers to ' . . . the dynamic interplay between tradition and innovation within the jazz community as improvisers transform its musical conventions and imbue them with deep personal meaning' (*ibid.*: 92). Armstrong, Parker and Coltrane, moreover, each inspired a host of followers, even imitators, as succeeding players sought to express themselves through the musical languages pioneered by these towering influences. Indeed, as in every other musical field, the great majority of players are not great innovators, seeking mostly to develop their own distinctive approach while accepting the constraints of the underlying musical model. Initially, this very often involves efforts to emulate a chosen mentor (see also Bailey, 1980: 69). It should also be emphasised that achieving an acceptable standard of performance is not simply a matter of obeying the rules in a technical sense, as Berliner's account makes clear (see p. 30 above); what established members of the jazz 'art world' communicate to neophyte improvisers are ways of shaping performance practices – even in their most detailed aspects – which are dictated not by musical requirements, nor by individuals' creative energies, but by the norms and values of an established 'interpretive community' (Fish, 1980). As with language more generally, and indeed all social interactions, the interests and idiosyncracies of individuals must somehow be reconciled with an existing 'form of life' (Wittgenstein, 1953: 11). This point will be developed in the next chapter.

Ingrid Monson has drawn out some of the implications of the recognition that jazz improvisation must be understood as embedded in the culture of a 'community of interpreters' (1994: 305), emphasising that, as in other African-American cultural traditions, performances are shaped through an interaction between musicians and audiences, who share an aesthetic frame of reference which allows them to make sense, and to take a critical view, of what is being played. Moreover, Monson emphasises that the actual contents of performances are also the outcome of ongoing interaction among the musicians; that is, they are fundamentally collaborative in a way which (pre)composed Western 'classical' music is not (1996: 74). As a consequence of these conventions, it may often be quite inappropriate to isolate the contribution of one individual for the purposes of analysis, or to treat the outcome as a 'text' similar to a composed score (*ibid.*: 80). Indeed, an important implication of Monson's examination of the interactive nature of jazz performances is the conclusion that analyses which restrict themselves to the notated 'text' can only yield a partial view of any music: ' . . . the formal features of musical texts are just one aspect – a subset, so to speak – of a broader sense of the musical, which also includes the contextual and the cultural'. A deeper understanding of music, Monson suggests, will require the development of an 'interactive, relational theory of music and meaning' (*ibid.*: 186) which will transcend the arbitrary distinction between musical structures and cultural contexts (*ibid.*: 190). This theme will be considered further in Chapter 9; its importance is evident in any attempt to examine the performance style of jazz players in the context of the art worlds in which they were situated. For present purposes, the career of Charlie Parker may serve as one brief illustration.

### Spontaneity and organisation: the work of Charlie Parker

The alto saxophonist Charlie Parker (1920–1955) was recognised as an outstanding musician by his contemporaries and associates, and by countless more who have only heard his playing on recordings. His work inspired a whole school of followers amongst saxophonists, and he was a major influence on players of all instruments. Indeed, Giddins has argued that he was ' . . . the only jazzman since Louis Armstrong whose innovations demanded a comprehensive reassessment of all the elements of jazz' (in Woideck, 1998: 5). Yet it is clear from what is known of his musical development that he did not emerge as a fully fledged virtuoso. On the contrary, as a teenager he was regarded as the 'saddest' member of one of the first bands he was in (Ramey in Woideck, 1998: 136) and is known to have experienced public humiliation on at least two occasions following his efforts to perform with established players. On one of these, probably in 1936, Count Basie's drummer Jo Jones threw a cymbal across the floor in protest at Parker's efforts (Russell, 1972: 83–85); the occasion is dramatised in Clint Eastwood's film *Bird* (1989). Such episodes are the stuff of legend, yet in the present context they may serve to illustrate two points. Firstly, the laughter and contempt which the young Parker endured give some indication of the informal, yet highly effective, ways in which the community of established players sought to uphold accepted technical and aesthetic standards. Secondly, by his own account (e.g. Woideck, 1998: 93) Parker's inadequacies had much to do with his lack of the conventional knowledge which was taken for granted within such communities, ranging from the etiquette surrounding when and with whom to 'sit in', to the fundamental musical knowledge of appropriate repertoire, keys, chord changes, and so on.

In other words, for all his immense talent Parker, like any other aspiring jazz player, had to work extremely hard to achieve mastery of both his instrument and the musical model on which conventional improvisation was based. In 1937 he accepted a summer job with George E. Lee's band up in the Ozark mountains primarily because it afforded the chance to practise and study. There he learned to play several of Lester Young's recorded solos note-for-note, and studied harmonic progressions with the guitarist Efferge Ware. When he returned to Kansas City, said the bassist Gene Ramey, 'the difference was unbelievable' (in Woideck, 1998: 136; Russell,1972: 93). It seems that Parker subsequently modelled himself on Buster Smith, then a leading local saxophonist (Woideck, 1998: 147), and was soon accomplished enough to impress bandleader Jay McShann, who recalled that Parker practised exercises constantly at this time (*ibid.*: 140).

The familiar details of Parker's meteoric musical career (and personal disintegration) will not be repeated here (see Reisner, 1962; Russell, 1972; Giddins, 1987;Vail, 1996; Woideck, 1996). What I wish to emphasise, however, are some of the ways in which Parker's difficult apprenticeship and later acceptance demonstrate the effectiveness of the jazz community as an established art world in shaping the expression of his undoubted, but initially unschooled, talent. In all fundamental respects, this process seems to have operated in Kansas City during the 1930s in much the same ways that Berliner documented in New York fifty years later. I have already noted the ways in which established musicians indicated their dismissal of the young Parker's perceived incompetence, his determination to over-come this rejection, and the intense, even obsessive efforts which he made to this end (Smith in Woideck, 1998: 151). Moreover, it seems that he quite consciously sought to emulate the playing of Lester Young, which he learned from records, and Buster Smith, with whom he worked in 1937–38. Such mentors feature prominently in the biographies of virtually all jazz musicians. It should also be apparent that the apprenticeship process is not simply one of acquiring musical skills in a technical sense; Parker learned to improvise on the foundations of the musical material in common use in Kansas City in the mid-1930s: 12-bar blues (in a quite restricted number of keys) and a selection of 'standard' songs, such as 'I Got Rhythm', 'Honeysuckle Rose', 'Body and Soul' and 'Cherokee'. He used this material as the basis of his repertoire for the remainder of his life (see Owens, 1995: 37–38). In all these ways then, the young Charlie Parker was inculcated by his elders into the aesthetic values and musical conventions of an established, and rich, musical tradition, a tradition which – despite the radical consequences of his own work – he never challenged.

Of course, by the early 1940s, when his personal style was approaching its mature period, Charlie Parker's playing was recognised by his peers, and several of the elders, as innovative and exceptional. There was an undeniable freshness about the unprecedented combination of his melodic inventiveness, harmonic sophistication, rhythmic poise, instrumental virtuosity, and the clear sense of structure which is evident in his solos. At the same time, it is apparent that Parker's work, far from constituting a challenge to the jazz tradition as it was evolving, was in fact a fundamental contribution to its development. As Martin Williams has suggested, Parker's work represented 'a truly organic growth for jazz', rather than the 'spurious impositions of a self-consciously "progressive" jazzman', and his conclusion was that 'What Parker and bebop provided was a renewed musical language (or at least a renewed dialect) with which the old practices could be replenished and continued' (in Woideck, 1998: 13). In doing this Parker reached the aesthetic summit of the jazz community: the reconciliation of tradition and innovation in a personal style, the seamless integration of conventional and individual elements.

So Parker's achievements, far from representing a challenge to the conventions of the jazz musicians' art world, were based on his supreme mastery of them. A similar point could be made about Parker's collaborator, the trumpeter Dizzy Gillespie; not initially a brilliant player, he became an instrumental virtuoso, a diligent student of harmony, and a master improviser (see Shipton, 1999). Partly because of his command of the idiom, and partly because of his own remarkable inventiveness, Parker was perceived as 'something else' by contemporaries. As one of the great creative minds of jazz, Parker sounded distinct and original from his very earliest recordings. As DeVeaux has argued, the 'gradual and altogether unexceptionable progression of musical style' was soon *perceived* as revolutionary, largely because the 'pace of evolutionary growth demanded of jazz at this juncture proved too brisk for the average listener to understand' (1997: 7). As the outcome of his explorations with Gillespie and others in their circle began to coalesce into the distinct 'bebop' style (with Gillespie, as ever, aware of the benefits of suitably tantalising publicity), opposition – and a measure of conflict – began to emerge. All this is consistent with Becker's account of the likely effects of innovation on established artistic communities (1982: 306ff). For some listeners, the emergence of bebop simply emphasised the extent to which jazz had departed from the stylistic conventions associated with its origins, giving rise to the dispute between 'traditionalists' and 'modernists', and adding impetus to the revival of the earlier New Orleans style. For many established musicians, the innovations and virtuosity of the bebop players were experienced as a real threat to their professional standing, both financially and aesthetically, so that 'older players of all colors reacted fiercely against the young innovators' (Peretti, 1992: 200). In time, of course, the new musical language of bop became widely accepted as the basis for 'modern' jazz in general (Owens, 1995: 4; DeVeaux, 1997: 2). Indeed in later decades it was itself referred to as 'mainstream' (e.g. Gioia, 1997: 216), often to differentiate it from jazz-rock and other forms of 'fusion'.

I have suggested that Charlie Parker's improvisations cannot be understood as the unmediated expression of intuitive genius (indeed his initial efforts were perceived as simply incompetent), that the form of expression which he developed was channelled and constrained by the conventions accepted by jazz players in 1930s Kansas City, and that his ultimate pre-eminence as an innovator derived not from his rejection of these conventions but from his capacity to master and transcend them. It remains, briefly, to consider his distinctiveness as an improviser, partly to illuminate the process of improvisation more generally, and partly because this helps to dispel the notion that by focusing on conventions and constraints the 'art world' perspective somehow effaces the character of individual artists. In fact it is precisely because of their outstanding creativity that Parker and Louis Armstrong have consistently been identified as the two supreme innovators whose influence was sufficient to transform the musical language of their day and the conventions of the jazz community, and whose work consequently sets them apart from the vast majority of players. (In more than half a century since Parker was in his prime, perhaps only John Coltrane has approached his influence as an improvising soloist.)

Moreover, although recent authors, with the benefit of hindsight, have rightly emphasised the extent to which Parker's work had deep roots in the jazz tradition, there is no doubt that his playing seemed to many contemporaries to be radical and disturbing. Ralph Ellison, who heard Parker and the other bop pioneers at the legendary jam sessions at Minton's during the early 1940s, recalled their new music as

> a texture of fragments, repetitive, nervous, not fully formed; its melodic lines underground, secret and taunting; its riffs jeering – 'Salt Peanuts! Salt Peanuts!' – its timbres flat or shrill, with a minimum of thrilling vibrato, its rhythms were out of stride and seemingly arbitrary, its drummers frozen-faced introverts dedicated to chaos. (1967: 203)

Moreover, this was intellectually demanding music, not the familiar, comfortable sounds that, as Ellison put it, 'give resonance to memory' (*ibid.* ). Indeed, as Thomas Owens has suggested, Parker's solos – despite their often breathtaking speed of execution – achieved a degree of 'internal logic and consistency' (1995: 35), a structural coherence, which only the greatest of players had previously attained. For Owens, this purposeful integration of elements was largely the result of Parker's habitual use of lengthy 'scalar descents' which underlie his fluctuating phrases, and impart a sense of movement towards a definite goal: 'this scalar organisation is a device that he brought into jazz, for his predecessors' music does not contain it'. It was this 'system of improvisation' which allowed Parker to create great solos so consistently, and which was absorbed, consciously or otherwise, by his many followers (*ibid.*: 36).

Through his exhaustive analyses of Parker's work, Owens has done much to explicate the essential features of his style:

Parker, like all important improvisers, developed a personal repertory
of melodic formulas that he used in the course of improvising . . . he
favoured a certain repertory of formulas for the blues in B♭, a slightly
different repertory for the blues in F, a much different one for *A Night
in Tunisia* in D minor, and so on. Some phrases in his vocabulary came
from swing, either unchanged or modified; others he created. But
whether using borrowed or original melodic formulas, his way of combining and organising them was his own. (Owens, 1995: 30)

Owens has identified sixteen such figures which form the basis of
Parker's approach, with the most common short phrases each occurring, on average, 'once every eight or nine measures' in his improvisations (*ibid.*: 31). These are, so to speak, the conjunctions and
prepositions of Parker's improvisational language, linking his more
extended figures. One of the latter which Owens identifies is of particular interest, in that through it we can glimpse something of the
way in which Parker transformed the tradition from within. In
measures 55–57 of his famous solo on 'Shoe Shine Boy' (recorded
on November 9th, 1936), Lester Young played a phrase (Buchmann-
Moller, 1990b: 4) which reappears as the opening two bars of
Parker's solo on Jay McShann's 'The Jumpin Blues', recorded on
July 2nd, 1942. The same phrase was then used by trumpeter Benny
Harris as the opening of his theme 'Ornithology' (itself a contrafact
on the chord changes of the standard 'How High the Moon'), which
was recorded by Parker on March 28th,1946. In the early career of
this little phrase, then, we can observe both Parker's creative appropriation of the work of one of his own mentors, and the way in
which Parker's own figures and formulae were rapidly taken up by
the 'modern' players of the day, contributing immensely to the
codification of bebop as a musical language.

Another aspect of Parker's work, which Owens identifies, is of
particular relevance to the present discussion. As the recordings of
his 'live' performances demonstrate, he was particularly fond of
introducing 'quotes' from the melodies of other pieces, so that to
Ralph Ellison his solos ' . . . added up to a dazzling display of wit,
satire, burlesque, and pathos' (1967: 223). All this is testament – if
it were needed – to Parker's dazzling imagination and matchless
instrumental skills. Yet besides the introduction of humour, or a sudden change of mood, into a performance, some of Parker's quotes
provide incontrovertible evidence of his profound immersion in the
jazz tradition. In the fifth chorus of 'Cheryl' (a 12-bar blues in C),

recorded at Carnegie Hall, New York City, on Christmas Eve of 1949, Parker produces an extraordinarily skilful paraphrase of Louis Armstrong's celebrated introduction to 'West End Blues', recorded twenty-one years earlier. Exactly eight weeks later, during a performance taped at the St Nicholas Ballroom in New York on February 18th, Parker played another of his blues lines, 'Visa' (also in C). Once again, the 'West End Blues' introduction is paraphrased, only this time Parker plays the first part of Armstrong's line to complete his fourth chorus, and uses most of the rest to form the beginning of his fifth. Again, too, it is a brilliant and astonishing transposition, but beyond that it is also the clearest possible demonstration of the way in which Parker – widely perceived at the time as the arch-modernist – drew on the resources of the jazz tradition. For this is not simply a short quote from some appropriate (or deliberately incongruous) pop song, but a quite complicated fragment which Parker – in the era before the availability of tape recorders – must have worked hard to master. It is tempting, but probably futile, to speculate on Parker's reasons for introducing this extract at a time when there was considerable animosity between certain traditional and modern elements in the jazz audience. What it does confirm is his deep roots in the tradition.

Parker's interpolation of the 'West End Blues' quote also illustrates the collaborative nature of jazz performances. In the third and fourth choruses of his solo on 'Cheryl', prior to the 'West End Blues' quote, Parker plays a series of figures which end on the off-beat prior to the third beat of every second bar. The drummer, Roy Haynes, soon picks up the pattern and plays the appropriate accents with Parker. Interestingly, a very similar pattern emerges on the 'Visa' performance, also prior to the quotation from Armstrong, only this time Haynes accents the first beat of every second bar, as well as the appropriate off-beat (as in a 'conga' rhythm). This sort of evidence from tapes of Parker's 'live' perfomances once again affords a fascinating glimpse of his improvisational method. In both solos, the conga-type rhythmic figures precede the Armstrong quote, as if something in the former suggested the latter to him. Moreover, both are clearly routines, drawn from his repertoire of such devices, which his fellow-musicians (on both occasions Haynes, pianist Al Haig, bassist Tommy Potter, and trumpeter Red Rodney) recognise and respond to as part of the collaborative process of creating the performances. Indeed, such considerations may act as a reminder of the analytical limitations inherent in examining an improvisation independently of the context in which it was produced, thereby neglecting the fact that, as Monson has put it, it must be understood as part of 'an interactive musical conversation in real-time perfomance' (1996: 185). Parker's brilliance may have ensured that his was the dominating voice in almost every group he played in as an adult, yet his work was made possible only by that of others and by the wider network of the jazz art world, with all its opportunities, challenges and constraints.

## Conclusion

Even a very brief consideration of some aspects of Charlie Parker's career suggests the relevance of Becker's 'art worlds' perspective on cultural production: the ways in which Parker was informally but forcefully disciplined by the community of musicians, his intense motivation and dedicated practice, his learning from mentors, his acceptance of established perfomance conventions, his integration of innovations into the tradition, the opposition to his work by conservative elements, the formation of a self-conscious school of innovators, the codification of their style and its gradual acceptance into the mainstream. Above all, it should be apparent that this perspective is not concerned simply to document the cultural and institutional circumstances within which Parker performed – thus perpetuating the distinction between the 'art work' and its 'social context' – but to demonstrate both the ways in which the 'work' is shaped and constrained by the social context and also the arbitrary nature of the distinction itself.

It seems, too, that the 'art world' perspective may prove a fruitful basis for the investigation of further ways in which the 'editorial moments' (Becker, 1982: 198ff) in which performers shape their solos are influenced by the context of their production. There is evidence, for example, that recordings made in studio settings are likely to exhibit less risk-taking, and more signs of pre-planning, than those made by the same players in 'live' performances, where the consequences of errors or accidents may be much less serious. Alternatively, soloists may work out ways of ensuring that the relatively brief time they have avaliable to them on a recording still allows them to shine; even Charlie Parker's 'famous alto break' on 'A Night in Tunisia' (recorded at Radio Recorders Studios in Hollywood on

March 28th, 1946), appears to have been 'a precomposed, memo-
rised phrase' since different 'takes' of the piece reveal that Parker's
'break' was 'virtually identical' on each (Owens, 1995: 43). By contrast, many 'live' recordings (including Parker's) often display a
degree of exuberance, spontaneity and risk-taking which studio settings may inhibit. Indeed, it could be argued that not the least of
the ways in which the conventions of the jazz world were changed
by the artistic modernism of Parker and his cohorts was to move
players away from a conception of solos as more-or-less planned
contributions intended to fit into a larger piece, and towards the idea
of the solo as an extended personal statement. Of course, this
process had been under way for some time, and – as DeVeaux (1997)
has shown – many factors were involved, notably the institutionalisation of 'jam session' procedures, and the rise of small-group jazz.
What is clear is that after bebop improvising soloists were firmly
established at the centre of the jazz 'art world', and that Louis
Armstrong's advice to stick with 'a certain solo that fit with the tune'
(quoted in Gushee, 1998: 313) was less and less heeded by the rising generation of players.

Despite this increased emphasis on spontaneity and personal
expression, I have argued that the art of the improviser is miscon-
strued if it is still regarded as idiosyncratic, unpredictable, or dependent on flashes of inspiration. On the contrary, an 'art-world'
approach is particularly well equipped to investigate the way in
which performers' decisions – even down to their finest details – are
shaped by their assessments of situational constraints, and the
process through which they take into account the expectations of
others. While the jazz solo is often described as an act of self-expression, and while such a view may be used to give aesthetic legitimation to jazz as a musical practice, it is nonetheless the case that a
variety of identifiable influences may bear upon the soloist in the
heat of the creative process. Deciding who the 'audience' is, for
example, is not a simple matter for either player or researcher. Is it
the more-or-less anonymous crowd on the other side of the stage
lights, who may be roused to appreciation with a few well-worn routines? Is it the other musicians in the group, who may think little of
this but will appreciate what they hear as more genuinely creative
work? Is it the bandleader, or the promoter, whose musical opinions
may be questionable, but whose approval is necessary for future
employment? Or is it some 'significant other' (a respected mentor,

or a lover perhaps), who is on hand at the time, or alternatively some other 'reference group' (Shibutani, 1962) – perhaps of players who are not present, but whose aesthetic ideals are respected? The point is that the player may (or may not) take account of any of these in formulating a course of action in performance, so that such influences are all possible contributors to the shaping of the musical 'text' which emerges.

As with all jazz players, then, the apparently uninhibited spontaneity of Charlie Parker's solos was expressed through the organised conventions and situational constraints of the art world in which he found himself. Many conventions he accepted, others he transformed as a result of his own virtuosity and remarkable creativity. But there was no sudden, unpremeditated flash of inspiration; rather, an intense and lengthy process of 'working on' the musical materials available to him, from his teenage years well into his twenties. The celebrated version of 'Ko Ko' (recorded on September 26th, 1945), which sounds as stunning now as ever, was the outcome of Parker's six-year exploration of its chord sequence – 'Cherokee' – and particularly its difficult 16-bar 'bridge' section, so that over this period of time he had 'developed some comfortable ways of moving through these chords' (Owens, 1995: 39–40). None of this should in any way be taken to diminish Parker's achievement – even today the piece presents formidable problems for aspiring players – but it is an indication of the way in which all capable players have over time built up what Berliner (1994) calls a 'storehouse' of devices on which they can draw when constructing improvised solos. Similarly, Tirro (1974) has demonstrated the way in which players devise 'constructive elements', for example specific ways of negotiating unfamiliar harmonic progressions, which they they employ in subsequent performances, and which may impart a distinctive, personal character to their work. As Berliner has observed, a jazz performance of a particular piece is very often just the latest realisation of work which has been in progress for a considerable time. Through the perpetual process of 'working on' material, then, players aim to ensure that their improvisations are well-organised in a specifically musical sense. In making use of the conventions of a particular art world, they affirm their commitment to a pattern of social organisation which both facilitates and channels their self-expression.

There are striking similarities, then, between the jazz world of 1930s Kansas City, in which the young Charlie Parker struggled to find his voice, and that of New York in the 1980s, which Paul Berliner explored in such fascinating detail. Increasingly since the 1970s, however, there have been profound changes in the jazz art world, as the informal apprenticeships of old have increasingly given way to formalised courses of study in colleges and universities. Already there have been dire warnings that the price of academic respectability – with its catalogue of canonic figures, standardised teaching methods and approved repertoire – may be the death of jazz as an individualistic, creative and spontaneous music (e.g. Marquis, 1999; Tomlinson, 1992). Such perils are real indeed. But before rushing to blame the educators for snuffing out the golden age of individualism, we should reflect that the social institutions which made such an age possible – the dance halls, night clubs, theatres, bars and cafes and their jam sessions, radio shows, touring circuits, and so on, where most of the music was actually played – have also disappeared. Moreover, even if there is not an Armstrong, a Parker or a Coltrane among us, there is no shortage of fine musicians with fresh ideas, and there can be no doubt that through their collective efforts, jazz musicians have revitalised the art of improvisation in Western music.

In this discussion, emphasis has been placed on the orderly and organised aspects of jazz improvisation. This should not, finally, be taken as in any way an attempt to diminish the creative accomplishments of its players. As Berliner has put it, 'a soloist's most salient experiences in the heat of performance involve poetic leaps of the imagination to phrases that are unrelated, or only minimally related, to the storehouse' (1994: 216–217). Indeed, it precisely in reconciling the tension between innovation and tradition, spontaneity and organisation, that players seek to achieve that integration of the individual and the collective which is at the heart of the jazz aesthetic.

# 8

# 'Hear me talkin'': art worlds, improvisation and the language of jazz

> It's like a language. You learn the alphabet, which are the scales. You learn sentences, which are the chords. And then you talk extemporaneously with the horn. It's a wonderful thing to speak extemporaneously, which is something I've never gotten the hang of. But musically I just love to talk just off the top of my head. And that's what jazz music is all about. (Stan Getz, quoted in Maggin, 1996: v–vi)

> I see it as a family, and we listen to one another, and kind of keep the language going. (Jim Hall, quoted in Stern, 1999: 34)

## Introduction

The argument of this chapter is that the practice of musical improvisation, which has often been considered as a result of the unusual talent of a few individuals, or as a problem for the psychology of creativity, may be productively analysed from a sociological point of view. Indeed, it may be suggested that this form of musical expression offers a specific challenge to sociological explanation of the same kind that Durkheim (1952), more than a century ago, found in suicide – which was then, as now, generally understood as the outcome of the subjective states of individuals. As such, it was regarded as the ultimate private, intimate and personal act, and so properly approached from the perspective of individual psychology. Similarly, what could seem more personal, even idiosyncratic, than the realisation in music of powerful emotions by jazz players in mid-solo flight, so to speak, their bodies tense and their faces contorted by the sheer physical effort of getting the music out of their instruments? Indeed, much of the ideology and mythology of jazz revolves around this image of the heroic individual struggling to express personal truths within, but against, an environment of uncomprehending conformity.

Yet, as Bourdieu once put it: 'Sociology's misfortune is that it discovers the arbitrary and the contingent where we like to see necessity, or nature . . . and that it discovers necessity, social constraints, where we would like to see choice and free will' (1990: 14). With this in mind, the above quotations from two celebrated jazz musicians may serve to introduce the main theme to be developed here: building on the perspective outlined in the previous chapter, it will be argued that jazz improvisation may be understood as a kind of natural language, a collaborative practice which can be sustained only in the context of an 'art world', and which depends for its realisation upon particular interactional situations.

## Studies of jazz improvisation

Perhaps because of the low status which it has generally enjoyed in the hierarchy of western music, there have been relatively few systematic studies of improvisation (Nettl, 1998: 4), and those tend to be based on individualistic presuppositions. Indeed, while academic discussions are few and far between, they display a remarkably wide range of psychologistic positions. Thus Kernfield makes a vague reference to the role of the 'unconscious' (1995: 130), while in Pike's phenomenological approach, by contrast, musical improvisation is a 'rational creative process' based on 'conscious inner perception', and certainly *not* the 'uninvited intrusions of the unconscious mind' (1974: 91). Another candidate is Pressing's model, which he described as an 'explicit cognitive formulation' (1988: 129), and is thus representative of much recent work in psychology. There are several useful aspects of Pressing's model, not least the way in which it effectively demystifies musical improvisation, treating it not as a mysterious gift given only to a few, but as a particular set of skills which in principle may be learned like any other.

However, this model appears to be based on the assumption that the process is a cognitive one in which *individuals* process information in an input–output sequence. Such an approach is sociologically unsatisfactory in that it not only decontextualises people (in the sense of abstracting them from the real situations in which they have to act), but also obscures the extent to which they are engaged in an essentially collaborative practice. Moreover, even in its own terms the cognitive approach seems problematic, in that – as Pressing himself recognises in a later paper – the limitations of human computational abilities would make it impossible for all the presumed stages of the input–output model to be carried out within the limits of the tiny time-spans available in real-life, real-time situations: ' . . . improvisation is critically shaped by often rather severe constraints on human information-processing and action' (Pressing, 1998: 51). Thus Pressing's 'theory of the improvisational generation of musical behaviour . . . does not spell out exactly how real-time constraints of memory and attention are to be accommodated' (*ibid.*: 56).

As a consequence of these constraints, Pressing suggests that real improvisers use 'certain tools . . . representing the results of deliberate practice' (1998: 51). These tools include a 'referent', which he defines as 'a set of cognitive, perceptual, or emotional structures (constraints) that guide and aid in the production of musical materials' (*ibid.*: 52), an 'associated knowledge base' (*ibid.*: 53), and an acquired 'specialist memory' (*ibid.*: 54). For present purposes, the interesting point is that in attempting to rescue the cognitive input–output model, Pressing was led to introduce elements clearly emanating from 'outside' the individual, such as constraints on performance practice, relevant knowledge, and a specialised memory. Where else could the 'referents' and the 'knowledge base' come from? For example, Pressing takes as an instance of an important 'referent' for jazz players 'the song form, including melody and chords' (*ibid.*: 52). I think it is indisputable that the 'song form' referred to here must be understood as an element of the wider musical culture, sustained by its normative authority and the collaborative activities of many musicians. Each of the 'tools' used to shape improvisational practice is, as Durkheim might have said, a collective property, in the sense that they are derived from the established practices and discourse of particular social groups.

The difficulties inherent in using the decontextualised individual as the basis for a model of musical improvisation should now be apparent, since the implication of Pressing's remarks is that in order to become a competent improviser, a musician must participate in, or at least be familiar with, the aesthetic and practical norms of a community of practitioners (and in order to exercise such competencies, the player must perform appropriately in situations of collaborative interaction). Indeed, what Pressing calls the 'referents', 'constraints' and appropriate 'knowledge base' for improvisers appear in many ways similar to what Becker (1982: 40ff) called the 'conventions' to which participants in an 'art world' orient their activities. These conventions constitute the basis of its normative organisation, and constitute its 'reality' for participants. As I suggested in the previous chapter, this view of improvisation is consistent with Nettl's fundamental idea of the 'model' of performance practices which can be seen to underlie improvisational traditions in all musical cultures (1974: 11). For present purposes the essential point is that these models are *cultural* products – collaboratively developed, sustained and changed – and as such must be regarded for analytical purposes as social rather than individual phenomena.

Two further aspects of Pressing's account are useful in redirecting analytical attention away from the individual, and towards the social, collective dimensions of musical improvisation. The first, which will only be mentioned here (for a fuller discussion, see Gibson 2002), is the recognition that through constant practice and frequent repetition, the activities of improvisers, right down to their finest details, become *embodied* as 'automatic', just like the activities of 'walking and eating' (Pressing, 1988: 139). The endless and sometimes obsessive instrumental 'practice' which Berliner (1994) has shown to be a necessary precondition to participation in the jazz 'art world' may be understood as the essential process through which musical knowledge, technical control of instruments, and particular kinds of aesthetic sensibility become embodied. This focus on the idea of embodied knowledge not only resonates with an increased awareness in recent sociology of the significance of 'embodiment', but also with the developing critique of 'cognitivism' as an approach to the explanation of human action. Indeed, insofar as sociologists have examined improvisational practices, their accounts emphasise the theme of embodiment; for Berliner (1994) and Sudnow (1978) it is a matter not just of doing things skilfully, but of developing an embodied aesthetic sense of 'rightness' and 'wrongness'. In Becker's terms, the conventions which give 'art worlds' their organisational form 'become embodied in physical routines, so that artists literally feel what it is right for them to do' (1982: 203).

Pressing also recognised that it is useful to speak of the 'language' of jazz improvisation, and it is this which will be the main focus of attention in this chapter. Of course, jazz players and listeners have long been accustomed to using linguistic metaphors in describing performances, and it has been argued persuasively that such usage is a direct reflection of a distinctive – and fundamental – aspect of the African-American aesthetic tradition (e.g. Jones [Baraka], 1963; Gates, 1988; Monson, 1996; Tomlinson, 1992). Phrases like 'telling it like it is', 'saying something' (or alternatively 'saying nothing'), and 'hear me talkin' to ya' (Shapiro and Hentoff, 1966 [1955]) have become associated with jazz soloists' playing in an artistic context which places high value on story telling, verbal dexterity, the elaboration of familiar terms in new ways, and – in marked contrast to the Western art-music tradition – the concept of performances as essentially collaborative, with a dialogic relationship between performers and audiences (Monson, 1996: 2). According to Berliner, the principles which guide jazz improvisers are often expressed in terms of ' ... perhaps the richest of their language metaphors, storytelling, whose multilayered meanings have been passed from generation to generation within the jazz community since its earliest days' (1994: 200–201).

Such considerations, once again, lead us to consider the collective aspects of jazz performance, particularly the implication that the learning of any language, whether spoken or musical, is a collaborative rather than an individual practice (Berliner, 1994: 95, 102). Before pursuing this, however, it is instructive to consider one further psychologistic approach, as outlined by Perlman and Greenblatt (1981) in a paper intriguingly titled 'Miles Davis meets Noam Chomsky: some observations on jazz improvisation and language structure'. As the title suggests, Perlman and Greenblatt accept the premisses of Chomsky's 'transformational grammar' as an approach to the analysis of language, and so presumably his postulation of a language 'faculty' which is innate in individuals (McGilvray, 1999: 56). For them, both conventional jazz playing and speech in a natural language 'are describable in terms of three levels of structure – deep, shallow, and surface' (*ibid.*: 169). The 'surface structure' is the improvised line as performed, the 'deep structure' is the underlying harmonic organisation (such as the 12-bar blues form), with the two linked by the 'shallow structure', that is 'the array of possibilities that the musician may choose from at any given point' (*ibid.*: 172). However, this concept of 'structure' is problematic, to say the least. Whereas there *is* a set of specifiable rules and conventions which serve to orient musicians using, say, the 12-bar blues form within a particular stylistic context, it has not been possible to show that there is a 'deep structure' underlying natural language use which individuals 'know' how to apply (Rorty, 1993: 337–338). As followers of Wittgenstein have argued, what *can* be found is a collection of acceptable uses and conventions which are grounded, sanctioned and normatively organised in particular linguistic communities. Similarly, Perlman and Greenblatt's notion of 'shallow structure' turns out to be not a structure at all, but in their words an 'array of possibilities' used by musicians 'according to conventions' (*ibid.*: 172).

Once again, the choice of terminology here is significant. Conventions, by definition, are *social* patterns, not (hypothetical) structures lodged somewhere in the brains of individuals, and a recognition of the role of conventional patterns in language use leads us away from an analytic preoccupation with cognitive processing, towards a focus on rule use, and the normative organisation of social life. Indeed, for Baker and Hacker, Chomsky's account of the language 'faculty 'is 'the acme of absurdity . . . a faculty, which is not really a faculty but a cognitive state (which is not really cognitive nor actually a state), turns out to be a system of hypothesised rules' (1984: 280, 282). In the present context, the essential element in Baker and Hacker's critique of Chomsky is their insistence that the understanding of language use requires a sociological, as opposed to a psychological, approach. As they put it:

> A language is a *normative* practice, a practice of using signs according to rules. It is also a *social* practice. It exists in the activities of language users in the community, surviving the demise of individual speakers. . . . The dubious 'totality' of rules and definitions of English is not extractable from the mind or the performance of any single speaker, but only from the linguistic practices of a speech community. (*ibid.*: 285)

From this perspective, it is not Perlman and Greenblatt's view of jazz improvisation as a kind of natural language which is at fault, but their (and Chomsky's) understanding of language. Indeed, their own description of *what jazz musicians actually do* (as opposed to what they are assumed to do), provides a much more useful starting point from which to consider an alternative, more sociologically satisfactory, account: 'the musician accomplishes his/her aims through mastery of and spontaneous resort to a basic vocabulary of musical figures, interspersed by quotes, and connected by scales and arpeggios . . . . The basic lexicon of jazz 'licks' is not large – there are perhaps two or three dozen that most players rely on' (Perlman and Greenblatt, 1981: 175–176). It is, as these authors say, the use of such well-known figures, and the way in which they are used, which contributes much to the distinctive and recognisably authentic sound of a jazz performance (*ibid.*: 175). For present purposes, however, the important point is that such figures (or 'licks'), are not the personal property of individuals (although they are often derived from the work of influential players), but are part of the common stock of phrases which jazz performers make use of in normatively organised ways, in the context of established stylistic paradigms. I will return to this topic later.

I have argued, then, that while Perlman and Greenblatt are basically correct in their brief remarks on what jazz players actually do in the course of improvisation, the musicians' actions and capacities cannot be satisfactorily explained by the assumption of an innate language faculty and a 'transformational grammar'. However, some more recent studies of language use suggest how a more satisfactory approach might be developed. As Mackenzie has argued, Chomsky's perspective accepts what has been called the 'poverty of the stimulus' argument: that while children have only 'limited and contingent exposure' (2000: 173) to linguistic usages, they nevertheless are soon able to use this restricted 'data' to compose and produce grammatically correct speech. This fundamental premiss, however, has been challenged. First, in doubting its empirical validity Hacker argues (in a way which goes to the heart of the issue) that 'the "data" are inadequate not for the child to learn a language, but for the linguist to construct a theoretical grammar'. In fact, our 'contacts with "the world" are not brief but lifelong, interrupted only by sleep' (1990: 141). Moreover, children's linguistic environment does not constitute 'data' to be deployed in 'theoretical reasoning'; learning a language is not a matter of attaching names to concepts already possessed (*ibid.*: 142). Rather, what we learn is how to use words in normatively appropriate ways, and the notions of correctness we derive from this usage are not determined by a syntactic 'system of knowledge in the "mind/brain"' (*ibid.*: 135; see also Heil, 1981). Rather, as Hacker puts it: 'Grammatical principles are *rules*, not descriptive laws of a science. They specify how something is to be done, constituting norms of correctness. They do not describe regularities, but stipulate standards for the use of signs' (*ibid.*: 137). It is this understanding of language use, I suggest, that is appropriate to the analysis of musical improvisation, especially since, as far as the question of 'how a person can act freely' is concerned, a person's 'linguistic behaviour' is no different from 'the rest of his intentional actions' (*ibid.*: 140).

Secondly, Mackenzie rejects the view that normal speech is composed through the selection of appropriate words and their combination according to known syntactic rules of application. Rather, it is a ' . . . case of deploying prefabricated, institutionalised, and fully contextualised phrases and expressions and sentence heads, with a grammatical form and a lexical content that is either wholly or largely fixed' (2000: 173). That is, in producing speech we utilise a vast store of fixed, prepatterned phrases' or 'institutionalized utterances' (*ibid.*) which, if empirically recognised, lead to a view of natural language use as 'formulaic' rather than involving the endless recombination of individual words. In developing this approach, Mackenzie draws on the work of Pawley and Syder and their contention that the vocabulary of native language speakers is relatively restricted – perhaps 'a few thousand' words for 'the average mature English speaker'. On the other hand, the number of 'lexical phrases' which may serve as 'institutionalized utterances' is 'much greater, running . . . into the hundreds of thousands' (1983: 210). Pawley and Syder's conclusion is that 'complex lexical items are much more numerous than has generally been conceded and that semi-productive grammatical patterns play an important part in the creation of new linguistic forms' (*ibid.*: 219). These authors provide convincing lists of 'lexical phrases' known to, and regularly used by, English speakers; what is of interest is the congruence of their argument with the approach to musical improvisation being developed here. Mackenzie himself takes up this topic, noting the parallels between idiomatic speech and (in this case Irish) traditional music making: ' . . . a traditional musician has a repertoire of tunes and knows the range of acceptable improvisational possibilities they permit, just as a native speaker has a repertoire of semifixed expressions and knows how they can be acceptably completed and how they can be playfully distorted . . . it is the acquisition of a large store of fixed and semifixed prefabricated phrases that enables linguistic novelty or creativity' (Mackenzie, 2000: 175). The terminology here is remarkably similar to that of Berliner in describing the acquired knowledge of jazz players, when he refers to the 'storehouses' (1994: 102) of musical effects and devices on which they rely in creating 'solos'.

A number of issues arising from these arguments are of particular salience here. First, it is clear that the pervasiveness of 'institutionalised utterances', 'formulaic language' (or musical devices) should not be seen as a denial of the creativity of the speaker (or player). Fluency in a language confers a knowledge of how these patterns can be used, and the ability on occasion to deploy them in new and innovative, yet acceptable, ways. Thus Mackenzie wishes to retain the notion of a 'generative element' (2000: 174), which 'ultimately allies this description of language with Chomsky's account of the abilities of native speakers' (*ibid.*: 175). However, as suggested above, others have drawn rather different conclusions, rejecting the dualism inherent in Chomsky's view of the 'language faculty' as a 'computational system' (Hacker, 1990: 135), and its implication that 'for every outward or physical utterance there is an inner mental predecessor to that utterance of a non-linguistic nature that gives the utterance its meaning'. On the contrary, for Hagberg the 'facts of practice' force a recognition of the performative, 'improvisatory' nature of both speech and musical improvisation in which 'the meanings of improvisational phrases are discovered and attended to as (and just after) they are created, and not – as the dualistic conception appropriated from linguistic dualism would suggest – before' (Hagberg, 1998: 480, 481).

This perspective on both everyday speech and musical improvisation echoes G.H. Mead's concept of emergence, and his emphasis on 'the *contingency* of improvisational interaction: although a retrospective examination reveals a coherent interaction, each social act provides a range of creative options, any one of which could have resulted in a radically different performance' (Sawyer, 2000: 152). Similarly, for Day, jazz improvisation is 'lived activity' (2000: 102) which must be understood as fundamentally collaborative, and cannot be grasped through an analytic model which abstracts individuals from their ongoing involvement in social interactions: 'the exemplary improviser is one who, unlike Descartes, resists the temptation to adopt towards his present experience the attitude of its being *given*, all-too-familiar' (*ibid.*: 110). Accordingly, Day refers to Sudnow's 'error' in pursuing his 'jazz identity in isolation, while still assuming that [his] experiences are representative of most competent jazz practitioners' (*ibid.*: 111; see also Martin, 1979).

There are, too, significant similarities between Pawley and Syder's (1983) account of language use and Becker's (1982) discussion of activities in art worlds, notably in relation to the notion of conventions and artists' efforts to be creative within the framework which they provide. By making use of the large 'store of familiar collocations' speakers are freed to 'attend to other tasks in talk-exchange' (Pawley and Syder, 1983: 192, 208), just as established conventions, for Becker, allow the artist to innovate in some ways while taking many other features of the situation for granted (1982: 40ff). It is significant, too, that both discussions take account of the socially sustained constraints and restrictions which set limits to what is acceptable. Pawley and Syder emphasise that only a small proportion of the potentially vast number of grammatically correct utterances which could be generated according to 'syntactic rules' are actually 'nativelike in form', that is, idiomatically appropriate or normatively acceptable (1983: 193). The issue, then, is that of 'nativelike selection' (*ibid.*). How do some patterns of speech become regarded as approved and appropriate, while others – apparently equivalent syntactically and semantically – are rejected or at best considered strange? In musical contexts, as both Becker (1995) and Brown (2000: 120) have shown, there are social pressures which may constrain players to stay within the limits of accepted conventions, and which may influence the fine details of performances. In general, as Becker has put it, 'even the most inventive jazz players work a small library of short phrases which they vary and combine endlessly' (1995: 304).

Once again, the use of the language metaphor is notable, as is the consistency of these discussions with Berliner's account of the ways in which musicians learn to play jazz, with its emphases on the tension between tradition and innovation, the use of the 'storehouse' of musical devices, and the idiomatic conventions which govern what can be played in a given style. It's useful also to recall again the jazz pianist Barry Harris's comment to his student: 'I have been listening to this music for over forty years now, and my ears tell me that that phrase would be wrong to play. You just wouldn't do it in this tradition' (Berliner, 1994: 249). Here Berliner is emphasising the role of authoritative mentors in inculcating a way of playing music, and the point may be generalised. As Hacker suggests, it is through such processes of hearing and showing and learning by experience that people acquire the ability to speak in appropriate, idiomatic ways and, more generally, to conduct themselves in appropriate ways. Once again, we are led to appreciate the ways in which both natural speech and jazz performances must be understood as improvised yet 'normal' modes of social action – 'a species of ordinary, unrehearsed activity' (Day, 2000: 102; see also Brown, 2000: 114).

There is an interesting anomaly here: while ordinary speech is usually treated as prosaic and unproblematic, musical improvisation tends to be regarded as exceptional or mysterious; so theoretical accounts of improvisation which treat it as, for example, arising through an exceptional 'heightened awareness state' (Sarath, 1996: 8) must themselves be regarded as problematic. Sawyer, too, emphasises that 'everyday conversation is creatively improvised' (2000: 149) and – of considerable significance here – goes on to argue that if this is the case, 'then everyday activities such as conversation become relevant to aesthetics, as both Dewey and Collingwood claimed' (*ibid.*: 150). Although the theme cannot be pursued here, this is an important point, drawing attention to what might be termed the aestheticisation of ordinary experience: the ways in which, in both speech and everyday conduct, socialisation leads us to appreciate the appropriate and idiomatic *ways* of doing things (and the various sanctions for perceived violations of such taken-for-granted procedures). In a more specifically musical context, this idea of the 'internalisation' of aesthetic norms helps to explain why, as both Becker and Berliner note, musicians' commitments to stylistic paradigms may be experienced so strongly, as essential elements of a player's musical identity. Moreover, as Sawyer points out, in their aesthetic theories both Collingwood and Dewey emphasised the collaborative nature of artistic production and the communal source of aesthetic norms. In Dewey's terms: 'Even the composition conceived in the head and, therefore, physically private, is public in its significant content, since it is conceived with reference to execution in a product that is perceptible and hence belongs to the common world' (Dewey quoted in Sawyer, 2000: 156).

Although they depart from different premisses, then, both the cognitive input–processing–output model and the approach deriving from Chomsky's 'transformational grammar' result in various kinds of difficulties in their efforts to explain language usage. The point to be emphasised here is that both presuppose that language is a matter of what *individuals* do and consequently that explanations of language can be formulated in terms of individuals, whether responding to their environment, or activating their innate language faculty. Both these approaches decontextualise the actions of real people and, as a result, they neglect the ways in which both speech and musical improvisation are fundamentally collaborative practices, engaged in as joint or 'collective action' (Becker, 1974). Through these practices we create and sustain the *interactional* encounters and situations which are the foundation of all social life. It follows that the explanation of such practices must be sought at a social rather than an individual level. Before pursuing this theme, however, it may be useful to consider an example of the kind of musical figure (or 'lick') which, as Perlman and Greenblatt suggested, has become part of the lexicon of phrases available to the jazz player.

### What gets played?

It is likely that rather than the 'two or three dozen' basic figures rather casually mentioned by Perlman and Greenblatt (1981: 176), there are more likely to be hundreds of basic phrases which occur and recur in improvised jazz solos, which can be recognised by knowledgeable players and listeners. As Becker has put it ' . . . these phrases are typically not invented by the people playing them, but are part of a vocabulary of such phrases that go back to the beginnings of jazz playing' (Becker, 1995: 304). Such phrases are often linked by other devices which, to the initiated, serve as the musical equivalents of conjunctions and prepositions (Berliner, 1994: 228). As I suggested in the previous chapter, many of the basic 'licks' are derived from phrases used by highly influential figures. At one time, practice books containing transcriptions of Louis Armstrong's characteristic phrases ('hot licks') were sold to aspiring players, and as we have seen Owens (1995: 30–34) has documented sixteen basic phrases used by Charlie Parker which formed the foundation of his distinctive approach to improvisation. Many other noted players have made use of 'trademark' phrases or devices in formulating their own approach, and many of these have entered the lexicon recognised by experienced players (and listeners). There is, too, an expanding number of books containing transcriptions of exemplary solos by noted performers, and collections of exercises which demonstrate effective ways of negotiating the harmonic sequences underlying most jazz improvisation. All of these are available to learners. There are various other ways in which the details of improvised solos can be heard to derive from generally known devices and

formulae, and I will return to these. First, though, it may be useful
to provide an example of a phrase which has become established in
the jazz language. (To facilitate comparisons, the following examples
are presented in concert pitch).

On August 9th, 1938, Lester Young, then a member of the Count
Basie Orchestra, recorded the above solo as part of a performance
of 'I Want A Little Girl' (a standard 32-bar song) by the Kansas City
Five, who were all members of the larger Basie band. Usually a saxophonist, Young played this piece on clarinet, and in going from bar
9 to bar 10 of his solo, he produced the eight-note phrase which I
wish to focus on here:

Taken out of context, the phrase itself is slight and unremarkable, and examples or variants of it can be found in a wide variety of musical styles. It is also a phrase which falls very easily under the fingers of saxophonists, trumpet and trombone players, and pianists, and this – together with Lester Young's enormous influence – may have contributed to its widespread adoption, documented by the evidence of countless recordings made in later years. Twenty-one years after Young's solo was recorded, for example, the trombonist Frank Rehak produced the following:

Here the phrase can be heard clearly, as can Rehak's use of it as the basis of his 'turnaround' from the first to the second eight-bar sections of his solo. By this time the phrase, and variants of it, were well established and can be heard in use by leading performers, and indeed as part of what Perlman and Greenblatt called the 'lexicon' of competent jazz players. In fact, the point could be documented endlessly. The following is a short extract from a solo played by trombonist Joshua Roseman on a recording from 1999:

Here, the seven notes are an almost perfect example of the phrase in use, before Roseman extends it briefly. It should be emphasised that this recording (Douglas, 2000) was made *sixty-one years* after Lester Young's version of 'I Want A Little Girl' and that the phrase itself continues to be heard regularly, on both recordings and 'live' performances. The pianist Keith Jarrett, for example, uses it as the basis for the second half of the 'bridge' section in his 1999 recording of George Shearing's 'Conception' (Jarrett, 2000) and the phrase forms part of the theme of 'Soul Bop', as recorded by its composer, saxophonist Bill Evans, in 2004 (Evans/Brecker, 2004). In general, then, the essential point is that the phrase *can be heard* being adapted for use over a period of more than seventy years by various different players, and in a variety of stylistic contexts. It seems reasonable to conclude that it has indeed entered the lexicon of experienced players as a recognisable 'lick' and as such may be regarded as part of the jazz 'language'. The phrase, however insignificant in itself, has become part of what Berliner has called the 'storehouse' of figures, patterns, devices, effects, etc., on which players can draw in fashioning their own statements. As such, the storehouse of phrases must be understood not as the idiosyncratic creations of isolated individuals, but as the collective 'property' of the community of jazz musicians: emerging, sustained, and being transformed in the development of a collaborative tradition.

Before leaving this example, however, it is appropriate to consider its origins. The most likely source is Duke Ellington's recording of 'Delta Serenade', made on January 9th, 1934, in which the now-familiar phrase is used as the basis for the melody.

Clearly, the phrase would have been familiar to New York musicians, and anyone who heard this record, from the early part of 1934 onwards. It is therefore interesting, and possibly significant, to note that Lester Young spent from late March to mid-July of that year in New York and on tour with Fletcher Henderson's Orchestra (Buchmann-Moller, 1990a: 49–53). Whether this was the context in which Young picked up the phrase is speculation; however, what can be documented is that it was current amongst musicians based in New York at the appropriate time. Once again, attention is drawn to the collaborative practices of a community of players rather than the inspiration of isolated individuals.

## Improvisation as language

I have suggested that musical improvisation in the jazz tradition must be understood in sociological rather than psychological terms, since what is involved in the activity is the collaborative participation of players in the context of an 'art world'. The example of the little phrase played by Lester Young illustrates how a musical figure can become part of the 'storehouse' of resources which experienced and knowledgeable players can draw on. They may do so when it seems appropriate or 'sounds right' to them at a particular moment; the point to be emphasised is that both knowledge of the phrase and the ability to decide on its appropriate use (or more accurately to feel it 'right') at a particular time (the 'definition of the situation') depend on prior involvement in, and orientation to, the collective procedures of an 'art world', and an acceptance of the aesthetic criteria of a particular stylistic 'reference group' (Shibutani, 1962). In fact, there is a striking parallel between Berliner's account of the ways in which improvisations are 'heard' in the jazz community, and socio-linguistic discussions of the ways in which the functions and meaning of language are dependent on 'speech communities'. There is evidence too, as with language use, of the familiar interpretive circle in which players learn the appropriate stylistic conventions and reproduce them (in their own ways), thereby sustaining and confirming the validity of conventional practices. In Berliner's words: 'Beyond providing models for melodic shape and phrasing, the absorption of conventional vocabulary patterns establishes the basis for the relationship between aspiring performers and their tradition' (*ibid.*: 249).

As the above remark suggests, the idea of jazz improvisation as a musical language which must be learnt thoroughly, and enacted in performance, runs through Berliner's book and – as the quotations at the start of this paper suggest – there is much evidence that musicians themselves often think and talk about improvisation as a kind of language. As Berliner puts it:

> The same complex mix of elements and processes coexists for improvisers as for skilled language practitioners; the learning, the absorption, and utilisation of linguistic conventions conspire in the mind of the writer or speaker – or, in the case of jazz improvisation, the player – to create a living work. Just as creative handling of jazz vocabulary bears analogy to language use, the methods by which improvisers cultivate their abilities bear analogy to language acquisition . . . On a larger scale, players eventually acquire the ability to tell stories, shaping ideas into a structure that conveys, in the language of jazz, a beginning, middle, and end. (*ibid.*: 492–493)

What these remarks suggest is that both musical improvisation and language use are public, collective phenomena which must be understood as collaborative practices. They also, once again, indicate some of the inadequacies of attempts to explain either improvisation or speech in terms of the characteristics of (decontextualised) individuals. Of course, it would be misleading to exaggerate the similarities between musical improvisation and natural language use; the former is a technically specialised skill and, as Schütz put it, is not tied to a 'conceptual scheme' in the way that speech is (1976: 23–24). Nonetheless, there are sufficient similarities, some of which have been noted above, to suggest the validity of a sociological approach to understanding improvisation in jazz, and as a consequence to approach the fundamental issue of *why people play what they do* at particular moments and in particular situations. It may be suggested, firstly, that this is simply a specific instance of the general question underlying all attempts to explain social action (Why do people do what they do?), and secondly that individualistic approaches – whether they derive from cognitive psychology or structural linguistics – are not well equipped to answer the questions which, from a sociological point of view, are analytically central: Why these words and not others? Why this action and not that? Why this musical phrase, or sound, or effect, rather than other possible ones?

Once again, Berliner's work suggests the potential of a sociological approach. Established musicians, Berliner points out, are not so much concerned to teach specific details of performance practice as to inculcate appropriate ways of going about things: ' . . . veterans who teach jazz vocabulary directly to students never suggest that phrases be ends in themselves. Instead, they represent their demonstrations as examples of the kinds of things you can do' (Berliner, 1994: 142). Indeed, Berliner's discussion of this point echoes a well-known, but earlier and purely theoretical consideration of the way in which rule-governed language use is in itself constitutive of a 'form of life':

> Learning how to do something is not just copying what someone does; it may start that way, but a teacher's estimate of his pupil's prowess will lie in the latter's ability to do things which he could precisely *not* have copied . . . . He has to acquire the habit not merely of following his teacher's example but also the realisation that some ways of following that example are permissable and others are not . . . . It involves *being able to go on*. (Winch, 1958: 58–59)

It is in exactly these ways that the norms of the jazz art world are internalised and embodied, and that experience is aestheticised so that particular 'feelings' about rightness and wrongness become part of the consciousness of the practitioner.

It should be emphasised at this point – in the hope of avoiding an all-too-familiar misunderstanding – that this reflexive view of the way in which the normative conventions and aesthetic values of the art world become part of the consciousness of the players does not entail a reductive or even deterministic view of their actions. Obviously, it would be absurd to regard the improvising musician as a 'judgemental dope' (Garfinkel, 1967: 68), 'who unthinkingly . . . "acts out" the institutional directives of the culture' (Heritage, 1984: 27), or as a puppet whose strings are pulled by social forces of one kind or another, especially as notions of innovation and creativity are at the very centre of the jazz world's aesthetics (Berliner, 1994: 486). Here, Becker provides the essential clarification by emphasising the ways in which art world practitioners *orient* their activities towards established conventions, or *take account of* them, in formulating their courses of action – or in Becker's terms, 'editing' what they do (Becker, 1982: 192ff). To be considered innovative or creative, it is not enough to act strictly according to conventions (although many artists do this, and may be regarded as perfectly competent practicioners). As Becker puts it: 'although artists ordinarily take into account the imagined responses of other members of the art world during the artistic moment, they learn to ignore them at times' (*ibid.*: 204). For the improvising musician, this refusal may be part of an effort to create distinctive, recognisably personal, statements, as in the case of Lester Young, referred to above. After a short period (in 1934), Young was forced to leave the Fletcher Henderson Orchestra because he deliberately refused to imitate the then-fashionable style of his predecessor, Coleman Hawkins. 'I had in mind what I wanted to play', he explained, and I was going to play that way' (Buchmann-Moller, 1990a: 50).

Berliner provides a more recent example of a player's simultaneous recognition of a convention, and rejection of it. In the transition from one soloist to the next, it is a common practice for the second player to begin by copying or paraphrasing the final phrase played by the first. Apart from demonstrating the aural skill of the player, this convention (often heard on recorded as well as 'live' performances) can convey a sense of continuity to listeners. Yet, like other such practices, its effect may diminish with use, and it may come to seem like the antithesis of creative playing. The saxophonist James Moody, reports Berliner, consciously seeks to eliminate such well-worn conventions from his work: 'I'll tell you something else that really gets on my nerves. It's when I hear a horn player who comes in playing the last phrase of someone else's statement. I never do that . . . . Let me do something else' (Moody quoted in Berliner, 1994: 403). (In the present context, it is again notable that Moody chooses to describe improvisation by using terms such as 'phrase' and 'statement'.)

In the act of producing improvised solos, then, jazz musicians seek to reconcile personal orientations and impulses, on the one hand, and socially sustained conventions, on the other. The crucial element is the process of reconciliation rather than the domination of one or the other: 'in those moments of simultaneous feeling and thinking what is being thought consists of a continual dialogue with the world relevant to the choices being made. The editorial and creative moment fuse in a dialogue with an art world' (Becker, 1982: 204). In a pioneering analysis, Tirro (1974) obtained data which allowed aspects of this process to be explicated. Tirro describes the technical task facing jazz improvisers, and their use of a 'model' or 'the schema which limits the probabilities allowable for a solo in a particular style' (*ibid.*: 289), developing the argument that as far as their musical content is concerned, solos by experienced players are not one-off, isolated events; rather, 'each improvisation has a history of similar, related performances' (*ibid.*: 296). Like composers of Western art music, jazz musicians aim to develop a personal, distinctive treatment of the material that confronts them – harmonic sequence, tempo, rhythm, and so on – within a particular stylistic framework, or set of conventions. There is much evidence of this on recordings, which show players working on and developing particular ideas, often over considerable periods of time, but Tirro's distinctive contribution was to record all the stages through which group of players rehearsed and eventually performed 'an unfamiliar and difficult piece' (*ibid.*: 297). The recorded evidence showed that on a specific passage chosen for analysis, the first two versions produced by the alto saxophonist (Bunky Green) 'bore little relationship to the eventually adopted pattern. Then, of the subsequent twenty versions, seventeen bear the imprint of the idea' (*ibid.*: 300). What the evidence shows, then, is the process through which Green selected a pattern which 'worked' for him, and then developed it in subsequent performances of the same piece over a two-month period. It is through the use of such 'constructive elements', Tirro suggests, that improvisers develop coherent, formally organised, musical statements in which individual inspiration and socially sustained conventions can be reconciled.

The implications of Tirro's analysis are consistent with those of Berliner. Far from being spontaneous, unpremeditated events, the solos played by mature improvisers are in an important sense 'work in progress'; the latest version is a revision, itself ' . . . the product of a reworking of formerly used syntactical elements' (Tirro, 1974: 297). In the present context, Tirro's use of the term 'syntactical' is once again worthy of note, as is his observation that the communication of meaning by improvisers depends on cultural resources shared by both musicians and those who listen to them: 'the audience is part of a larger jazz community which can be assumed to know the standard repertory' (*ibid.*). Tirro's work, then, lends support to the contention that musical improvisations in the jazz tradition are normatively organised within a context of social conventions, and can be described in terms of natural language use in a speech-community. If so, then it should be evident that such improvisations must be understood as specifically sociological rather than psychological phenomena, and analysed accordingly. Moreover, I hope that enough has been said to dismiss any lingering suspicion that this perspective involves a sociologistic denial of individual autonomy or a reduction of action to the outcome of larger social 'forces'. On the contrary, analysis focuses precisely – as in interactionism more generally – on the ways in which particular individuals, with unique biographies and projects, must nonetheless collaborate in the context of the social 'worlds' which their actions both sustain and reproduce. After all, in an important sense natural language is itself improvised; normally what we say is not rehearsed but formulated 'as we go along', often using ritualised formulae, usually taking account of the unfolding dynamics of situations, sometimes requiring conscious effort, sometimes proving very difficult. The essential point is that irrespective of what things we are saying, the linguistic resources with which we attempt to formulate them – our words, phrases, intonation, concepts and so on – are drawn from and reproduce the collective practices of speech communities. In this respect (although not in all others), jazz improvisation may be understood in the same way as 'natural language'.

## Implications

Before concluding, it may be useful to consider three implications of the argument that jazz improvisation is essentially a collaborative practice, and as such may be best understood from a sociological perspective.

### *The jazz aesthetic*

I have noted the extent to which jazz musicians themselves, and those who write about them, have used the metaphor of language in describing the practice of improvisation (e.g. Berliner, 1994: 95ff), and sometimes extended this to try and capture the reflexive process in which appropriate courses of action are formulated. Drummer Max Roach, for example, talked about developing an improvisation in this way: 'From the first note that you hear, you are responding to what you've just played. It's like language: you're talking, you're playing, you're responding to yourself. When I play, it's like having a conversation with myself' (Berliner, 1994: 192). Roach's words (which, incidentally, echo G. H. Mead's concept of the reflexive self) nicely link the 'outer' and the 'inner' aspects of the process, the effort to use the 'vocabulary' of the music in appropriate yet distinctive ways. Indeed, these two aspects are the basis for two of the fundamental themes in the ideology of the jazz world: the language metaphor, which I have emphasised, representing the public, collective, communal traditions of music-making; and, in apparent contrast, the private, individual creativity of players celebrated for their unique qualities of inspiration. As Berliner put it: 'On the grand scale of judging the overall contribution of the artist to jazz, a fundamental criterion is originality . . . ' (*ibid.*: 273). Yet it would be a mistake to regard these 'outer' and 'inner' ideological themes as contradictory. On the contrary, they are derived from the two basic imperatives of the improviser's situation – the public and the private, so to speak. It has been argued in this paper that effective use of the 'language' of jazz depends on a reconciliation of the two, just as participation in social life more generally involves what Schütz (1964: 161) called 'tuning-in' to the taken-for-granted features of the *inter*subjective world, and the achievement of ' actual simultaneity . . . of separate streams of consciousness' (Schütz, 1972: 163).

*Styles as conventions*

A consideration of these 'taken-for-granted' features leads to the possibility of specifying for specific improvisers in particular situations just what it is that they are 'oriented to' or 'attending to' as they make the 'editorial' choices which determine the outcome of their work. So far I have referred rather loosely to the 'jazz tradition', yet as suggested in the previous chapter it is clear that this tradition is itself differentiated into various stylistic orientations – bebop, Dixieland, swing, hard bop, fusion, New Orleans, and others – each with its own aesthetic and associated patterns of things that sound 'right' and 'wrong'. Within each of these 'schools', moreover, there are further distinctions (for example, between 'hot' and 'cool' approaches: Armstrong/Beiderbecke, Hawkins/Young, Brown/ Baker, and so on), and the picture is further complicated by the considerable influence of players who have achieved iconic status and of those, equally influential if less well-known, who have been the mentors of particular performers. So it would be quite wrong to reify the various 'styles' of playing, or to exaggerate the strength of the boundaries between them. On the other hand, from an analytical point of view styles may be usefully conceptualised (in this and other traditions of music) as configurations of conventions, in Becker's (1982) sense of the term. It is precisely an orientation to what improvisers take to be the conventions of a particular style that lead them to make the 'editorial' choices that they do. In the jazz art world, there are conventions about not only, for example, the appropriate instrumentation for a given style, its repertoire and the keys in which pieces are to be played, but also about how players *ought* to sound in particular contexts. Ways of playing – even small details – which are encouraged and approved in one style may be dismissed as 'corny' or otherwise inappropriate in another. To repeat, these conventionalised ways of doing things constitute and reproduce the aesthetic values of a stylistic orientation, which become part of the consciousness of practitioners, and allow us to identify patterns of normative organisation embedded in the practices of improvisers.

This point will be pursued below. First, though, it is worth noting one implication of regarding styles as configurations of conventions: the idea that since much 'improvised' jazz conforms quite closely to a stylistic paradigm, it may be regarded as 'normal', in the sense that Kuhn used the term 'normal science' (Sharrock and Read, 2003).

That is, a great deal of what musicians play in conventional settings – for example, saxophone-led quartets, big bands, piano trios, traditional bands, and so on, can be accounted for in terms of their orientation to known conventions and their reproduction of devices which successfully reproduce them. Of course, almost all players, as suggested above, will try to do these things in their own way and achieve a distinctive 'voice'. Yet the extent to which they achieve this is variable, with some players (even quite well-known ones) content to emulate the sounds of an admired mentor, while others consistently try to develop a unique and recognisably original approach. The important point is that while most seek to 'express' themselves musically, to 'say something' in what they play, they have to do so through the medium of an established stylistic 'language' – just as in everyday speech.

## The 'internal dialogue'

As noted above, Becker's account of the 'editorial' process involved in the creation of artworks draws on Mead's model of the reflexive self, able to respond to itself as to another, and to formulate actions through an 'internalized dialogue' (Becker, 1982: 198, 200). Yet it might be objected that this postulation of an 'inner conversation' (Baldwin, 1986: 80) raises difficulties similar to those faced by the cognitivist approach criticised above. While it is true that Mead's model does not decontextualise the individual – indeed, it was developed specifically to demonstrate that 'mind' must be understood as a *social* process (Mead, 1934: 224) – the idea of the internalised dialogue might be said to depend on the postulation of 'internal' mental processes and states which, as in the cognitive model, are hypothetical and empirically unobservable. Coulter, for example, has argued that the notion of an 'internalised dialogue' is both 'highly mentalistic' and ultimately metaphysical (1989: 57, 58). Most actions in most situations are not preceded or accompanied by information-processing, decision-making or interpretation. As Baker and Hacker put it, for most of the time we do not need to engage in 'silent soliloquies' in order to understand what is going on (1984: 349). Situations are intelligible, just as the sounds of language are comprehensible, because we have been socialised into an acceptance of the ways of a particular cultural community, into a 'form of life'. Consequently there is no need to postulate an 'internalised dialogue' in order to explain action; as Coulter puts it, 'intelligibility is intersubjective' (1989: 68), not a matter of subjective interpretation.

Clearly, full consideration of this challenge to 'mentalistic' perspectives is beyond the scope of this chapter. In relation to the conceptualisation of musical improvisation, however, certain themes emerging from recent studies seem to suggest a way forward. It is notable that despite the theoretical gulf between cognitive psychologists and their critics, there is a clear convergence in accounts of the empirical processes through which improvised musical conduct becomes embodied practice. The following is from Pressing, who as we have seen, developed an 'explicit cognitive formulation' (1988: 129):

> By the time advanced or expert stages have been reached, the performer has become highly attuned to subtle perceptual information and has available a vast array of finely timed and tuneable motor programmes. This results in the qualities of efficiency, fluency, flexibility, and expressiveness. All motor organisation functions can be handled automatically (without conscious attention), and the performer attends almost exclusively to a higher level of emergent expressive control parameters. (*ibid.*: 139)

The description of the activity here is in many ways consistent with Sudnow's account of his own experiences in learning to become a competent improviser, and his eventual realisation that the whole process involved *eliminating* the distinction between 'thinking' and 'doing' that the very notion of decision-making presupposes. As his abilities improved, Sudnow reports, the deliberate formulation of plans of procedure receded from consciousness: 'there was no need to find a path, [or] image one up ahead' (1978: 94). In fact deliberate planning had the effect of inhibiting the essential activity he sought to sustain, the ability to 'sing' on his instrument. The metaphor of 'singing' is useful here, not only because it is a musical one, but also because it implies the transcendence of two distinctions – between player and instrument, and between thinking and doing. Here Sudnow anticipated a more recent concern in social thought by insisting that both knowledge and action must be understood as embodied: 'To *define* jazz (as to define any phenomenon of human action) is to *describe* the body's ways' (*ibid.*: 140).

Both Pressing and Sudnow, although they represent very different theoretical positions, suggest that the learning process through which someone becomes a competent improviser involves overcoming the initial conscious focus on possible courses of action and moving towards a stage in which appropriate 'ways of the hand' are simply felt, when a separation between conscious 'thinking' and 'doing' actually obstructs competent performances. It is significant that the theme of embodiment – like that of language – also emerges in Berliner's discussion, when players describe how their fingers 'find' phrases for them, without any conscious 'choice' occurring. It is important to recognise, too, that they are guided by their absorption of aesthetic norms, and that their musical responses are more than simply intellectual ones: 'through its motor sensory apparatus, [the body] interprets and responds to sounds as physical impressions, subtly informing or reshaping mental concepts' (Berliner, 1994: 190). Moreover, the enormous amount of practice which jazz musicians undertake may be understood as the process by which skills and knowledge become 'embodied'. It may be suggested, then, that the notion of 'embodied knowledge' which emerges from these (and other) studies may go some way towards disposing of the difficulties raised by the term 'internalised dialogue'. Certainly, it is clear that Becker does not take this term to imply the priority of mental processes. The conventions which, he maintains, serve to give art worlds their organisational form ' . . . become embodied in physical routines, so that artists literally feel what is right for them to do' (1982: 203).

## Conclusion

Jazz improvisers fashion their musical statements through a recognisable musical language which is shaped by the established conventions of the art worlds in which they operate. Such a view, however, does not entail the substitution of a deterministic sociologism. On the contrary, the 'embodied knowledge' acquired by improvisers does not dictate what they do so much as allow them to engage in a 'dialogue' (Becker, 1982: 204) with an art world organised around specific aesthetic norms. There are evident parallels between this account of the jazz community as an art world and Fish's analysis of the ways in which readings of texts are not determined by the texts themselves, but in the 'interpretive communities' in which they are generated and sustained (Fish, 1980: 171). So a further implication of this perspective on the production of art works is that the distinction between text and context becomes analytically problematic, and that, contrary to some recent arguments (e.g. Zangwill, 2002), a sociological approach not only has much to contribute to explaining the production of all sorts of works and artefacts, but may also be indispensable. This theme will be developed in the following chapter.

# Text, context and the cultural object

## Introduction

A notable aspect of the development of the social sciences in recent years – some would say *the* most notable aspect – has been the enormous increase in concern with the analysis of culture. The reasons for this 'cultural turn' are complex, and a full consideration of them is far beyond the scope of this chapter, but I don't think that anyone would seriously dispute that it has occurred. Within sociology, it has been suggested that this reorientation of the research agenda reflects a fundamental change in capitalist societies themselves during the twentieth century: from an earlier period in which people's sense of their own and other identities was closely linked to the kind of work they did and when sociological thought was much influenced by the notion of human beings as producers, to an era in which both identities and sociologists' interests were shaped by a concern with acts of consumption (e.g. Chaney, 2004: 41). Clearly, this reorientation brings with it a new focus on commodity consumption, lifestyles, and the effects of the mass media, although it should be remembered that, from the 1930s on, the critical theorists of the 'Frankfurt School' anticipated many of these concerns in their analyses of the effects of mass culture in modern societies, and their despair over the increasing dominance of the 'culture industry' (Adorno and Horkheimer, 1979).

Parallel to these developments within sociology, relatively new fields have been opened up, with the formalisation of cultural and media studies as specialisms in their own right – although describing matters in this way is somewhat misleading, since the growth of academic interest in cultural analysis has led to a blurring of disciplinary boundaries and a renewed interest in interdisciplinary studies. One consequence is that, just as there has been a 'cultural turn' in the social sciences, so in the humanities a 'turn to the social' is apparent, with scholars in, for example, the fields of literature, the visual arts, and music displaying a concern not only to rediscover the social contexts of the creation and reception of artworks, but also to show how the works themselves bear the imprint of the social circumstances of their production. In this, of course, analysts are following the path taken many years ago by Adorno, and much of the recent renewal of interest in his work may derive from his view that 'authentic works of art give us true knowledge of the contemporary sociohistorical totality' (Zuidervaart, 1991: 43). As far as Adorno was concerned, music in modern societies was mostly 'affirmative', a commodity produced for the market, serving both to yield profits and to 'conceal alienation by mystifying the true character of the relations of production . . . ' (Paddison, 1993: 103). Alternatively, for Adorno, the 'radical "serious" music of the avant-garde' (a small sub-set of all musical production) can act as a 'negation', expressing alienation and refracting 'the contradictions of society immanently, in terms of its own material and structure' as in the case of 'Schoenberg and the Second Viennese School' (*ibid.*: 103–104). In what follows, I will consider some of the implications of this perspective for what may be termed called the 'social analysis' of music, an approach which is echoed in much of the work of the 'new' musicologists but one which, as I have suggested, is problematic from a sociological point of view. An alternative perspective will be outlined, using the process of jazz improvisation as an example of how a more satisfactory analysis of cultural objects may be realised.

## Cultural objects as 'sedimented geist'

It should be said immediately that there is much of interest in the works of the 'new' musicologists, and much that resonates with sociological concerns (as I have argued in Chapters 2 and 3). In particular, the new musicologists have – rightly – argued for the broadening of their discipline to include all kinds of musical production and consumption, and against its continuing preoccupation with the 'canon' of great composers and their works. Thus popular styles are to be regarded as worthy of serious analytic attention, since for the new musicologists they are an expression of the social-structural location and ideological commitments of the groups of people who create them. Contrary to Adorno's dismissal of popular music styles as nothing more than affirmative commodities, it follows that for the new musicologists popular music *can* express rebellion or resistance, or in Adorno's terms act as a 'negation' of the ideology of mass society. This is the essence, for example, of Shepherd's explanation of the popularity in the latter half of the twentieth century of rock styles, their counter-cultural messages driven by the oppositional force of the black music in which they are rooted (1991: 143ff; see also the argument of Bradley, 1992). Such analyses have begun to free academic musicology from the grip of the Western 'classics', showing how the boundary between 'serious' and 'popular' music is socially constructed (and so may be contested), and demonstrating the limitations of Adorno's view of music as either 'affirming' or 'negating' the oppressive culture of mass society.

However, it will already be apparent that another, perhaps even more fundamental, aspect of Adorno's analytic approach has been retained by the 'new' musicologists; indeed it has been taken by them as constitutive of the 'social analysis' of music. This is the idea, touched on above, that cultural objects in general, and music in particular, must be understood as a 'crystallization of history' – that is, as bearing within their form traces of the social circumstances in which they were created, or, as Adorno put it, representing 'sedimented *Geist*' ([1949]: 38). This notion, as I have argued, is implicit in Shepherd's concept of the 'structural homology' between forms of music and forms of social organisation. Similarly, it has been suggested that McClary's interpretations also presuppose a 'homology' between music and society, which depends on 'an equation between conformance to or subversion of normative patterns in music on the one hand and in society or ideology on the other' (Cook, 2001: 172). Indeed, the importance of the music–society 'homology' to this mode of analysis is emphasised by Cook: 'Take away the homology and the interpretation loses its plausibility as an interpretation *of* the music rather than one imposed *on* it; it becomes, in a word, arbitrary' (*ibid.*).

There are a number of important issues here, but in this chapter I will be concerned in particular with the analytic and theoretical *consequences* of the assumption that cultural objects are representations of the social context of their production, so that 'microcosmic analysis' will reveal the generality of social relations within the 'concrete particular' (Buck-Morss, 1977: 74). It seems to have been Walter Benjamin whose ideas influenced Adorno to adopt this position (*ibid.*), but I will say no more about the assumption itself, other than to point out that in the view of several commentators, Adorno was unable actually to specify *how* musical forms are able to represent social ones (Jay, 1984, 271–272; Middleton, 1990: 61; Subotnik, 1991: 247; Zuidervaart, 1991: 97–98; Paddison, 1993: 277; Martin, 1995: 117), and to suggest that the new musicologists have been no more successful in demonstrating this relationship. What I do want to explore, however, is the immediate consequence that this way of approaching the 'social analysis' of music retains both the idea that for analytic purposes music may be treated as a cultural object or 'work', separable from the circumstances of its production, and also that this analysis will necessarily involve an interrogation of music as a cultural 'text' so as to disclose its inherent (social) meaning. This is certainly Adorno's *modus operandi* (Buck-Morss, 1972: 139), it underlies Shepherd's readings of music as 'social text' (1991), and it appears to be the basis of McClary's assumption that 'social knowledge' is inscribed in musical 'conventions' (2000: 5–6). However, as I have argued above (pp. 18–19), like the other social analysts of music McClary is not able to specify *how* musical conventions have the powerful effects she claims (2000: 6–7); her own analysis consists of readings of musical texts abstracted from the social contexts in which they are played and heard. She says little or nothing, for example, about actual processes of reception, the uses to which music may be put, the various ways in which it may be appropriated, and so on.

On this basis, like many an 'old' musicologist, McClary and the others appear to retain the notion that music has some kind of inherent meaning, a commitment which is difficult to reconcile with both their own espousal of social constructionism, and any sociological approach which takes seriously the premiss that the meanings of cultural objects are not intrinsic but are generated in the process of collaborative interaction (Blumer, 1969: 69). To repeat, I am not primarily concerned here to debate the nature of musical meaning (on this see Martin, 1995: 25ff), but with the retention in these so-called 'social' analyses of the idea of a 'text' or a 'work' which is somehow independent of the circumstances of its realisation. In what follows it will be argued that, *from a sociological perspective*, this idea is problematic, and that it rests – though these presuppositions are usually tacit – on the reification of both 'text' and 'context', and on an essentialist ontology which has been largely discredited in

contemporary sociological work. In pursuing this theme, it is useful
to recall Blumer's purpose in considering the social constitution of
cultural objects, which was to develop some of the implications of
G.H. Mead's philosophy for sociological analysis: ' . . . for Mead
objects are human constructs and not self-existing entities with
intrinsic natures. Their nature is dependent on the orientation and
action of people toward them' (Blumer, 1969: 68). Certain quite
fundamental consequences follow from these apparently straightforward points. Firstly, despite the claims of the musicological analysts mentioned above, the idea that a musical 'text' (or any other
cultural object) can have an 'intrinsic' meaning is decisively rejected:
the *sociological* focus of analytic interest is on the ways in which
such 'texts' are interpreted, defined, appropriated and variously
used. (As Rorty has pointed out, interpretation is itself a kind of use
to which a text may be put; 1999: 134, 144). Secondly, it follows
that 'texts' and other cultural objects are *themselves* the outcome of
human interactional work – they do not exist 'out there', so to
speak, but are constituted by people on the basis of their cultural
relevancies (what they have learned to 'take for granted') and individual interests. In fact the persistent failure to specify the 'real'
nature of musical 'works' is a fine example of a debate premised on
the reification of the 'text' and the search for its 'essence'. As I shall
suggest, from a sociological point of view what one can observe in a
musical performance are people engaged in various social practices,
simultaneously orienting themselves to each other and to cultural
'objects' relevant to their purposes: perhaps scores or chord
sequences, maybe a conductor or bandleader, certainly instruments,
with luck an audience, and so on. At the same time, I will be considering some of the implications of Rorty's contention that 'All that
it takes to be an object is to be talked about in a reasonably coherent
way' (1999: 85).

## The constitution of social worlds

As Blumer points out, the implications of Mead's perspective,
though simply expressed, are quite profound:

> This analysis of objects puts human group life into a new and interest-
> ing perspective. Human beings are seen as living in a world of mean-
> ingful objects – not in an environment of stimuli or self-contained
> entities. The world is socially produced in that the meanings are fabri-

cated through the process of social interaction. Thus, different groups come to develop different worlds – and those worlds change as the objects that compose them change in meaning. Since people are set to act in terms of the meanings of their objects, the world of objects of a group represents in a genuine sense its action organisation. (Blumer, 1969: 69)

In fact, the sociological approach which Mead's ideas open up departs quite radically from many established and orthodox assumptions in the social sciences. As Blumer indicates, it invalidates any attempts to explain human behaviour in terms of prior 'stimuli', and shows how 'meaningful objects' are not 'self-contained entities' which can be objectively defined. Instead, and in keeping with Mead's pragmatist orientation, the perspective takes cultural objects to be produced and reproduced through processes of collaborative interactions, which are the primary and inescapable site of human communication. This does *not*, however, imply that the conduct or outcomes of interactions are unpredictable, open-ended or subject to the whims of individuals; on the contrary, the collective constitution of cultural objects, for Blumer, generates and sustains 'worlds' of meaning which – as Durkheim said of 'social facts' – are external to individuals and constrain them (Durkheim, 1982 [1895]). But whereas for Durkheim, and the tradition of 'structural' sociology which he inspired, such 'social facts' (such as *rates* of crime or suicide) describe societies and social structures which are real 'entities' with causal powers – such as the 'normal' rate of crime or the 'suicidogenic current' (Durkheim, 1952 [1897]) – from Mead's perspective such conceptions of society or social structure are treated as abstractions, which by definition cannot have causal powers. Instead, the orderliness of social life and the pattern of relationships (including, it must be said, such matters as inequities in wealth, power and prestige), in other words the 'sheer force' and the 'facticity' of social institutions (Berger and Luckmann, 1991: 78) are to be conceived as the *outcomes* of the 'collective action' (Becker, 1974) which is the normal condition of human life. The perspective thus entails a decisive rejection of a positivist ontology in the human sciences, and with it the idea that human action may be explained in terms of causes and effects – as well as the notion that 'objects' have inherent qualities or intrinsic meanings.

In what follows, I will be mainly concerned to illustrate some of the ways in which this alternative tradition of sociological thought, inspired partly – though not wholly – by Mead and the symbolic interactionists, can both overcome the sorts of difficulties listed above and demonstrate the value – indeed the indispensability – of sociological thought in developing our understanding of music as social practice. Doing so initially involves a reconsideration of the premisses on which the social analysis of music is to be carried out, and in particular an analytic reorientation which involves moving away from a focus on the musical 'work' isolated from its social context. Such a move is consistent with Mead's project of overcoming the false dualisms – such as individual/society (or, in this case, text/context) – which he saw as obstructing the development of a properly scientific understanding of social life (Baldwin, 1986). Instead, Mead developed a view of human social life as processual, essentially collective, and collaborative; one in which cultural objects are treated not as 'self-contained entities' but as *constituted* in the constant interactions among members of society. Although coming from a different theoretical background, Middleton has nicely captured some of the implications of this view for the social analysis of music, asking: 'Is the individual song the only, or even the basic unit of meaning, rather than the larger discursive categories (genre, style, performers, album, radio programme, and so on) and the context provided by social practices (dancing, driving, partying, discussing)?' (Middleton, 1990: 114). What is entailed here is a view of music as an element in wider configurations of social interaction and as realised by people in specific social situations, rather than as a 'self-contained entity', and it is a view which I will consider further. First, though, it should be said that this does not in any way invalidate the practices of musicologists in separating 'pieces' of music from their social contexts for the purpose of, say, analysing their internal structure or documenting their history. What it does suggest, though, is the divergent analytic interests of musicologists and sociologists of music, and the consequent differences between the discourses in which they operate; in recent times, sociologists have increasingly begun to ' . . . focus on how people make and do things with music, [and] have sought to move beyond the music/society dichotomy . . . ' (DeNora, 2003: 155). In the contemporary sociological discourse, music is thus 'decentred', so to speak, and seen as an aspect of more general social practices; but in itself this is no reason for musicologists also to make this move, or to stop what they are accustomed to doing.

## Musical works as cultural objects

Having argued for a recognition of the distinctiveness of musicological and sociological discourses, and the contrasts between them, it seems reasonable to give some indication of the nature of contemporary sociological approaches, and of the particular contribution which they can make to an understanding of music in social life. A useful initial orientation has been provided by Becker, in noting that 'the very idea of "the work itself" is empirically suspect' (1999: 1). By this, Becker explains, he means only

> to indicate the empirical reality that lies behind what we could call the Principle of the Fundamental Indeterminacy of the Art Work. That is, it is impossible, in principle, for sociologists or anyone else to speak of the "work itself" because there is no such thing. There are only the many occasions on which a work appears or is performed or is viewed, each of which can be different from all the others. (Becker, 1999: 2)

In everyday, common-sense ways of thinking, and indeed within much musicological discourse, such a claim appears radical, even absurd. *Of course* there is 'something' that we may call 'Mahler's Fifth Symphony' or 'Swing Low, Sweet Chariot', or Cole Porter's 'Love for Sale'. And in everyday situations, so there is – which is precisely Becker's point, for such commonsense assumptions depend on collective definitions as to what is to count as the 'work' on any particular occasion, and on the purposes and interests which people bring to such situations. Such definitions and purposes normally remain unstated and taken-for-granted, but nevertheless, as Becker puts it, we 'can only distinguish "the work itself" by invoking some convention as to what – which of the many forms it takes from moment to moment – counts as the "real", "basic" work, and which kinds of variation don't matter' (*ibid.*). (Moreover, it is worth noting at this point that academic efforts to move beyond 'commonsense' notions, and to specify the natures of musical 'works', soon run into difficulties; see Talbot, 2000: 3ff for a discussion of these).

The examples above may serve to illustrate the general point. Even if experts were to agree on a definitive score for Mahler's symphony, this could hardly qualify as 'the work' since scores are silent, consisting only of instructions to musicians as to how to proceed on occasions when it is to be performed. But there are equally strong objections to the idea that the essential 'work' consists only of its performances, which, as Becker points out, may all be very different.

Such difficulties have led to disputes among philosophers and musicologists over the question of ' . . . what sort of thing is the musical work'? (Dodd, 2000: 424). From the perspective being considered here, this is the wrong question, because it conflates the concerns of people in everyday situations with those of the sociological analyst. The error derives from what Whitehead called the 'fallacy of misplaced concreteness' (1925: 52) – the idea that because we have a word for something, and a common-sense notion of what it can refer to, the word must therefore correspond to a 'thing', the qualities of which may be precisely defined. But there need be no such 'thing' as a musical work, any more than social 'classes' (Martin, 1987: 94), 'minds' (Coulter, 1979), or for that matter 'voices' (*ibid.*: 4), are objective 'self-contained entities'. Such concepts do not refer to 'things' with essential qualities, yet are useful, indeed indispensable, in the context of particular discourses; as Becker puts it, people normally accept such taken-for-granted, conventional usages as a result of 'their participation in the social organization of the world in which works of that kind are made' (1999: 2). In the case of the Mahler symphony, this pattern of social organisation is likely to revolve around a discourse in which terms like 'score', 'composer', 'conductor', 'critic', 'orchestra', 'audience', and others, are likely to be taken as unproblematic. Such discourses and their conventionally established concepts reflect the interests and purposes of particular groups of people, and reveal much about them to the sociological analyst. It does not follow, however, that the concepts which are fundamental to such discourses correspond to 'real' entities capable of ultimate definition. Rather, from a sociological perspective such terms reveal much about the ways in which people and things are *represented*: for example, the concept of 'conductor' is not an ultimate, exhaustive description of a particular person, but in the context of a symphony concert, it is a term which illuminates the purposes and interests of those who participate in this sort of 'art world' and is a useful 'shorthand' way of describing one person's expected role and how it should be carried out. There are many other ways in which the person could be described, all of them relevant to other situations, other discourses, other 'worlds' (Rock, 1979: 84). The person who in certain places and times is indisputably the 'conductor' may also, in other contexts, be a 'father', 'the accused', 'high coronary risk', 'board member', and so on. That is, there is no single, privileged or ultimate way of describing this

person independently of the discursive contexts in which a particular mode of representation takes place. This instance should also
serve to illustrate why such modes of representation may, by illuminating specific social worlds and the purposes of their participants,
be so revealing from a sociological point of view. I will return to this
point below.

Similar observations may be made about the other examples given
above. What is the essential work 'Swing Low, Sweet Chariot'? The
piece as performed in a religious setting or in a formal concert, perhaps by an African-American choir, and harmonised according to
the conventions of nineteenth-century European art music? Or the
versions regularly produced by thousands of English rugby union
fans (who have adopted the song) at international matches? Some
might argue that the former is a 'real' or 'correct' rendition, citing
the performance history of the song, and the traditions of black
music. Yet, firstly, such an argument nicely illustrates Becker's point
that ' . . . the general choice of the convention by which works will
be recognised results from a political process which is continuous,
and never settled for good' (Becker, 1999: 3). In order to argue that
one particular instance of a work (as opposed to others) is 'authentic', it has to be represented in a particular way, a context provided,
competing claims rejected, and so on (on the social production of
musical 'authenticity', see Peterson, 1997a and Vianna, 1999). It is,
as Becker says, a 'political process' in which particular interests and
commitments are in contention, each with the aim of establishing
their version of reality. Secondly, the 'real' or essential nature of the
'work' is neither self-evident nor can be disclosed through analysis
of it; what is sociologically important are the ways in which it may
be represented, the purposes of those engaged in the process, and
the always-contestable conventions which emerge from it. Thus the
singing of 'Sing Low, Sweet Chariot' has become customary, and no
doubt meaningful to English rugby fans, at international games. The
phenomenon is thus of some sociological interest: the song has
become one element in a more general configuration of social practices, and this is the case irrespective of the song's history, intended
meaning, or the claims made for it by others. In other words, this use
of the song is no more and no less authentic, no more or less sociologically 'real', than any other. Indeed, it is an interesting example
of the use of music in everyday life by people who are neither
specialists nor (if the results are any indication) music-lovers.

The career of 'Love for Sale', a song written by Cole Porter for the 1930 Broadway musical *The New Yorkers* may also serve to illustrate the general theme which, I hope, is emerging: the idea that 'works' are instantiated and occasioned according to the needs and interests of particular groups of people, in the context of the conventions established within specific 'art worlds'in particular times and places. The original show revolved around low-life and underworld characters, and in order to placate 'the critics and other censorious people' (McBrien, 1998: 137) who objected to a song about a prostitute, the original white singer of 'Love for Sale' (Kathryn Crawford) was 'replaced by a "coloured girl"' (Elizabeth Welch), and the scene altered to become a depiction of the Cotton Club. For years after, the lyrics could not be broadcast on American radio (*ibid.*). Already, it is apparent that the 'work' was modified and transformed according to the perceived needs and constraints of different situations, and further changes were required fifteen years later for 'Night and Day', the film biography of Cole Porter (*ibid.*: 296). In time, though, the song became a 'standard', often performed independently of its theatrical origins, with words and music reunited. This does not, however, make it any easier to define the essence of the work itself. Consider the very different versions recorded by jazz musicians 'Cannonball' Adderley and Miles Davis in 1958 (Adderley, 1958) and by the Buddy Rich Orchestra in 1967 (Rich, 1967). Given the difficulties which the song's lyrics had provoked earlier, the first notable feature of these versions is that neither uses the words at all. Equally significant, however, are the contrasting treatments which 'Love for Sale' receives. The Adderley/Davis version involves (among other things) a paraphrase (by Davis) of Porter's original melody and serves primarily as a vehicle for Adderley's improvised solo; it has subsequently become something of a classic of small-group jazz. On the other hand, Rich's band, playing an arrangement by Pete Myers, produces an up-tempo transformation of the 'work' into a climactic showpiece which has become a staple item in the big-band repertoire. Indeed, the contrasts between these two versions of the 'same' song are an effective illustration of the sort of thing Becker has in mind when speaking of the 'conventions' (1982: 40ff) which shape artistic choices in the process of producing 'works'. To put the matter concisely, the instrumentation, modes of playing and aesthetic aims apparent in these versions differ enormously – yet both succeed within the framework of the taken-for-granted assumptions on which each group of musicians operated.

So where is the essential 'Love for Sale' in all this? As I have suggested, different versions have had different lyrics or no lyrics at all, and sometimes the melody has been abandoned. It could be argued that what remains common to all is the harmonic structure of the original song, yet to suggest that a series of chord symbols constitutes the 'real' 'Love for Sale' invites the same sort of objections as the contention that the essence of a symphony is its 'score'. On its own, a chord sequence is simply a silent succession of symbols on paper, which, to the initiated, serve as indications about to how to proceed. Yet in this response we can detect the basic guidelines for a sociological analysis of the patterns of social organisation through which the various versions of 'Love for Sale' are produced. Consider four actual situations in which versions of the 'work' have been realised: the original 1930–31 production of *The New Yorkers* on the Broadway stage, where the show had 168 performances (McBrien, 1998: 136); the countless treatments of the song over the subsequent 50 years or so by singers in cabarets, bars and nightclubs; the small-group jazz of the Adderley/Davis recording; and the big-band swing of the Buddy Rich treatment. In each of these situations, we can identify an 'art world' in a specific time and place, in which the 'collective action' of various specialists through an established division of labour, and the conventions which guide their artistic choices, enable the production of performances. What is sociologically significant is the extent to which the conventions, the established discourse, the 'rules of the game', the aesthetic commitments of participants, and so on, all lead to *decisively different* patterns of artistic choices in each of these cases. And while participants in each of these 'art worlds' *may* have some notion of the nature of the 'work' they are creating, it is likely that such notions will vary considerably, according to the conventions of each.

The idea of a 'real' or 'essential' work, then, is simply unnecessary for the purposes of sociological analysis, which will focus on such patterns and processes of social organisation as conventions and their effects on choice-making by art-world participants. It is likely that people in these worlds will have very strong beliefs about what it is they are doing and how it should be done, as well as powerful aesthetic commitments and regular ways of working, and all these constitute the ethnographic data from which an understanding of the art world can emerge. By now, the distinctive character of a sociological approach to these sorts of phenomena should be apparent: above all else, it is concerned with identifying and describing the patterns of collaboration which constitute the 'collective action' necessary to create not only an 'artwork', but any kind of cultural product. For this purpose, it is unnecessary – indeed irrelevant – to abstract the concept of a 'work' from this configuration of interactions, and then to reify it by asserting (or seeking) its essential qualities. Empirically, what is observable is a number of people doing things together, orienting their activities to established ways of working, which the analyst may term a 'division of labour'.

It should now also be clearer how a sociological approach, in this case to the production of musical performances, differs from other possible perspectives. The concern of musicologists – whether 'old' or 'new' – to analyse the technical aspects of a piece or to discover things about its history, which is what most musicologists have done most of the time, is not only unproblematic from a sociological perspective, but likely to produce much valuable information. What is problematic, however, is the attempt to identify the 'inherent' qualities of some music, or the 'real' meaning of a song, and so on; such acts of decoding or deciphering, outside any actual context of production or reception, is inconsistent with a sociological focus on the ideas, aims, beliefs, emotions and reactions of real people in specific situations. The sociologist's analytic orientation respects, in a word, the polysemic nature of music and rests on no presuppositions as to its 'real', 'intrinsic' or 'essential' meaning. Thus, to return to one of the examples above, the song 'Love for Sale' was re-staged and given to a black singer so that it would be 'heard' in ways more acceptable to white Broadway audiences (as well as critics and censors) in the early 1930s (McBrien, 1998: 137). But the 'same' song has been performed on innumerable occasions by jazz musicians who have no interest at all in its words, but who are committed to very different aesthetic and stylistic conventions – perhaps concerned with the imaginative ways in which soloists can use the basic harmonic structure of the song, or with the technical skills needed to bring off a convincing performance of Pete Myers' arrangement. To repeat, then, sociological analysis does not seek to discover a 'real' meaning in music, but to identify and describe the ways in which it is heard on the occasions of its production and use. In this respect, the concerns of sociologists and musicologists may diverge, although the *claims* made about music, by listeners, critics, DJs – and musicologists – may be valuable data for the sociologist, seeking to examine the perpetual process through which the meanings of music are asserted and contested (Martin, 1995: 67).

For the sociologist, then, there is no need to seek the ultimate or transcendental essence of a musical 'work'. From a philosophical perspective, however, this has been a serious quest, with scholars divided, apparently, between those who regard musical works as 'abstract objects which have sound-sequence-occurrences as instances', and those who identify the 'work' with 'the set of its occurrences' (Dodd, 2000: 424). Both views, however, lead to problems. In the latter case, since sets are essentially 'constructed out of their instances' and a musical work can have more or less 'occurrences than it has in fact had', it is illogical to conceive of it as a set (*ibid.*: 424–425). Yet the former view, that musical works are 'eternal types', appears to rest on the claim that an 'infinite number of sound structures' already exists, from which 'the composer' makes a creative selection. Musical works cannot be created by their composers, since it is held that 'abstract objects cannot be created' (*ibid.*: 431). Thus sound structures ' . . . exist eternally, not because they can have instances at any time, but because they are types, and a type, if it exists at all, exists at all times'. This all leads to the result that 'musical works, if they are types of any kind, pre-exist their composition' (*ibid.*: 436). So from this point of view Mahler's Fifth Symphony existed prior to the orchestras and instruments which are used to perform it; he did not create it but, rather, 'placed something within our culture that was not there before' (*ibid.*: 430), and thus made it possible for there to be instances – tokens – of the general, eternal, type. By analogy, 'in 1900 the type which is the Ford Thunderbird, the abstract entity, existed, but could not have had any tokens at this time' (*ibid.*: 438).

Doubtless there are impeccable philosophical arguments leading to these conclusions; from a sociological point of view, however, they are somewhat frustrating. It is tempting to ask, somewhat prosaically, precisely *where* these 'eternal types' actually 'exist' – where, for example, was Mahler's Fifth (or the Ford Thunderbird) in 1066? The argument seems to depend on the assumption of some metaphysical realm, independent of real people and the situations in which they interact. Such difficulties, as I have suggested above, may well derive from the *a priori* assumption that there are such 'things' as musical 'works', the essential qualities of which must then be determined. Not all philosophers, of course, subscribe to these ideas; recently Richard Rorty, for example, has argued forcefully against the assumptions that we can understand the world in terms of objects with essential qualities, and that language functions to represent such objects. Rorty makes a crucial distinction between this conception of language as representational, and what, in his view, people really do, which is to use language to describe things (1999: 63). In his words:

> we should think of the word 'language' not as naming a thing with an intrinsic nature of its own, but as a way of abbreviating the kinds of complicated interactions with the rest of the universe which are unique to the higher anthropoids. These interactions are marked by the use of strings of noises and marks to facilitate group activities, as tools for coordinating the activities of individuals. (Rorty, 1999: 64).

Underlying these remarks is a view of human existence in many ways consistent with the sociological perspective considered here, a view which takes as primary the 'life-world' (Schütz, 1964: 3) in which all our experience occurs, and the processual, collaborative nature of human activities.

## Art worlds and cultural production

I have considered above some of the ways in which a sociological approach to understanding the processes and practices through which music is produced and heard differs from perspectives driving from the discourses of musicology and philosophy. It remains to illustrate the analytic benefits of such an approach – the sociological 'payoff', so to speak, which is yielded when music-making is conceptualised in terms of collaborative interactions in the context of particular art-worlds. Indeed, far from neglecting or ignoring the actual process through which artistic creation takes place (Zangwill, 2002: 208), the approach developed by Becker 'goes to the heart of what a work of art is. You could call it a genetic approach, since it focuses on how the work is made' (Becker, 1999: 3–4). It is important to emphasise that Becker is concerned neither to make claims, as some of the 'social' analysts of music have done, about the ways in which musical styles 'articulate' or 'represent' the values of social groups or whole societies, nor to accept the inevitable reifications entailed by this. Instead, and once again directly contrary to Zangwill's (2002) view of the sociology of art, Becker's approach involves a primary focus on the collaborative activities through which 'works' are realised, and in particular on the sequence of 'choices' (Becker, 1999: 4; 1982: 194ff) which result in performances or finished 'works' taking the specific form that they do. Zangwill insists that 'aesthetic considerations play a role in determining choices and hence in determining what gets produced' (2002: 213), and that sociologists neglect this role. His view, however, seems to derive from a particularly impoverished understanding of sociological analysis; what I am suggesting is that, far from effacing the central processes of cultural production, as Zangwill claims, Becker in fact emphasises them, and provides a method for understanding 'what gets produced' through investigating the circumstances of its production.

In view of Zangwill's criticisms of the sociology of art, two important aspects of Becker's 'art worlds' approach should be emphasised. First, for Zangwill, Becker's work leads only to 'superficial' descriptions, since it lacks any 'reference to mental content, or any fine-grained details of mental content' (2002: 208). In fact, and directly to the contrary, Becker's model of artistic production is derived from, and is an application of, Mead's analysis of mind as an essentially social process, in which human interaction is based on the process of 'taking the role of the other' (Becker, 1982: 200). So the production of 'works' is seen here as a continuous decision-making process, a sequence of choices which – if abstracted from the flow of consciousness – Becker terms 'editorial moments':

> During the editorial moment, then, all the elements of an art world come to bear on the mind of the person making the choice, who imagines the potential responses to what is being done and makes the next choices accordingly. Multitudes of small decisions get made, in a continuous dialogue with the cooperative network that makes up the art world in in which the work is being made. (*ibid.*: 201)

From this it should be clear that Zangwill's assertion that Becker fails to consider 'mental content' is simply false. However, and of even greater importance, it should also be evident that in basing his analysis on Mead's conceptualisation of mental processes, Becker is proposing a model of artistic production in which social processes are central, rather than the questionable individualistic presuppositions which underlie, for example, aestheticians' notion of the 'creative artist' or cognitive psychologists' tendency to treat individuals in isolation from the social situations in which they act. As Fowler has argued, Zangwill also accepts 'an old-fashioned liberal assumption of the separation of the individual and the "external" social' (Fowler, 2003: 364). This kind of assumption presupposes the validity of the individual–society duality, and, as Fowler suggests, regards the latter as 'only an external constraint' (*ibid.*: 365). By contrast, in Becker, as in Mead, social life is understood as 'collective action' (Becker, 1974). It is a vision of human life which decisively rejects the individual–society dualism, and one in which 'mental content' must be understood as arising from, and flowing back into, the intersubjective worlds in which we participate, and which are the source of all our experience.

A second salient aspect of Becker's model concerns the aesthetic commitments of participants in art worlds. For Zangwill, there is another serious deficiency in the sociology of art here: in his view, those who produce and appreciate art do so primarily because of the aesthetic value they derive from it, while 'the sociologically minded refuse to recognize' the reality of this aesthetic aspect (2002: 211–212). (It appears not to matter to Zangwill that Becker devotes an entire chapter of *Art Worlds* to the topic of 'Aesthetics, Aestheticians, and Critics' or that the theme of the aesthetic motivations of artists runs right through the book). The central issue here, though, is the way in which the 'sociologically minded' are likely to conceive of the 'aesthetic'. For Zangwill, 'sociological' analyses have the effect of effacing the quality of the aesthetic, rendering it illusory or epiphenomenal, and reducing artists and their listeners to a state of 'false consciousness', because (he believes) such approaches take art objects to be merely the reflections or expressions of prior social forces. From such a position it appears that 'art has some other social property that really moves [people] to make and perceive it' (Zangwill, 2002: 208). To the extent that the social analysis of art can be reductionist in this way, Zangwill is right to reject it; but it is quite wrong of him to assert that such reductionism is inherent in, or characteristic of, contemporary sociological analyses. On the contrary, it is precisely this kind of reductionism which has been seen as sociologically deficient. As Blumer put it: 'In such approaches the human being becomes a mere medium through which such initiating factors operate to produce given actions' (Blumer, 1969: 73). In reorienting analysis towards the forging of collective action in inter-subjective 'worlds', the effect of Blumer's argument is to render problematic much of the work of the 'social' analysts of music: for example, in their efforts to specify the 'genuine social knowledge' which is 'articulated and transmitted' (McClary, 2000: 5) by musical 'texts' (Shepherd, 1991: 109). For Becker, a proper sociological concern is not to find the 'secret meanings' of artworks 'as reflec-tions of society' (1989: 282), but to identify the ways in which such works are shaped by the fact of artists' participation in networks of 'collective action', and their inevitable involvement in art worlds in which specific aesthetic standards and practices have been established.

Again in direct contrast to Zangwill's assertions about the sociol-ogy of art, it should be apparent that far from offering 'no explana-tion at all of art-making' (Zangwill, 2002: 208), Becker is concerned above all to place this process at the heart of his analysis, in expli-cating the sequence of 'choices' which must be made by every artist; choices which are constrained – though not determined – by the art-world context in which the 'work' is produced. And in the present context, such choices may be understood as decisions which, con-sciously or not, artists make in the light of their particular aesthetic commitments. Understanding the aesthetic values of individual artists or the aesthetic ideologies of 'schools', or whole 'movements', is thus an essential part of sociologists' work, for it is only by doing so that they will be able to offer an explanation of the 'choices' which are involved in the production of any 'work'. Moreover, far from ignoring the aesthetic motivations of art-world participants, as Zangwill claims, sociologists will focus on these as fundamental to artists' 'definition of the situation' (Rock, 1979: 83ff) and on the ways in which such aesthetic commitments – whatever they happen to be – are likely to be deeply felt by them. Indeed, just as in other areas of social life, an individual's immersion in the culture of an art world is likely to be a profound experience of socialisation, in which established aesthetic criteria and practices (or, possibly, opposition to them) become deeply engrained in the 'habitus' of individuals, and effective ' . . . in conditioning artists' feel for the game' (Fowler, 2003: 367). Becker emphasises the ways in which established conventions can become 'part of' individuals' aesthetic awareness; in the case of the jazz pianist, for example, ' . . . conventions of the craft get embodied in the tiniest details of the artist's physical experience . . . ' (Becker, 1982: 203). This approach, then, far from effacing the aesthetic dimension of artistic production, is concerned to demonstrate how such a 'sense' of rightness and wrongness is inculcated in individuals, and more generally to examine the aestheticisation of experience in art-world contexts.

To illustrate the potential of this mode of sociological analysis Becker refers to three recent studies (Berliner, 1994; Monson, 1996; DeVeaux, 1997) of jazz improvisation which document how the collaboration of individuals in specific art worlds enables the production of instrumental 'solos', which exhibit particular stylistic and formal features. Becker's point is that through an accumulation of the sort of 'detailed knowledge' displayed in these studies it is possible ' . . . to make a sociological analysis of particular works "in themselves"' (1999: 6). Indeed (and contrary to Zangwill's assertions), it is an acceptance of the aesthetics of the jazz world in general, and of specific stylistic conventions, which motivates players both to devote themselves to the arduous process of developing their musicianship, and to produce the kinds of 'works' that they are aiming at: 'Selecting from their varied options, artists pursue the goal of designing an imaginative, graceful version of the [chord] progression that clearly delineates the piece' (Berliner, 194: 86). In the situation of actual performance, players 'perpetually make split-second decisions about suitable materials and their treatment' (*ibid.*: 497). Moreover, attachment to the 'options' inherent in stylistic conventions can be profound: particular ways of doing things become not only 'felt' as right or wrong, but literally embodied, so that, as Becker argues, it is a mistake to talk in terms of conceptual and physical aspects of the activity as if they were separate things. In his words, artists ' . . . experience conventional knowledge as a resource at a very primitive level, so deeply ingrained that they can think and act in conventional terms without hesitation or forethought. They experience choices as acts rather than choices' (Becker, 1982: 204). In such ways the aesthetic norms of an art world become part of the embodied consciousness of participants.

The detailed studies of jazz musicians to which Becker refers provide a huge volume of evidence indicating ways in which sociological analysis can contribute not only to an understanding of the context of artistic production, but to the creation of the 'works' or 'texts' themselves. Such studies have shown how certain aesthetic commitments become ingrained in the players, and how stylistic

conventions are internalised so as to become significant aspects of
their social selves: habitual, unconscious ways of doing things which
nevertheless are expressions of the norms of an art world. In performance, these factors influence their choices of notes, phrases,
timbres and so on – in other words, the 'editorial moments' concerning what sounds to make – as does the unfolding process of their
real-time interaction with co-performers, and the response of audiences and 'significant others' who may influence the performance
whether present or not. The work, the musical 'text', must therefore
be understood as emerging through the moment-to-moment collaboration of players as they respond to each other's contributions.
Monson's study (1996) includes a detailed analysis of ways in which
members of a 'rhythm section' work together in the co-production
of performances, aiming to achieve an integration of their efforts,
yet all the while remaining open to new ideas or possibilities as these
may emerge, or to restoring order when things go wrong. In terms
of the perspective outlined here, Monson's conclusion is significant,
suggesting that the isolation of a musical 'text' from this process –
for example, the transcription of a 'solo' – may, by decontextualis-
ing it, obscure as much as it reveals: 'the formal features of musical
texts are just one aspect – a subset, so to speak – of a broader sense
of the musical, which also includes the contextual and the cultural
(*ibid.*: 186).

In another study, such 'contextual' features become apparent as
musicians indicate some of the ways in which their own 'definitions
of the situation' have an effect on what it is that they choose to play.
On some occasions, for example, they may opt to play safe with
short solos and familiar repertoire: 'If I go into a wine bar of course
I'm gonna honour the fact that people aren't gonna want to hear a
load of totally abstract stuff'. On the other hand, 'If you're in front
of a jazz audience who're all sitting listening, like really listening,
then it has to make a big difference to your playing. You've got to
keep the whole of their interest up' (Gibson, 2002: 184–185). Elsewhere, Monson has emphasised the importance of recognising the
distinctive aesthetic tradition from which jazz developed, and the
interpretive contexts in which its players work – the 'community of
interpreters (which includes both performers and audiences)' – since
'a sonic detail becomes socially meaningful and actionable only in an
at least partly shared context of use' (Monson, 1994: 305). These
points are important in illustrating both the limitations of extracting

a notated musical 'text' from the processual collaboration of musicians in specific situations, and the relevance of a sociological perspective in which their activities are viewed as ongoing interactions.

However, and this is the point I wish to emphasise, a focus on 'ongoing interaction' makes it very difficult to sustain the familiar distinctions between 'text' and 'context' or between 'the work' and its 'social environment'. Studies of the collaborative production of jazz performances have provided particularly good examples of the process of artistic production, but the implication of Becker's analysis (and Mead's conception of mind as a social process) is that in *all* forms of cultural production the choices made by practitioners are shaped by their socialisation into the norms and values of particular 'worlds'. Another way of putting the matter is to say that while it is perfectly legitimate for a 'work' or a 'text' to be isolated for consideration, perhaps by a musicologist, or a philosopher, or an historian, or a critic, *for the purposes of sociological analysis* this separation, and the act of decontextualisation on which it depends, is highly problematic. The disciplinary aims and commitments of, say, musicologists and sociologists, resting on different conceptions of their tasks, are once again revealed as quite divergent.

## Conclusion

It has been argued that the assumptions made by some musicologists as to what constitutes the 'social' analysis of music are not necessarily shared by contemporary sociologists, indeed to the latter these assumptions may appear problematic – as with the identification of 'texts' or 'works', their abstraction for analytic purposes, and the persistence of the distinction between 'works' and the 'social context' in which they are produced. I have suggested that from a sociological point of view this distinction is not sustainable: drawing on Mead's conception of mind and the social self, Becker has shown how the culture of the art world, mediated through the actions of practitioners, enters into the production of 'works'. Studies of the practices of jazz musicians provide an excellent illustration of this sort of process, in which the sounds which may be called 'the work' emerge over time through the interactional collaborations of the players. Thus it may be suggested that there is a clear analytical 'payoff' in adopting the sort of sociological perspective which can contribute a great deal to an understanding of precisely why the cultural objects which may be designated as 'works' come to take the form that they do. Indeed, and in direct contradiction to those, such as Zangwill, who assert that the sociology of art has nothing to say about 'works themselves' (2002: 211), the implication of the foregoing discussion is that a sociological approach may be useful, indeed indispensable, in arriving at a satisfactory understanding of the relations between 'texts' and their 'contexts', and in demonstrating their indivisibility.

It should be said, finally, that an awareness of this point is evident in the work of some scholars whose concern with popular music has led them of be wary of the work-concept as it is encountered in the European 'classical' music tradition (on the latter, see Goehr, 1992). In many popular music styles, for example, the idea of the 'work' is simply irrelevant, and the aim of art-world participants is the production of performances, whether 'live' or recorded. Thus for Horn, 'the popular music event is structured around an interactive nexus of performer, performance, and performed . . . . The potential event is one in which much is negotiable, according to a variety of conventions, generic and otherwise' (2000: 29). Similarly Middleton, drawing on the work of Goehr, argues for a conception of music as 'process' rather than 'product', and for analysis which ' . . . attempts to "un-work" the practice, so to speak' (Middleton, 2000: 86). Not all musicologists, then, remain attached to the idea that 'social' analysis involves deciphering the musical 'text'. Indeed, Small recommends that the term 'music' be treated as a verb rather than as a noun, in order to emphasise the idea that making music involves a process of collaboration among people, and to encourage the abandonment of the idea of music as a reified 'thing'. For Small: 'There is no such thing as music . . . . Music is not a thing at all but an activity, something that people do. The apparent thing "music" is a figment, an abstraction of the action, whose reality vanishes as soon as we look at it closely' (1998: 2). The convergence between these ideas and the perspective outlined here will, I hope, be apparent.

Part IV

# Coda

# 10

# Everyday music

## Introduction

One of the arguments for which Wittgenstein is most celebrated is his contention that linguistic meaning is not inherent in words, phrases, sentences and so on, but depends on the ways in which they are *used* (1972: 20). At first sight, this seems contrary to common-sense notions of how we communicate, and also to alternative theories of language which are based on the assumption that words represent states of affairs. After all, what could be more straightforward than a sentence like 'The grey geese are flying east', which seems to describe – indeed, may evoke a picture – of a group of birds travelling in a particular direction. And this may, of course, be exactly what the sentence is intended to convey. However, as Wittgenstein's argument suggests, things are rarely so simple, and a moment's reflection suggests various other ways in which the same sentence might be used to mean very different things – it could, for example, function as a 'password' allowing a spy to pass on infor-mation, or allowing access to an exclusive club. Or it could be the 'punch-line' of a joke, among other possibilities. The point is that hearing the sentence is not enough to decide its meaning; to do this it is necessary to know something of the context in which it is used, the intentions of the speakers, the conventions of their situation, and so on.

As Rorty has suggested, this analytical reorientation from a focus on meaning to a concern with usage also entails abandoning the notion of 'language' as a specific subject: 'Wittgenstein was coming to see "language" as referring simply to the exchange of marks and noises among human beings for particular purposes' (1993: 350). That is, speaking, listening, discussing and so on are to be regarded not as special modes of communication which are independent of the circumstances in which they occur, but as a part (albeit a vital one) of the collaborative social practices which create and sustain the world of human experience. As I suggested in the previous chapter, the conventional distinction between the linguistic 'text' and the 'context' of its production becomes problematic once analytic attention is redirected to the collaborative work through which orderly interactions are realised. Clearly, such a conception of language as social action also entails a move away from the study of 'languages' as abstract systems, towards the investigation of the actual speech practices of real people in particular linguistic communities as they go about getting things done (Goffman: 1964). As such, the study of language becomes part of, and inseparable from, the sociological concern with the production and reproduction of social order.

In this chapter, I want to consider some of the implications of these arguments for our understanding of music, since there are significant parallels between the move from 'meaning' to 'use' in studies of language, and the more recent reorientation evident in sociological studies which have been concerned to investigate ways in which music is *used* in social situations, rather than to define its meaning in some ultimate, decontextualised sense. As I suggested in Chapter 3, a good deal of work carried out under the auspices of the 'new' musicology is disappointing in this respect – indeed, somewhat paradoxically, the 'new' musicologists often seem committed to a distinctly 'old' conception of sociology. In any case, as Becker has argued, recent sociologists of music are not much interested in pursuing a quest for 'meaning' (1989: 282). Rather, they regard the creation, performance, reception and appropriation of music as instances of collective action in which the musical elements are defined by, and reflexively confer meaning on, wider configurations of social activity; in this respect, sociological perspectives have come to converge with those of the ethnomusicologists who have always insisted that music must be understood as part of more general cultural complexes.

In what follows, some of the implications of an analytical focus on the 'everyday usage, function and meaning of music' (Edstrom, 1997: 19) will be considered, with particular attention to some of the sociological themes which are raised. It should be said immediately that such a discussion inevitably moves away from certain topics which have been considered central to orthodox musicology. Once again, the differences between musicological and sociological discourses become evident. Sociologists are likely to approach music with questions and concerns which are derived from a rather different academic discourse, in which matters such as social organisation, interaction, identity, lifestyles, and the processes of mass mediation may be of more fundamental interest. Moreover, a sociological perspective is likely to deprive music of its 'aura', of that special – even magical – quality which attracted musicologists (and many others) to it in the first place. However, it should also be said that this sort of demystification is the typical outcome of good sociology, which can demonstrate not only the social organisation of all kinds of human activities, but also do much to illuminate the social basis of even the most intense individual experiences – such as those which music can evoke. Some examples of this will be considered below. A further consequence of putting music on the sociological agenda, so to speak, is that this brings into analytical focus a wide range of music which, to the musicologist, may be of little interest, or even seem distasteful. But if we are serious about understanding the cultural significance of everyday music, we need to bring into the analysis *all* the music which people create, experience and make use of in their daily lives, and not just that which fulfils certain aesthetic criteria. McClary, for example, has done as much as anyone to spread the ideas of the 'new musicology' and to take seriously the matter of the effects of music, a topic often avoided in orthodox musicology (McClary, 1991: 4). In this, she has done much to reinvigorate the field. Yet in arguing – I believe rightly – for a broadening of the scope of musical studies and the abandonment of the traditional cultural hierarchy, McClary nevertheless betrays a commitment to the aesthetic criteria of traditional musicology:

> My history of Western music contains Bach, Mozart and Beethoven, but it also includes Stradella and the Swan Silvertones, Bessie Smith and Eric Clapton, k.d. lang, Philip Glass, and Public Enemy. And it treats all of them as *artists* who have negotiated with available conventions and in particular historical circumstances to produce *musical artifacts of exceptional power and cultural resonance.* (McClary, 2000: 30; emphasis added)

Now there is no reason why all kinds of 'artists' who produce music of 'exceptional power and cultural resonance' should not be studied, and many good reasons why they should. However, as Leppert has argued, 'the popular musics typically celebrated by scholars represent something of a mass-culture avant-garde' (2002: 345), and what I am concerned to establish here is that this sort of focus, and the aesthetic ideology which underlies it, are quite distinct from a sociological concern with everyday music. For one thing, the very use of the term 'artist' tells us a good deal about the social organisation of 'art worlds'. More generally, in considering musical production, contemporary sociologists are 'less interested in genius and in rare works and more interested in journeymen and routine work' (Becker, 1989: 282). And as far as consumption is concerned, it may well be that it is the music of least interest to the musicologist – simple, manufactured, mass-mediated pop songs, for example, or advertising 'jingles' on TV – which is of sociological interest precisely *because* of the part they may play in the everyday lives of real people. Moreover, although the topic can only be hinted at here, this perspective implies a considerable widening of the definition of 'music', certainly beyond that considered normal in academic contexts – people whistling while they work, or humming along with the radio, or arguing about when a particular record was in the 'charts', and so on, are all engaged in activities which may be of interest to the sociologist. Indeed, while it is easy to understand Adorno's despair over those he called the 'humming millions', their submission to the 'culture industry', and its standardised products, sociological investigations into the role of music in contemporary culture need to take these matters very seriously – after all, such studies are concerned with the everyday lives of 'millions' of people.

## Studies of everyday music

In considering music sociologically, then, we are led to consider not only music which is 'exceptional' but also that which may be mundane and prosaic, perhaps embedded in the normal, taken-for-granted routines of daily life. Of course, as DeNora has suggested, Adorno knew this very well (2003: 153). While he was largely uninterested in popular music, and relatively little of his enormous scholarly output is concerned with it, Adorno – like other members of the 'Frankfurt School' – anticipated the later 'cultural turn' in sociology in understanding the importance of consumption and the mass mediation of cultural products in modern capitalist societies. And although the cultural pessimism which pervades the Frankfurt School interpretation of mass culture has not always been shared by later authors – some emphasising the potential for resistance and liberation (as opposed to oppression) in popular music (e.g. Paddison, 1996) – it is the themes of consumption and mass mediation which are the foundations for much recent research, as well as providing a theoretical context for sociological studies of everyday music.

To some, of course, the very idea of the 'consumption' of music, just like washing powder or cans of beans, is anathema precisely because, as suggested above, this destroys its 'aura'; similarly, to speak of the 'use' of music may seem to reduce it to a merely functional level. But as I have also suggested, this sort of demystification is typical of good sociological work, and some recent studies have begun to demonstrate ways in which music can play a part in the constitution of everyday settings – that is, neither imposing a 'meaning' on its listeners, nor reflecting an existing emotional state, nor representing an already formed taste pattern, but as an element in the process through which people actively engage in the ongoing flux of events. The availability of 'hardware' which enables us listen to music in private, as opposed to public, settings, and to choose what to play, is a relatively recent, yet culturally consequential, development. Thus, for example, DeNora has explored some of the ways in which music may be used as a 'technology of self' (2000: 46ff), in which ' . . . the ostensibly "private" sphere of music use is part and parcel of the cultural constitution of subjectivity, part of how individuals are involved in constituting themselves as social agents' (*ibid.*: 47). Clearly, the topic is a sociologically significant one in the context of wider concerns with the achievement of a stable sense of identity in conditions of rapid social change, and with the 'presentation of self' (Goffman, 1959) through the series of discontinuous encounters which are also taken to be typical of modern – or post-modern – patterns of social organisation. Almost all of the women interviewed by DeNora 'were explicit about music's role as an ordering device at the personal level, as a means for creating, enhancing, sustaining and changing subjective, cognitive, bodily and self-conceptual states' (*ibid.*: 49). Moreover, some of DeNora's interviewees described ways in which music could be used to provide an appropriate 'background' to a situation in which something else, such as studying, was of primary importance. Here again we have a good example of how the sociological agenda may be seen to diverge from the musicological one: the interview data provide examples of how the works of 'canonical' composers such as Bach, Beethoven, Schubert, Mozart and Sibelius are deliberately *not* attended to, and treated entirely functionally, as an aid to concentration (*ibid.*: 59). But however pragmatic and prosaic, such use of music is sociologically significant, in this case allowing a person to configure her environment in a particular way, so as to accomplish a particular activity.

Just as music may be used by individuals in private domains, so it enters into and often sustains collaborative social practices – DeNora examined some of the ways in which music can be used to regulate and 'entrain' the body, as when highly rhythmic children's songs or the structured routines of an aerobics class are effective in synchronising individuals' activities (*ibid.*: 89ff). Music may also be used to provide an appropriate 'atmosphere' for either intimate encounters or such public spaces of shopping malls or superstores. In considering these and other uses of music, DeNora emphasises that it should not be regarded simply as a 'stimulus' which produces particular 'effects'; rather, she emphasises the *active* role of people in appropriating the music in particular ways, investing it with emotions, ideas, memories, intentions, and so on, and experiencing it in terms of these. Moreover, the ways in which music 'works' cannot be disclosed through abstract, decontextualised analysis, but through the detailed examination of real people as they interact in real situations. Once again, the idea is of music as one element in a wider configuration of activities, with the music receiving much of its 'meaning' from these, and *vice versa* (*ibid.*: 41ff).

A similar emphasis on the active role of individuals in the production of musical experiences is evident in Hennion's (2001) discussion of 'music lovers', which aims to avoid the reductionism implicit in studies which take cultural 'tastes' to be little (or nothing) more than the manifestation in individuals of 'external determinisms' such as the 'social origins' of the listener or the presumed 'aesthetic properties of the works' (*ibid.*: 1). In keeping with much of Hennion's previous work, his focus is on the process of mediation – in this case, the activities which come, inevitably, *between* the music and the experiences which it is held to produce, allowing us 'to see the music lover as the co-producer of the work, instead of always assuming that she is an unquestioning admirer, in mind and body' (*ibid.*: 11). In other words, Hennion is concerned to examine precisely those activities which are usually taken for granted in everyday situations, and rendered invisible in much sociological work – including that of Bourdieu – which takes people's tastes and dispositions to be the consequences of (prior) variables such as social class, education, gender or ethnicity (*ibid.*: 3). This sort of understanding of tastes (and attitudes) – as interactionist sociologists have always argued – effaces the very phenomena which ought to be at the centre of sociological analysis, namely the actions and interactions of real people in everyday situations (Abbott, 1997).

Hennion's fundamental point, then, is that neither musical 'tastes' nor the 'aesthetic' experiences which contribute to them are simply the outcome of prior social factors, but must be understood as emerging in and through the particular activities that 'music lovers' engage in. Thus musical experiences and their concomitant emotions are not simply 'effects', but must be understood as *produced* in the course of actions and interactions. This is why Hennion speaks of taste as 'performance' (2001: 1): not as an attribute of isolated individuals, but as emerging from social practices which are often collaborative. It is an understanding of music listening as an active rather than a passive process, which 'entails seeing music not as a static product, on a score, on disc or in a concert programme, but as an unpredictable event, a real-time performance, an actual phenomenon generated by instruments, machines, hands and actions' (*ibid.*: 2). Hennion's analytical reformulation of the sociology of musical 'taste' as an active, collaborative process, can thus accommodate the otherwise uncomfortable fact that, as shown in Chapter 5, the relationship between demographic variables and musical tastes is far 'looser' that has generally been supposed. More positively, Hennion's discussion is consistent with the tradition of sociological work which understands social life as produced and sustained through the collaborative practices of real people in real situations, and not as the effect of prior social 'forces' or underlying 'structures' (Martin, 1995: 167ff).

In the present context, then, Hennion's study of 'music lovers' is particularly valuable for the ways in which it illuminates not only people's 'use' of music, but the specifics of the activities, practices, habits, rituals, routines and so on which are part of, indeed indispensable to, making the experience of music a meaningful, emotionally rich one. Moreover, Hennion also draws attention to the transformations in music-use that have been made possible by the invention of sound recording and subsequent technological developments (2001:

15), so that experiencing music is no longer tied to a particular location in which others are present. On the contrary, Hennion's research led him to emphasise ' . . . the meticulous care with which music lovers construct an area devoted to personal listening, and the importance of a space like this, which puts them in the right frame of mind and enables them to find what they are looking for' (2001: 6–7). And 'what they are looking for' often involves the creation and reinforcement of narratives concerning personal identity; alternatively, music may serve for some people as 'the binder of relations with those around them' (*ibid.*: 8), by either listening or playing together. Moreover, and here there is a significant concurrence with the argument developed by Frith (1996b: 18–19), these 'uses' of music and their effectiveness do not depend on either the 'type' or indeed the 'quality' of the music itself. In his own terms, Hennion's concern with the 'performative and reflective' practices which constitute musical experience as a 'ceremony of pleasure' are likely to 'demolish the hierarchy of the genres', since such practices are common to music-lovers right across the stylistic spectrum. Moreover, this focus on the creation of 'identity and taste through a series of common practices' (*ibid.*: 17–18) also entails the re-contextualisation of music: it is taken to be an important element, but one element nonetheless, in a wider configuration of social activities. Thus Hennion draws our attention to 'a heterogeneous body of practices for attaining a state of emotional intensity' (*ibid.*: 19), irrespective of musical *genre*, while Frith argues that:

> too often attempts to relate musical forms *to* social processes ignore the ways in which music is *itself* a social process . . . . [. . .] The critical issue . . . is not meaning and its interpretation – musical appreciation as a kind of decoding – but experience and collusion: the "aesthetic" describes a kind of self-consciousness, a coming-together of the sensual, the emotional, and the social *as* performance. In short, music doesn't represent values but lives them. (1996b: 270, 272)

Again, the difference between sociological and musicological discourses becomes apparent, with different research questions and analytic frameworks coming into play. If we are interested in the role of music in, for example, sustaining a sense of personal identity, or in strengthening ties of sociability, then music is important not as a cultural object in itself, but for its 'affordances' (DeNora, 2003: 48), for what it enables people to do. From this point of view, sociological interest is not primarily in the music itself (either in its technical characteristics, or in what it may be claimed to 'articulate'), but in its qualities as a 'resource for getting things done' (*ibid.*: 46). Indeed, even for those with a 'passion for music', Hennion argues that it is above all 'a means . . . of reaching certain states'; indeed, in this context, he speaks of musical experience as the 'secularisation of the sublime' in contemporary culture:

> the gradual formation of a specific, highly sophisticated ability, developed collectively to attain through music . . . states of emotion that are "sublime" (or "out of this world", or "cool": the words change, or are lacking, depending on the genre of music, but not their target). (Hennion, 2001: 11)

Hennion sees something of a paradox in all this, in that the aim of the 'meticulous activity' (*ibid.*: 13) undertaken by music-lovers is the attainment of *passivity* – 'a loss of control, an act of surrender' (*ibid.*: 12). For present purposes, the important point is that even for those with a 'passion' for music, it is viewed here as a *means* to an end, as *used* by people to achieve 'sublime' states. Moreover, Hennion's analysis is consistent with, and a timely reminder of, a tradition of sociological work which has investigated the social bases of individual experience, examining some of the ways in which states of mind which are experienced as deeply personal are nevertheless dependent on our participation in organised social practices. A further implication of Hennion's perspective, as I have noted, is to place the analysis of situated activities at the top of the sociologist's research agenda, in an effort to avoid the artificial separation of social practices, on the one hand, and musical 'works' on the other: in this, as Hennion puts it, 'places and times are essential' (2001: 18). There is also a convergence here with the work of DeNora on music sociology, as when she argues for ' . . . a symmetrical approach in which we pay equal attention to musical materials and to the circumstances in which these materials are heard and integrated into social experience in real time' (DeNora, 2003: 155).

In *The Hidden Musicians* (1989), Finnegan has demonstrated the ways in which this sort of research orientation, although taking music-making as its starting point, both diverges from the standpoint of musicology, and develops a sociological understanding of how musical activities may be embedded in wider patterns of social activity. Irrespective of the style of music involved, or its position in the cultural hierarchy, Finnegan shows how people were involved in communities of interest, in which their social relationships derived meaning and significance from the music, and *vice versa*. Indeed, from this perspective, musical distinctions of *genre* are important not because of their technical aspects or presumed qualities, but because, as Frith notes, 'it is through its generic organisation that music offers people, even passive stay-at-home listeners, access to a social world, a part in some sort of social narrative, offers them what Finnegan calls "social pathways"' (Frith, 1996b: 90). As far as the development of a sociology of musical practices is concerned, two points follow from this. Firstly, as Frith's reference to the 'stay-at-home listeners' suggests, even for solitary listeners music's meanings and effects depend on their orientation to an 'implied community' (*ibid.*: 90–91) – that is, their involvement in some way in a wider network which is socially structured in terms of the rules and expectations of particular *genres*. For Frith, the pleasures which music affords 'have to be related to the stories it tells about us in our genre identities' (*ibid.*: 90). Like Hennion, Frith argues that the meaning of music is neither inherent in the music itself, nor is it in the social practices of its consumption; rather, its meaning for us emerges when the two come together in the moments of our engagement with it, in the context of 'background' assumptions and expectations related to *genres* (*ibid.*: 94). It is in this engagement that we can *be* certain sorts of people, and can affirm our identities both to ourselves and others. It is quite clear that for Finnegan the 'pathways' which an engagement with musical activities provides are consequential and significant – for the ways in which they afford relationships with other people, and a sense of self in the context of the wider society. These are important matters for the sociologist (or anthropologist) concerned with social order and social organisation, though not necessarily for the musicologist.

Secondly, it is evident that Frith's emphasis on the concept of *genre* leads to an analytical framework very similar to that used by Finnegan – that is, the 'art worlds' perspective elaborated by Becker (1982). Indeed, the terms used by Frith to describe 'how genre rules integrate musical and ideological factors' are similar to those of Becker: Frith speaks, for example, of the 'conventions' (of appropriate sounds, performance practices, and packaging) and of the 'embodied values' which involvement with musical *genres* generates and sustains (Frith, 1996b: 94). This approach to the analysis of musical practices is distinctively sociological, in the sense that *all* those involved in the 'art world' (and not just composers or performers) must be included in the analysis: the notion of a *genre*, for example, entails a recognition of the collaborative activities not just of musicians and listeners, but promoters, publicists, truck drivers, sound engineers, instrument makers, managers, critics, broadcasters and so on, in short all those whose 'collective action' (Becker, 1974) is necessary for the idea of a *genre*, its practices and its ideology, to be sustained.

A good example of an 'art world' which is organised around musical performance, and which is of considerable sociological interest, is that of karaoke (a topic which many musicologists, and 'serious' music-lovers, might prefer to ignore). Yet as Drew (2001) shows in his ethnographic study, karaoke bars are the focal point for local activities which, though primarily organised around singing, inevitably draw people into wider networks of association – both in terms of personal contacts at the event and the 'narratives' of identity which may be constructed around their experiences. And, as in other studies of musical practices which have adopted an anthropological as opposed to a musicological approach, such as those of Finnegan (1989) or Cohen (1991), it is the social relationships among participants rather than purely musical matters which are at the centre of the analysis: karaoke bars are 'sites of everyday music making and everyday interaction, where songs form but one thread of the drama, one current in the flow of communication' (Drew, 2001: 25). Indeed, Drew's work is exemplary in demonstrating how music-making which quite clearly violates some established cultural expectations about what music is supposed to be, can nevertheless be an important element in the world of those who participate. Running through his discussion is a contrast between the authoritative professional/national criteria which are conventionally used to evaluate music, and the amateur/local practices evident in the karaoke bars. The latter, for example, clearly violate the widespread assumption that most people 'can't sing' (Drew, 2001: 31) and that professional standards are what really matters. Karaoke music, too, challenges deep-rooted Western notions about the importance of the 'text' (as opposed to performances) and of 'innovation' (in contrast to imitation) (*ibid.*: 51).

However, Drew is not concerned to refute the criticism of karaoke which is derived from these widely held assumptions.

Although some karaoke singers are very good at what they do, many *are* inadequate when judged by 'professional' standards. Performances *are* indeed derivative, and often repetitive. Yet for Drew evaluations based on such observations are, in an important sense, irrelevant: 'what draws people to local music scenes is the promise of a music that touches their daily lives and relationships' (*ibid.*: 16). While 'stars' are remote, local performances are immediate and involving, even in their imperfections, and the imitative, repetitive aspects of performance – which from the point of view of 'professional' music may render them wholly uninteresting – are, from the perspective of karaoke singers and their audiences, opportunities to reassert personal and collective identities (*ibid.*: 52). Certain songs and performers become 'crowd favourites',. which vary according to the venue and the preferences of audiences; what they have in common, Drew argues, 'is that they seem to crystallise the experience of the people who celebrate them, and as a result, to constitute these people as members of a common culture' (*ibid.*: 56).

Drew's discussion thus leads him, like other ethnographers of music use, to emphasise the ways in which participants can experience a sense of self, security, and social solidarity (e.g. Bennett, 1997). The point need not be elaborated, other than to remark, once again, on the way in which such studies demonstrate the divergence between musicological and sociological perspectives. Yet Drew warns against seeing the popularity of karaoke as a return to an earlier era of participatory, communal singing: 'Rather than a premodern, folk mode of music making, karaoke points to a fully modern mode, one that comes to terms with our implacable drive for individual agency, creativity, and pleasure in modern society' (*ibid.*: 125). The activity itself depends on quite sophisticated technology; moreover the 'texts' which the singers appropriate are all products of the mass media.

Similar considerations emerge from Bull's ethnography of the use of personal stereos by people in a big-city environment. Bull argues that most discussions of urban experience prioritise visual aspects at the expense of auditory ones (2000: 2–3) and he shows how the use of a 'Walkman' enables people to adopt effective strategies, not only to sustain a sense of stable identity in the face of the contingencies of their everyday experiences, and potentially hostile surroundings, but to reconfigure the physical environment, geographical space and clock-time – to impose a degree of control over their situation by imposing an alternative narrative on it (*ibid.*: 154). It is, of course, by allowing their music, rather than the external environment, to structure their 'inner', private realm of experience that the personal-stereo users can achieve this reconfiguration, and, significantly in the present context, Bull suggests that it is the process of attending to the music, rather than any particular 'type' of music, which is crucial to the 'construction and transformation of experience' (*ibid.*: 14). Thus, like Drew, Bull provides a further example of how individuals' private pleasures and sense of self – their protection, so to speak, from the vicissitudes of the world that confronts them – are nevertheless bound up with the use of quite advanced technology to provide them with the music which facilitates their narratives.

The use of personal stereos is also distinctively modern in the sense that it represents a further retreat from a communal mode of living in which communication is primarily through face-to-face interaction, and may be regarded as part of the inexorable movement towards the 'individualisation' of experience, or what Bull, in a later paper, calls the 'privatised everyday lifeworld of urban citizens' (2004: 244). Just as personal stereos may be used to effect a clear demarcation between the 'interior world of control and the external one of contingency and conflict' so car drivers may use sound systems to create for themselves 'a safe and intimate environment in which the mobile and contingent nature of the journey is experienced precisely as its opposite' (*ibid.*: 251). For Bull, this is part of the process in which, because of the availability of appropriate technology, 'urban citizens' have been able 'to make the "public" spaces of the city conform to a notion of a "domestic" or "intimate" private space' (*ibid.*: 255); and, following Adorno's usage, he contrasts the 'warmth' of the latter with the 'chill' of the former. In the present context, my concern is primarily with the ways in which music, delivered by a variety of technologies, is used to generate and sustain this 'warmth'. Yet, as Bull suggests, there is something of a paradox here, in that the inner, subjective realms of individual experience are being seen as sustained, indeed protected, by what Adorno called the products of the 'culture industry' – both the high-tech 'hardware' which enables us to use music in unprecedented ways, and the 'software' of media messages generated by the 'culture industry'. Writing long before the advent of karaoke machines, personal stereos or in-car sound systems, Adorno was concerned with the ways in which music ' . . . contributes ideologically to the integration which modern society never tires of achieving in reality . . .

It creates an illusion of intimacy in a totally mediated world' (Horkheimer and Adorno, quoted in Bull, 2004: 254). Ideas of the 'illusion of intimacy', and the permeation of our deepest experiences by the products of the 'culture industry', are at the heart of the critical theorists' diagnosis of the pathology of the 'totally mediated world'. But for present purposes, the point to be emphasised is the way in which *music* is held to be central to these processes, inviting a further consideration of how, and why, it is useful and effective in producing the sorts of experiences – the emotional states, the memories, the structuring of experiences, the sense of self and belonging, and so on – which were mentioned above.

## Tuning in and synchronicity

I have argued that there are very good reasons for the investigation of the uses of music in everyday contexts, but that in doing this the research agenda and analytical focus of the sociologist may diverge from those of the musicologist. This need not be thought of as a bad thing: it is simply one illustration of the rather different preoccupations and theoretical commitments of these discourses. Yet just as there has been a reluctance on the part of musicologists to engage with music which does not appear to them in some way interesting or innovative, so sociological research has only just begun to look at the use of music by people who are *not* involved in a musical 'world' in some way or another. Finnegan (1989) demonstrated the many ways in which participation in a music 'world' – even peripherally, and irrespective of the music's 'quality' – could nevertheless provide people with both social and aesthetic satisfactions. Hennion quite explicitly focused on the activities of 'music lovers' (2001), while the karaoke enthusiasts studied by Drew, and Bull's personal-stereo users, were evidently people who had a deep attachment to 'their' music, whatever style or genre they preferred. (Indeed, one of the strengths of Bull's study derives from the fact that he was not concerned with what 'type' of music his interviewees liked, but – consistent with Frith's argument – was interested in how they were able to use it, and what it did for them in terms of the personal narratives they were able to create around it (1996b: 275).) Similarly, for the women studied by DeNora, the private use of music 'turned out to be one of the most important features of the constitution and regulation of self' (DeNora, 2000: 49).

Clearly, music played a big part in these women's lives, and DeNora's study shows how it 'worked' for them in various ways. However, what I am suggesting is that if we are to pursue the issues arising from a concern with the use of music in everyday contexts, it is essential to move *beyond* the investigation of those who already have a significant involvement with, or attachment to, music – just as we have to broaden the scope of research to include music which may *not* be interesting, innovative, or even 'serious' from the point of view of the academic specialist, but which may nonetheless be important in, for example, the ongoing constitution of identity or the organisation of social situations. (Musicologists may not find much to interest them in such 'works' as 'The Teddy Bears' Picnic', 'The Grand Old Duke of York', or 'When Santa Got Stuck Up The Chimney', but their importance in the context of, say, children's parties is hard to deny.) From a sociological perspective, what becomes important is to understand *how* music, of any kind, 'works' for people (and not only 'music lovers') in various situations and contexts, and here some of DeNora's studies do indeed constitute a decisive move in the right analytical direction – in her concept of the 'musical event' (2003: 94, 155), and in her accounts of how music is used 'to configure and reconfigure bodies and emotional-cognitive modalities' over the course of aerobic sessions (2000: 102, 159), or is used as a therapeutic agent helping a blind, mute person to come 'into closer co-ordinated activity with another person' (*ibid.*: 15).

Indeed, the latter example is particularly suggestive of the way in which we may develop a sociological understanding of how music can be effective in 'everyday' situations: in speaking of the way music can help to bring about 'closer co-ordinated activity', DeNora's analysis converges with that of Alfred Schütz in his emphasis on the 'mutual tuning-in relationship' which he takes to be the basis of human communication (Schütz, 1964: 161). Schütz's paper on 'Making Music Together' dates from 1951, and is fairly well known (although its implications have not always been fully appreciated). Two aspects of his analysis seem of particular relevance here: first, his demonstration that prior participation in a 'musical culture' (*ibid.*: 166) of some kind provides us with the general background knowledge and expectations which allow us to make sense of all 'types' of music, and secondly his more specific analysis of musical relationships themselves. For Schütz, the meaning and content of music can only be grasped 'polythetically', that is, in a step-by-step, gradually developing process. Thus the essence of musical communication consists in the synchronisation of participants' 'inner time':

> this sharing of the other's flux of experiences in inner time, this living through a vivid present in common, constitutes . . . the mutual tuning-in relationship, the experience of the 'We', which is at the foundation of all possible communication. (*ibid.*: 173)

The idea, then, is that by virtue of its polythetic nature music provides a basis for the synchronisation of individuals' consciousness – the process, developing through time, in which the discrete and disparate subjectivities of participants are brought into alignment, or 'tuned in' as Schütz puts it, as they attend to the flow of musical sounds.

It is evident that what Schütz mainly had in mind was the familiar scenario in which performers (who must synchronise their activities in 'inner' *and* 'outer' time) interpret the works of composers either for themselves or in the presence of listeners; indeed he refers to 'chamber musicians' who ' . . . share not only the inner *durée* in which the content of the music played actualises itself; each, simultaneously, shares in vivid present the Other's stream of consciousness in immediacy' (*ibid.*: 176). But as these remarks suggest, and as Schütz makes explicit, this analysis may be applied to *all* forms of 'making music together' – to 'people sitting around a campfire and singing to the strumming of a guitar or a congregation singing hymns under the leadership of the organ' as much as to choirs and orchestras, and to 'accomplished jazz players' as much as to 'the performance of a string quartet' (*ibid.*: 177). For Schütz, then, music-making (and listening) – which involves attending to the polythetic flow of organised sounds – provides an exemplary model of the general process of human communication in social interaction; he discovers in music-making an excellent demonstration of the way in which the 'mutual tuning-in relationship', the 'simultaneous partaking of the partners in various dimensions of inner and outer time' (*ibid.*: 178) is the real foundation of *all* forms of human communication.

In the present context, as Schütz's own remarks suggest, an important implication of this analysis is the basis it provides for an understanding of the effectiveness of 'everyday music'. Various studies, including those considered above, have demonstrated some of the ways in which music may be used by people to achieve social ends of one kind or another. Schütz's analysis, I suggest, enables us to go further, and to develop an understanding of *how* music as a particular kind of medium can be effective in, for example, providing a personal 'narrative', sustaining a sense of identity, or creating a feeling of 'belonging'. Although in his paper Schütz was primarily concerned with the process of communication, it is important to pursue the idea that 'mutual tuning-in' involves not only cognitive orientations, but *also* the emotional and physical sensations which music as a specifically sonic medium can convey to members of particular 'musical cultures'. This sort of idea is evident in DeNora's discussion of what music 'affords': ' . . . the concept of affordance highlights music's potential as an organising medium, as something that helps to structure such things as styles of consciousness, ideas, or modes of embodiment' (2003: 46–47). Moreover, any analysis of how music 'works' for people in these ways inevitably involves an examination of the social relationships which provide the context for their actions and their experiences. As Frith put it, there is a contrast between studies of musical 'meaning and its interpretation' and those which focus on 'experience and collusion' (1996b: 272): 'music is especially important for our sense of ourselves because of its unique emotional intensity – we absorb songs into our own lives and rhythm into our own bodies (*ibid.*: 273). Frith's distinction, it should be said, again suggests something of the divergence between musicological and sociological concerns.

Although their interests and projects differ, it is notable that the arguments of the sociologists DeNora, Frith and Hennion all converge on the notion of the social practices in which music is embedded, suggesting that the particular effectiveness of music as a medium derives from the ways in which it provides a means for people to link individual consciousness and collective membership – in Schütz's terms to create a 'We' by 'tuning in' to an intersubjective world of common experience. Moreover, as Schütz's remarks suggest, all 'types' of music may be effective in this way – Frith uses the examples of jazz, rap, and nineteenth-century chamber music (1996b: 273) to emphasise the ways in which these may be effective in generating a sense of community, a feeling of belonging to a wider collectivity – whether real or 'imagined' (Anderson, 1983). In their explorations of these sorts of themes, it becomes evident why sociologists may be concerned with music that is of little interest (or

value) to musicologists, and why they believe that it must be studied
in the contexts of its use (rather than as 'works' which may be
analysed independently of any realisation). As I suggested above,
this does not in any way invalidate the traditional concerns of musicologists – although it may help to make the disciplinary presuppositions of both sociologists and musicologists more explicit. Indeed,
as DeNora argues, there is much to be gained from 'a new type of
interdisciplinary project that transcends the traditional boundaries
of both' (2003: 154).

Sociologists, then, have been led to take very seriously the kind of
settings and situations which are constituted by the 'social practices
in which music is embedded', and I have suggested that Schütz's idea
of the 'mutual tuning-in relationship' provides a useful basis for this
sort of analysis. It remains, finally, to render these points a little less
abstract by providing a few examples of situations in which participation in music involves the synchronisation of individuals' 'stream'
of consciousness so as to create and sustain a sense of collective
belonging. Most obviously, there are those occasions on which
groups of people are encouraged to sing together – the singing of
'national anthems', for example, or the 'bonding' which is supposed
to result from singing the 'company song'. Indeed, the apparent
decline of 'community singing' at large-scale sporting events would
be interpreted by some as further evidence of the trend towards individualisation and the privatisation of experience in modern societies. On the other hand, the spontaneous singing or chanting which
regularly occurs among football crowds is good evidence of one way
in which the co-orientation of participants can strengthen a sense of
collective identity. There are numerous occasions – parties and other
celebrations, for example – in which music is used in a ritual way for
the same purpose, and many religious ceremonies are organised
around music which is found to be effective in generating the sense
of 'We' which Schütz described. The tradition of active congrega-
tional participation which developed during the nineteenth century
in the Black churches of the southern USA is perhaps the most obvious example; it is also interesting to note that in considering the
church music of eighteenth-century England, Brewer notes the 'tension' between the idea of 'the church as a place for performing "art
music"' (1997: 556), and those who 'wanted a religion of the spirit
and who believed that music should be a means for all worshippers
to express their deeply felt piety' (*ibid.*: 555). The contrast between

'art music', which requires the attention of a passive audience, and a collective, participatory mode of involvement is evident here, as are the different conventions governing art music and everyday music. (Yet we should keep in mind Schütz's point that the effectiveness of *both* depends on synchronisation, on 'mutual tuning-in').

The above examples are all instances in which people participate actively in 'everyday' music. In contemporary societies, of course, everyday musical environments are far more likely to be 'mediated' in some way, as in the situations discussed by DeNora, where music was used as a 'device of social ordering' – 'a means of organising potentially disparate individuals so that their actions may appear to be intersubjective, mutually oriented, co-ordinated, entrained and aligned' (2000:109) – in both private and public spaces. In such contexts as parties, bedrooms and shopping malls, or through the use of karaoke machines, personal stereos and in-car sound systems, the availability of recorded music and a range of technologies with which to play it have given people an unprecedented degree of control over their aural environments, and as a consequence there are interesting sociological issues concerning not only the ways in which people use music to configure their own experiential states, as we have seen, but also the efforts of some to exert control over others. The essential point is that through 'mutual tuning-in', whether deliberate or not, individuals participate in an intersubjective reality: even the solitary listener, attending only to sounds from a headset, is immersed in a musical culture of some kind.

## Conclusion

It will be readily apparent that much of the foregoing discussion has led us some distance away from the orthodox concerns of musicology. When we begin to consider children's parties, football chants, karaoke bars, church services and so on, the committed musicologist might be forgiven for objecting that, as Hullot-Kentor put it when writing of Adorno, 'the music itself is not interesting' (1991: 109). However, these blunt but memorable words are helpful in illuminating the differences between the disciplinary discourses of musicology and sociology, and particularly in leading us to appreciate why contemporary sociologists of music have come to insist so strongly on the importance of understanding the many ways in which music is used, and the configuration of social relationships within which such usage takes place. For this purpose, the type, style or *genre* of music is irrelevant, as are its technical interest or quality – except insofar as the social process through which *genres* are created, the emergence of a hierarchy of styles, and claims about the meaning or quality of music are *themselves* topics for sociological investigation. I have argued, too, that sociological studies of 'every-day' music use will not only have to be much more stylistically inclusive, but will inevitably have to go beyond a concern with people who are already 'music lovers' or those for whom music has some special significance. The sociological concern is not to establish the value, or quality, or interest of music in some transcendental sense, nor to advocate any particular 'reading' of it. It is, rather, is to understand how music 'works' for all sorts of people in all sorts of situations, and how it may be said to do things for them in their everyday lives.

# Bibliography

Abbott, Andrew (1997) 'Of time and space: the contemporary relevance of the Chicago school', pp. 1149–1182 in *Social Forces* (75/4).

Adderley, Julian 'Cannonball' (1958) *Somethin' Else* Blue Note BNST 81595 (LP).

Adlington, Robert (2000) *The Music of Harrison Birtwistle* (Cambridge and NewYork: Cambridge University Press).

Adorno, Theodor W. (2002 [1941]) 'On popular music', pp. 437–469 in Leppert (ed.), *Teodor W. Adorno*.

Adorno, Theodor W. (1992 [1960]) 'Mahler', pp. 81–110 in *Quasi Una Fantasia* (London and New York: Verso).

Adorno, Theodor W. (1991) *The Culture Industry: Selected Essays on Mass Culture*, ed. J. M. Bernstein (London: Routledge).

Adorno, Theodor W. (1978 [1932]) 'On the social situation of music', pp. 128–164 in *Telos* (35).

Adorno, Theodor W. (1967) *Prisms* (London: Neville Spearman).

Adorno, Theodor W. (1958 [1949]) *Philosophie der Neuen Musik* (Tubingen: Mohr).

Adorno, Theodor W., and Horkheimer, Max (1979 [1944]) *Dialectic of Enlightenment* (London: Verso).

Allis, Wilfred (1995) 'The Manchester Gentlemen's Concerts'. Unpublished M.Phil. dissertation, Department of Sociology, University of Manchester.

Anderson, Benedict (1983) *Imagined Communities* (London: Verso).

Atkinson, Paul, and Housley, William (2003) *Interactionism* (London: Sage).

Attali, Jacques (1985) *Noise* (Manchester: Manchester University Press).

Bailey, Derek (1980) *Improvisation: Its Nature and Practice in Music* (Ashbourne: Moorland Publishing).

Baker, G. P. and Hacker, P. M. S. (1984) *Language, Sense and Nonsense* (Oxford: Blackwell).

Baldwin (1986) *George Herbert Mead: A Unifying Theory for Sociology* (Beverly Hills: Sage).

Bayles, Martha (1994) *Hole in Our Soul: The Loss of Beauty and Meaning in American Popular Music* (Chicago: University of Chicago Press).

Becker, Howard S. (1999) 'The work itself', at http://home.earthlink.net/~hsbecker (accessed 8 December 2005).

Becker, Howard S. (1995) 'The power of inertia', pp. 301–309 in *Qualitative Sociology* (18/3).

Becker, Howard S. (1989) 'Ethnomusicology and sociology: a letter to Charles Seeger', pp. 275–286 in *Ethnomusicology* (33/2).

Becker, Howard S. (1982) *Art Worlds* (Berkeley: University of California Press).

Becker, Howard S. (1974) 'Art as collective action', pp. 767–776 in *American Sociological Review* (39/6).

Bennett, Andy (2000) *Popular Music and Youth Culture: Music, Identity and Place* (Houndmills: Macmillan).

Bennett, Andy (1999) 'Subcultures or neo-tribes? Rethinking the relationship between youth, style and musical taste', pp. 599–617 in *Sociology* (33/3).

Bennett, Andy (1997) 'Going down the pub! The pub rock scene as a resource for the consumption of popular music', pp. 97–108 in *Popular Music* (16/1).

Berger, P., and Luckmann, T. (1991 [1966]) *The Social Construction of Reality* (London: Penguin).

Berliner, Paul (1994) *Thinking in Jazz: The Infinite Art of Improvisation* (Chicago and London: University of Chicago Press).

Berman, Russell A., and D'Amico, Robert (1991) 'Popular music from Adorno to Zappa', pp. 71–77 in *Telos* (87).

Blumer, Herbert (1969) *Symbolic Interactionism: Perspective and Method* (Berkeley: University of California Press).

Bourdieu, Pierre (1993) *The Field of Cultural Production: Essays on Art and Literature* (Cambridge: Polity Press).

Bourdieu, Pierre (1990) *In Other Words: Essays Towards a Reflexive Sociology* (Cambridge: Polity Press).

Bourdieu, Pierre (1984 [1979]) *Distinction: A Social Critique of the Judgement of Taste* (London: Routledge).

Bourdieu, Pierre (1977) *Outline of a Theory of Practice* (Cambridge: Cambridge University Press).

Bradley, Dick (1992) *Understanding Rock 'n' Roll: Popular Music in Britain 1955–64* (Buckingham: Open University Press).

Brewer, John (1997) *The Pleasures of the Imagination: English Culture in the Eighteenth Century* (London: HarperCollins).

Brown, Cecil (2003) *Stagolee Shot Billy* (Cambridge, MA: Harvard University Press).

Brown, Lee B. (2000) '"Feeling my way": jazz improvisation and its vicissitudes – a plea for imperfection', pp. 113–123 in *Journal of Aesthetics and Art Criticism* (58/2).

Broyles, Michael (1992) *'Music of the Highest Class': Elitism and Populism in Antebellum Boston* (New Haven, CT: Yale University Press).

Broyles, Michael (1991) 'Music and class structure in antebellum Boston', pp. 451–493 in *Journal of the American Musicological Society* (44).

Brunkhorst, H. (1999) *Adorno and Critical Theory* (Cardiff: University of Wales Press).

Buchmann-Moller, Frank (1990a) *You Just Fight For your Life: The Story of Lester Young* (New York: Praeger).

Buchmann-Moller, Frank (1990b) *You Got to Be Original, Man: The Music of Lester Young* (New York and Westport, CT: Greenwood Press).

Buck-Morss, Susan (1977) *The Origin of Negative Dialectics* (Hassocks: Harvester Press).

Buck-Morss, Susan (1972) 'The Dialectic of T. W. Adorno', in *Telos* (14).

Bull, Michael (2004) 'Automobility and the power of sound', pp. 243–259 in *Theory, Culture and Society* (21/4–5).

Bull, Michael (2000) *Sounding Out the City: Personal Stereos and the Management of Everyday Life* (Oxford and New York: Berg).

Burchell, Jenny (1996) *Polite or Commercial Concerts? Concert Management and Orchestral Repertoire in Edinburgh, Bath, Oxford, Manchester and Newcastle, 1730–1799* (New York and London: Garland Publishing).

Button, Graham (ed.) (1991) *Ethnomethodology and the Human Sciences* (Cambridge: Cambridge University Press).

Calhoun, Craig (1993) 'Habitus, field, and capital: the question of historical specificity', pp. 61–88 in Calhoun, LiPuma and Postone (eds.), *Bourdieu*.

Calhoun, C., LiPuma, E., and Postone, M. (eds.) (1993) *Bourdieu: Critical Perspectives* (Cambridge: Polity Press).

Carey, John (2005) *What Good Are The Arts?* (London: Faber).

Chanan, Michael (1994) *Musica Practica: The Social Practice of Western Music from Gregorian Chant to Postmodernism* (London and New York: Verso).

Chaney, David (2004) 'Fragmented culture and subcultures', pp. 36–48 in A. Bennett and K. Kahn-Harris (eds.) *After Subculture: Critical Studies in Contemporary Youth Culture* (Houndmills and New York: Palgrave Macmillan).

Cicourel, A. V. (1993) 'Aspects of structural and processual theories of knowledge', pp. 89–115 in Calhoun, LiPuma and Postone (eds.), *Bourdieu*.

Cicourel, A. V. (1964) *Method and Measurement in Sociology* (New York: Free Press).

Citron, Marcia J. (1993) *Gender and the Musical Canon* (Cambridge:

Cambridge University Press).

Clarke, Donald (1995) *The Rise and Fall of Popular Music* (London: Viking).

Clayton, Martin, Herbert, Trevor, and Middleton, Richard (eds.) (2003) *The Cultural Study of Music: A Critical Introduction* (New York and London: Routledge).

Cohen, Sara (1991) *Rock Culture in Liverpool* (Oxford: Oxford University Press).

Collins, Randall (1986) *Weberian Social Theory* (Cambridge: Cambridge University Press).

Cook, Nicholas (2001) 'Theorising musical meaning', pp. 168–195 in *Music Theory Spectrum*.

Cook, Nicholas (1998) *Music: A Very Short Introduction* (Oxford and New York: Oxford University Press)

Cook, Nicholas (1990) *Music, Imagination and Culture* (Oxford: Oxford University Press).

Cook, Nicholas, and Everist, Mark (eds.) (1999) *Rethinking Music* (Oxford: Oxford University Press).

Coulter, Jeff (1989) *Mind in Action* (Cambridge: Polity Press).

Coulter, Jeff (1979) *The Social Construction of Mind* (London: Macmillan).

Crossley, Nick (2002) *Making Sense of Social Movements* (Buckingham and Philadelphia, PA: Open University Press).

Crowther, P. (1994) 'Sociological imperialism and the field of cultural production: the case of Bourdieu', pp. 155–169 in *Theory, Culture and Society* (11).

Dahlhaus, Carl (1989) *Nineteenth Century Music* (Berkeley and Los Angeles: University of California Press).

Dawe, Alan (1970) 'The two sociologies', pp. 207–218 in *British Journal of Sociology* (21/2).

Day, W. (2000) 'Knowing as instancing: jazz improvisation as moral perfectionism', pp. 99–111 in *Journal of Aesthetics and Art Criticism* (58/2).

Dennis, Alex and Martin, Peter J. (2005) 'Symbolic interactionism and the concept of power', pp. 191–213 in *The British Journal of Sociology* (56/2).

DeNora, Tia (2003) *After Adorno: Rethinking Music Sociology* (Cambridge and New York: Cambridge University Press).

DeNora, Tia (2000) *Music in Everyday Life* (Cambridge and New York: Cambridge University Press).

DeNora, Tia (1995) *Beethoven and the Construction of Genius* (Berkeley: University of California Press).

DeNora, Tia (1991) 'Musical patronage and social change in Beethoven's Vienna', pp. 310–346 in *American Journal of Sociology* (97/2).

DeNora, Tia (1986) 'How is extra-musical meaning possible? Music as a place and space for "work"', pp. 84–94 in *Sociological Theory* (4).

Denzin, Norman (1969) 'Problems in analysing elements of mass culture: notes on the popular song and other artistic productions', pp. 1035–1038 in *American Journal of Sociology*, 75 (1969).

DeVeaux, Scott (1997) *The Birth of Bebop: A Social and Musical History* (Berkeley and Los Angeles: University of California Press).

DiMaggio, Paul (1992) 'Cultural boundaries and structural change: the extension of the high-culture model to theatre, opera and the dance, 1900–1940', pp. 21–57 in Lamont and Fournier (eds.) *Cultivating Differences*.

DiMaggio, Paul (1982) 'Cultural entrepreneurship in nineteenth century Boston: the creation of an organisational base for high culture in America', pp. 33–50 and 303–322 in *Media, Culture and Society* (4).

DiMaggio, Paul, and Mukhtar, T. (2004) 'Arts participation as cultural capital in the United States, 1982–2002: signs of decline?', pp. 169–194 in *Poetics* (32).

Dodd, Julian (2000) 'Musical works as eternal types', pp. 424–440 in *British Journal of Aesthetics* (40/2).

Douglas, Dave (2000) *Soul on Soul* BMG/RCA 09026 63603 2 (CD).

Douglas, Jack D. (ed.) (1971) *Understanding Everday Life* (London: Routledge and Kegan Paul).

Drew, Rob (2001) *Karaoke Nights: An Ethnographic Rhapsody* (Walnut Creek, CA, and Oxford: Alta Mira Press).

Dreyfus, Hubert, and Rabinow, Paul (1993) 'Can there be a science of existential structure and social meaning?' pp. 35–44 in Calhoun, LiPuma and Postone (eds.), *Bourdieu*.

Durkheim, Emile (1982 [1895]) *The Rules of Sociological Method* (London: Macmillan).

Durkheim, Emile (1952 [1897]) *Suicide* (London: Routledge).

Eagleton, Terry (1991) *Ideology* (London: Verso).

Edström, Olle (1997) 'Fr-a-g-me-n-ts: a discussion of the position of critical ethnomusicology in contemporary musicology', pp. 9–68 in *Svensk Tidskrift for Musikforskning* (79).

Ehrlich, Cyril (1985) *The Music Profession in Britain Since the Eighteenth Century: A Social History* (Oxford: Clarendon Press).

Elias, Norbert (1993) *Mozart: Portrait of a Genius* (Cambridge: Polity Press).

Ellison, Ralph (1967) *Shadow and Act* (London: Secker and Warburg).

Eva, Philemon (1997) 'Popular Song and Social Identity in the Victorian City'. Unpublished Ph.D. thesis, University of Manchester.

Evans, Bill, and Brecker, Randy (2004) *Soul Bop* BHM 1003–2 (CD).

Finnegan, Ruth (1989) *The Hidden Musicians* (Cambridge: Cambridge University Press).

Fish, Stanley (1980) *Is There a Text in the Class? The Authority of Interpretive Communities* (Cambridge, MA: Harvard University Press).

Foucault, Michel (1991[1975]) *Discipline and Punish: The Birth of the Prison* (London: Penguin).

Foucault, Michel (1974 [1966]) *The Order of Things: An Archaeology of the Hunan Sciences* (London: Tavistock).

Fowler, Bridget (2003) 'A note on Nick Zangwill's "Against the Sociology of Art"', pp. 363–374 in *Philosophy of the Social Sciences* (32/2).

Fox, Nick J. (1998) 'Foucault, Foucauldians and sociology', in *British Journal of Sociology* (49/3).

Francis, Dave (1987) 'The great transition', pp. 1–35 in R. J. Anderson, J. A. Hughes and W. W. Sharrock (eds.) *Classic Disputes in Sociology* (London: Allen and Unwin).

Frisby, D., and Featherstone, M. (eds.) (1997) *Simmel on Culture* (London: Sage).

Frith, Simon (1996a) 'Music and Identity', pp. 108–127 in S. Hall and P. DuGay (eds.) *Questions of Cultural Identity* (London: Sage).

Frith, Simon (1996b) *Performing Rites: On the Value of Popular Music* (Oxford and New York: Oxford University Press).

Garfinkel, Harold (1967) *Studies in Ethnomethodology* (Englewood Cliffs, NJ: Prentice-Hall).

Gates, Henry L. (1988) *The Signifying Monkey: A Theory of Afro-American Literary Criticism* (New York: Oxford University Press).

Gibson, William J. (2002) 'The collaborative process of jazz improvisation'. Unpublished Ph.D. thesis, University of Manchester.

Giddens, Anthony (1987) 'Structuralism, poststructuralism, and the production of culture', in A. Giddens and J.H. Turner (eds.) *Social Theory Today* (Cambridge: Polity Press).

Giddins, Gary (1998) 'Bird Lives!', pp. 3–9 in Woideck (ed.), *The Charlie Parker Companion*.

Gilmore, Samuel (1990) 'Art worlds: developing the interactionist approach to social organisation' in H. S. Becker and M. M. McCall (eds.) *Symbolic Interaction and Cultural Studies* (Chicago: University of Chicago Press).

Gioia, Ted (1997) *The History of Jazz* (New York and Oxford: Oxford University Press).

Goehr, Lydia (1992) *The Imaginary Museum of Musical Works* (Oxford: Clarendon Press).

Goffman, Erving (1964) 'The neglected situation', pp. 133–136 in J. Gumperz and D. Hymes (eds.) *The Ethnography of Communication* (*American Anthropologist Special Edition* (66/6).

Goffman, Erving (1959) *The Presentation of Self in Everyday Life* (New York: Doubleday).

Green, Lucy (1997) *Music, Gender and Education* (Cambridge: Cambridge

University Press).

Gunn, Simon (1999) 'The middle class, modernity and the provincial city: Manchester c1840–1880', pp. 112–127 in Kidd and Nicholls (eds.), *Gender, Civic Culture and Consumerism*.

Gunn, Simon (1997) 'The sublime and the vulgar: the Hallé concerts and the constitution of "high culture" in Manchester, c1850–1880', pp. 208–228 in *Journal of Victorian Culture* (2).

Gushee, Lawrence (1998) 'The improvisation of Louis Armstrong', pp. 291–334 in Nettl and Russell (eds.), *In the Course of Performance*.

Habermas, Jurgen (1992 [1962]) *The Structural Transformation of the Public Sphere* (Cambridge: Polity Press).

Hacker, P. M. S. (1990) 'Chomsky's problems', pp. 127–148 in *Language and Communication* (10/2).

Hagberg, G. (1998) 'Jazz improvisation', pp. 479–482 in M. Kelly (ed.) *Encyclopaedia of Aesthetics, Vol. 2*. (New York: Oxford University Press).

Hallé, Charles (1896) *Life and Letters of Sir Charles Hallé* (ed. C. E. Hallé) (London: Smith, Elder).

Harrison, Bernard (1979) *An Introduction to the Philosophy of Language* (London: Macmillan).

Haslam, Dave (1999) *Manchester, England: The Story of the Pop Cult City* (London: Fourth Estate).

Heil, John (1981) 'Does cognitive psychology rest on a mistake?', pp. 321–342 in *Mind* (90).

Hennion, Antoine (2001) 'Music lovers: taste as performance', pp. 1–22 in *Theory, Culture and Society* (18/5).

Hennion, Antoine (1997) 'Baroque and rock: music, mediators and musical taste', pp. 415–435 in *Poetics* (24).

Hennion, Antoine (1990) 'The production of success: an anti-musicology of the pop song', pp. 159–193 in S. Frith and A. Goodwin (eds.) *On Record: Rock, Pop and the Written Word* (London: Routledge).

Hennion, Antoine (1989) 'An intermediary between production and consumption: the producer of popular music', pp. 400–424 in *Science. Technology and Human Values* (14).

Hennion, Antoine, and Meadel, C. (1986) 'Programming music: radio as mediator', pp. 281–303 in *Media, Culture and Society* (8).

Herbert, Trevor (ed.) (1991) *Bands: The Brass Band Movement in the 19th and 20th Centuries* (Buckingham: Open University Press).

Heritage, John (1984) *Garfinkel and Ethnomethodology* (Cambridge: Polity Press).

Hirsch, P. M. (1971) 'Sociological approaches to the pop music phenomenon', pp. 371–388 in *American Behavioural Scientist* (14).

Hodeir, André (1956) *Jazz: Its Evolution and Essence* (New York: Grove Press).

Honneth, Axel (1995) *The Fragmented World of the Social* (Albany: State University of New York Press).

Honneth, Axel (1993) 'Max Horkheimer and the sociological deficit of critical theory', pp. 187–214 in S. Benhabib, W. Bonss and J. McCole (eds.) *On Max Horkheimer: New Perspectives* (Cambridge, MA: MIT Press).

Horkheimer, M., and Adorno, T (1973 [1956]) *Aspects of Sociology* (London: Heinemann).

Horn, David (2000) 'Some thoughts on the work in popular music', pp. 14–34 in M. Talbot (ed.), *The Musical Work*.

How, Alan (2003) *Critical Theory* (Houndmills: Palgrave Macmillan).

Hughes, M., and Stradling, R. (2001) *The English Musical Renaissance, 1840–1940: Constructing a National Music* (Manchester: Manchester University Press).

Hughes, J. A., Sharrock, W. W., and Martin, P. J. (2003) *Understanding Classical Sociology: Marx, Weber, Durkheim* (London: Sage).

Hullot-Kentor, R. (1991) 'The impossibility of music: Adorno, popular and other music', in *Telos* (87).

Hyland, William G. (1995) *The Song is Ended: Songwriters and American Music* (New York: Oxford University Press).

Jackson, Travis A. (2003) 'Jazz performance as ritual: the blues aesthetic and the African diaspora', pp. 23–82 in Ingrid Monson (ed.) *The African Diaspora: A Musical Perspective* (New York and London: Routledge).

Jarrett, Keith (2000) *Whisper Not* ECM 1724/25 (CD).

Jay, Martin (1984) *Adorno* (London: Fontana).

Jay, Martin (1973) *The Dialectical Imagination: A History of the Frankfurt School and the Institute of Social Research* (Berkeley: University of California Press).

Jenkins, Richard (2002) *Foundations of Sociology* (Houndmills: Palgrave-Macmillan).

Jenkins, Richard (1992) *Bourdieu* (London: Routledge).

Johnson, James H. (1995) *Listening in Paris: A Cultural History* (Berkeley: University of California Press).

Jones, Leroi (Amiri Baraka) (1963) *Blues People* (New York: William Morrow).

Kargon, Robert H. (1977) *Science in Victorian Manchester: Enterprise and Expertise* (Baltimore and London: Johns Hopkins University Press).

Keil, Charles (1995) 'The theory of participatory discrepancies: a progress report', pp. 1–19 in *Ethnomusicology* (39/1).

Kennedy, Michael (ed.) (1972) *The Autobiography of Charles Hallé* (London: Elek Books).

Kennedy, Michael (1960) *The Hallé Tradition: A Century of Music* (Manchester: Manchester University Press).

Kernfield, Barry (1995) *What to Listen for in Jazz* (New Haven and London:

Yale University Press).

Kidd, Alan (1993) *Manchester* (Keele: Ryburn).

Kidd, Alan, and Nicholls, David (eds.) (1999) *Gender, Civic Culture and Consumerism: Middle-Class Identity in Britain, 1800–1940* (Manchester: Manchester University Press).

King, Anthony (2004) *The Structure of Social Theory* (London: Routledge).

Kofsky, Frank (1998) *Black Music, White Business: Illuminating the History and Political Economy of Jazz* (New York: Pathfinder).

Kolb, Bonita M. (2001) 'The effect of generational change on classical music concert attendance and orchestras' responses in the UK and US', pp. 1–35 in *Cultural Trends* (41).

Kuhn, Thomas S. (1970) *The Structure of Scientific Revolutions* (Chicago: University of Chicago Press).

Lamont, M. and Fournier, M. (eds.) *Cultivating Differences: Symbolic Boundaries and the Making of Inequality* (Chicago: Chicago University Press).

Lemann, Nicholas (1991) *The Promised Land: The Great Black Migration and How it Changed America* (London: Macmillan).

Leppert, Richard (ed.) (2002) *Teodor W. Adorno: Essays on Music* (Berkeley: University of California Press).

Leppert, Richard (1988) *Music and Image: Domesticity, Ideology and Sociocultural Formation in Eighteenth Century England* (Cambridge: Cambridge University Press).

Levine, Lawrence W. (1988) *Highbrow/Lowbrow: The Emergence of Cultural Hierarchy in America* (Cambridge, MA, and London: Harvard University Press).

Longhurst, Brian (1995) *Popular Music and Society* (Cambridge: Polity Press).

Longhurst, Brian, and Savage, Mike (1996) 'Social class, consumption and the influence of Bourdieu: some critical issues', pp. 274–301 in S. Edgell, K. Hetherington and A. Warde (eds.) *Consumption Matters* (Oxford: Blackwell).

Lopes, P. (1992) 'Innovation and diversity in the popular music industry, 1969–1990', pp. 56–71 in *American Sociological Review* (57).

Lord, Albert B. (2000 [1960]) *The Singer of Tales* (Cambridge, MA, and London: Harvard University Press).

Lyotard, Jean-Francois (1984 [1979]) *The Postmodern Condition: A Report on Knowledge* (Manchester: Manchester University Press).

McBrien, William (1998) *Cole Porter: A Biography* (New York: Alfred A. Knopf).

McClary, Susan (2000) *Conventional Wisdom: The Content of Musical Form* (Berkeley and Los Angeles: University of California Press).

McClary, Susan (1991) *Feminine Endings: Music, Gender and Sexuality*

(Minneapolis: University of Minnesota Press).

McGilvray, J. (1999) *Chomsky: Language, Mind and Politics* (Cambridge: Polity Press).

McNay, L. (1994) *Foucault: A Critical Introduction* (Cambridge: Polity).

McVeigh, Simon (1993) *Concert Life in London from Mozart to Haydn* (Cambridge: Cambridge University Press).

Mace, Nancy A. (2004) 'Charles Rennett and the London music-sellers in the 1780s: testing the ownership of reversionary copyrights', pp. 1–23 in *Journal of the Royal Musical Association* (129).

Mackenzie, Ian (2000) 'Improvisation, creativity, and formulaic language', pp. 173–179 in *Journal of Aesthetics and Art Criticism* (58/2).

Maggin, Donald L. (1996) *Stan Getz: A Life in Jazz* (New York: Quill/William Morrow).

Marquis, Alice Goldfarb (1999) 'Jazz goes to college: has academic status served the art?', pp. 117–124 in *Popular Music and Society* (22/2).

Martin, Peter J. (forthcoming) 'The music business in capitalist society' in H. de la Motte-Haber and H. Neuhoff (eds.) *Handbuch der Systematischen Musikwissenschaft,* Vol. 4: *Musiksoziologie* (Berlin: Laaber-Verlag).

Martin, Peter J. (2004) 'Culture, subculture and social organisation', pp. 21–35 in A. Bennett and K. Kahn-Harris (eds.) *After Subculture: Critical Studies in Contemporary Youth Culture* (Houndmills: Palgrave-Macmillan).

Martin, Peter J. (2000) 'Music and the sociological gaze', pp. 41–56 in *Svensk Tidskrift for Musikforskning* (82).

Martin, Peter J. (1995) *Sounds and Society: Themes in the Sociology of Music* (Manchester: Manchester University Press).

Martin, Peter J. (1987) 'The concept of class', pp. 67–96 in R. J. Anderson, J.A. Hughes and W. W. Sharrock (eds.) *Classic Disputes in Sociology* (London: Allen and Unwin).

Martin, Peter J. (1979) Review of D. Sudnow, *Ways of the Hand*, pp. 562–563 in *Sociology* (13/3).

Marx, Karl, and Engels, Frederick (1974 [1845]) *The German Ideology* (London: Lawrence & Wishart).

Mead, George Herbert (1934) *Mind, Self and Society* (Chicago: University of Chicago Press).

Messinger, Gary S. (1985) *Manchester in the Victorian Age: The Half-Known City* (Manchester: Manchester University Press).

Meyer, Leonard (1970) *Emotion and Meaning in Music* (Chicago: Chicago University Press).

Middleton, Richard (2000) 'The popular music intertext', pp. 59–87 in M. Talbot (ed.), *The Musical Work.*

Middleton, Richard (1996) Review of P. J. Martin, *Sounds and Society*, in *Music and Letters* (November).

Middleton, Richard (1990) *Studying Popular Music* (Buckingham: Open University Press).

Mills, C. Wright (1959) *The Sociological Imagination* (New York: Oxford University Press).

Monk, Ray (1991) *Ludwig Wittgenstein: The Duty of Genius* (London: Vintage).

Monson, Ingrid (1996) *Saying Something: Jazz Improvisation and Interaction* (Chicago and London: University of Chicago Press).

Monson, Ingrid (1994) 'Doubleness and jazz improvisation: irony, parody and ethnomusicology', pp. 283–313 in *Critical Inquiry* (20).

Murray, Albert (1978 [1976]) *Stomping the Blues* (London: Quartet Books).

Neal, Mark Anthony (1999) *What the Music Said: Black Popular Music and Black Public Culture* (New York and London: Routledge).

Nettl, Bruno (1998) 'An art neglected in scholarship', pp. 1–23 in Nettl and Russell (eds.), *In the Course of Performance*.

Nettl, Bruno (1974) 'Thoughts on improvisation: a comparative approach', pp. 1–19 in *Musical Quarterly* (60).

Nettl, Bruno and Russell, Melinda (eds.) (1998) *In the Course of Performance: Studies in the World of Musical Improvisation* (Chicago and London: University of Chicago Press).

Negus, Keith (1999) *Music Genres and Corporate Cultures* (London: Routledge).

Owens, Thomas (1995) *Bebop: The Music and its Players* (New York: Oxford University Press).

Paddison, Max (1996) 'Adorno, popular music and mass culture', pp. 81–105 in *Adorno, Modernism and Mass Culture* (London: Kahn and Averill).

Paddison, Max (1993) *Adorno's Aesthetics of Music* (Cambridge: Cambridge University Press).

Parsonage, Catherine (2005) *The Evolution of Jazz in Britain, 1880–1935* (Aldershot: Ashgate).

Pawley, A., and Syder, F. H. (1983) 'Two puzzles for linguistic theory: nativelike selection and nativelike fluency', pp. 191–225 in J. C. Richards and R. W. Schmidt (eds.) *Language and Communication* (London and New York: Longman).

Peretti, Burton W. (1992) *The Creation of Jazz: Music, Race and Culture in Urban America* (Urbana and Chicago: University of Illinois Press).

Perlman, A. M., and Greenblatt, D. (1981) 'Miles Davis meets Noam Chomsky: some observations on jazz improvisation and language structure', in W. Steiner (ed.) *The Sign in Music and Literature* (Austin: University of Texas Press).

Peterson, Richard A. (1997a) *Creating Country Music: Fabricating Authenticity* (Chicago and London: University of Chicago Press).

Peterson, Richard A. (1997b) 'The rise and fall of highbrow snobbery as a status marker', pp. 75–92 in *Poetics* (25).

Peterson, Richard A. (1990) 'Why 1955? Explaining the advent of rock music', pp. 97–116 in *Popular Music* (9/1).

Peterson, Richard A., and Kern, R. M. (1996) 'Changing highbrow taste: from snob to omnivore', pp. 900–907 in *American Sociological Review* (61/5).

Peterson, Richard A., and Simkus, Albert (1992) 'How musical tastes mark occupational status groups', pp. 152–186 in Lamont and Fournier (eds.) *Cultivating Differences.*

Pike, Alfred (1974) 'A phenomenology of jazz', pp. 88–94 in *Journal of Jazz Studies* (2/1).

Pressing, Jeff (1998) 'Psychological constraints on improvisational expertise and communication', pp. 47–67 in Nettl and Russell (eds.), *In the Course of Performance.*

Pressing, Jeff (1988) 'Improvisation: methods and models' in J. A. Sloboda (ed.) *Generative Processes in Music: The Psychology of Performance, Improvisation, and Composition* (Oxford: Clarendon).

Rabinow, P. (ed.) (1991 [1984]) *The Foucault Reader: An Introduction to Foucault's Thought* (London: Penguin).

Reisner, Robert (1962) *Bird: The Legend of Charlie Parker* (London: Quartet Books).

Rich, Buddy (1967) *Big Swing Face* United Artists SLS 50174 (LP).

Robinson, J. and Hirsch, P. M. (1972) 'Teenage response to rock 'n' roll protest songs', pp. 222–231 in R. S. Denisoff and R. A. Peterson (eds.) *The Sounds of Social Change* (Chicago: Rand-McNally).

Rock, Paul (1979) *The Making of Symbolic Interactionism* (London: Macmillan).

Rorty, Richard (1999) *Philosophy and Social Hope* (London: Penguin).

Rorty, Richard (1993) 'Wittgenstein, Heidegger, and the reification of language', pp. 337–357 in C. B. Guignon (ed.) *The Cambridge Companion to Heidegger* (Cambridge: Cambridge University Press).

Rose, Arnold M. (ed.) (1962) *Human Behaviour and Social Processes* (London: Routledge and Kegan Paul).

Rosselli, John (1991) *Music and Musicians in Nineteenth Century Italy* (London: Batsford).

Russell, Dave (2000) 'Musicians in the English provincial city: Manchester c1860–1914', pp. 233–253 in *Music and British Culture, 1785–1914* (Oxford: Oxford University Press).

Russell, Dave (1997) *Popular Music in England, 1840–1914: A Social History* (Manchester: Manchester University Press).

Russell, Ross (1972) *Bird Lives! The High Life and Hard Times of Charlie 'Yardbird' Parker* (London: Quartet Books).

Sarath, E. (1996) 'A new look at improvisation', pp. 1–38 in *Journal of Music Theory* (40/1).

Savage, Mike, Barlow, James, Dickens, Peter, and Fielding, Tony (1992) *Property, Bureaucracy and Culture* (London: Routledge).

Sawyer, R. Keith (2000) 'Improvisation and the creative process: Dewey, Collingwood, and the aesthetics of spontaneity', pp. 149–161 in *Journal of Aesthetics and Art Criticism* (58/2).

Scott, Derek B. (1989) *The Singing Bourgeois: Songs of the Victorian Drawing Room and Parlour* (Milton Keynes: Open University Press).

Schuller, Gunther (1968) *Early Jazz: Its Roots and Musical Development* (New York: Oxford University Press).

Schütz, Alfred (1976) 'Fragments on the phenomenology of music', pp. 23–71 in F. J. Smith (ed.) *In Search of Musical Method* (London: Gordon and Breach).

Schütz, Alfred (1972 [1932]) *The Phenomenology of the Social World* (London: Heinemann).

Schütz, Alfred (1964 [1951]) 'Making music together: a study in social relationship', pp. 159–178 in *Collected Papers II: Studies in Social Theory* (The Hague: Martinus Nijhoff).

Sennett, Richard (1998) *The Corrosion of Character: The Personal Consequences of Work in the New Capitalism* (New York: Norton).

Sennett, Richard (1992 [1974]) *The Fall of Public Man* (New York and London: Norton).

Shapiro, Nat, and Hentoff, Nat (eds.) (1966 [1955]) *Hear Me Talkin' To Ya* (New York: Dover Publications).

Sharrock, Wes, and Read, Rupert (2003) *Kuhn: Philosopher of Scientific Revolution* (Cambridge: Polity Press).

Shepherd, John (2003) 'Music and social categories', pp. 69–79 in Clayton, et al (eds.), *The Cultural Study of Music*.

Shepherd, John (1991) *Music as Social Text* (Cambridge: Polity Press).

Shepherd, John (1987) 'Towards a sociology of musical styles', pp. 56–76 in A. L. White (ed.) *Culture, Style, and the Musical Event* (London: Routledge).

Shibutani, Tamotsu (1962) 'Reference groups and social control', pp. 128–147 in A. M. Rose (ed.) *Human Behaviour and Social Processes* (London: Routledge).

Shipton, Alyn (1999) *Groovin' High: The Life of Dizzy Gillespie* (New York and Oxford: Oxford University Press).

Simmel, Georg (1997 [1903]) 'The metropolis and mental life', pp. 174–185 in Frisby and Featherstone (eds.), *Simmel on Culture*.

Simmel, Georg (1997 [1911]) 'The concept and tragedy of culture', pp. 55–75 in Frisby and Featherstone (eds.), *Simmel on Culture*.

Small, Christopher (1998) *Musicking: The Meanings of Performing and*

*Listening* (Hanover and London: Wesleyan University Press).

Small, Christopher (1987) 'Performance as ritual: sketch for an enquiry into the true nature of a symphony concert', pp. 6–32 in A. L. White (ed.), *Lost in Music*.

Small, Christopher (1984) 'No meanings without rules', in *Improvisation: History, Directions, Practice* (London: London Association of Improvising Musicians).

Smith, R. J., and Maughan, T. (1997) 'Youth culture and the making of the post-Fordist economy: dance music in contemporary Britain' (London: Royal Holloway Discussion Paper 97/2).

Stern, C. (1999) 'The emperor of cool', *Jazz Times* (August).

Subotnik, Rose R. (1991) *Developing Variations* (Minneapolis: University of Minnesota Press).

Sudnow, David (1978) *Ways of the Hand* (London: Routledge and Kegan Paul).

Sudnow, David (1972) *Studies in Social Interaction* (New York: Free Press).

Swade, Doron (2000) *The Cogwheel Brain: Charles Babbage and the Quest to Build the First Computer* (London: Abacus).

Tagg, Philip (1998) 'The Goteborg connection: lessons in the history of popular music education and research', pp. 219–242 in *Popular Music* (17/2).

Talbot, Michael (ed.) (2000) *The Musical Work: Reality or Invention?* (Liverpool: Liverpool University Press).

Tawa, Nicholas, E. (1989) 'Philadephia: a city in the New World', pp. 368–382 in N. Zaslaw (ed.) *The Classical Era* (Houndmills: Macmillan).

Thornton, Sarah (1995) *Club Cultures: Music, Media and Subcultural Capital* (Cambridge: Polity Press).

Tirro, Frank (1974) 'Constructive elements in jazz improvisation', pp. 285–305 in *Journal of the American Musicological Society* (27).

Tomlinson, Gary (1992) 'Cultural dialogics and jazz: a white historian signifies', pp. 64–94 in K. Bergeron and P. Bohlmann (eds.) *Disciplining Music* (Chicago: University of Chicago Press).

Vail, Ken (1996) *Bird's Diary: The Life of Charlie Parker, 1945–1955* (Chessington: Castle Communications).

Van Eijck, Koen (2001) 'Social differentiation in musical taste patterns', pp. 1163–1185 in *Social Forces* (79/3).

Van Eijck, Koen (2000) 'Richard A. Peterson and the culture of consumption', pp. 207–224 in *Poetics* (28).

Veblen, Thorstein (1994 [1899]) *The Theory of the Leisure Class* (New York: Dover Publications).

Vianna, Hermano (1999) *The Mystery of Samba: Popular Music and National Identity in Brazil* (Chapel Hill and London: University of North Carolina Press).

Ward, Brian (1998) *Just My Soul Responding: Rhythm and Blues, Black Consciousness and Race Relations* (London: University College London Press).

Warde, Alan (1996) 'Afterword: the future of the sociology of consumption', pp. 302–312 in Edgell, Hetherington and Warde (eds.) *Consumption Matters.*

Weber, Max (1978) *Economy and Society* (Berkeley: University of California Press).

Weber, Max (1930 [1904–5]) *The Protestant Ethic and the Spirit of Capitalism* (London: Allen and Unwin).

Weber, William (2001) 'From miscellany to homogeneity in concert programming', pp. 125–134 in *Poetics* (29).

Weber, William (1994) 'The intellectual origins of musical canon in eighteenth-century England', pp. 488–519 in *Journal of the American Musicological Society* (47).

Weber, Willam (1992) *The Rise of Musical Classics in Eighteenth-Century England: A Study in Ritual, Canon and Ideology* (Oxford: Clarendon Press).

Weber, William (1977) 'Mass culture and the reshaping of European musical taste, 1770–1870', pp. 5–22 in *International Review of the Aesthetics and Sociology of Music* (8).

Weber, William (1975) *Music and the Middle Class* (London: Croom Helm).

White, A. L. (ed.) (1987) *Lost in Music: Culture, Style and the Musical Event* (London: Routledge).

Whitehead, Alfred N. (1925) *Science and the Modern World* (New York: Mentor).

Whitfield, Roy (1988) *Frederick Engels in Manchester: The Search for a Shadow* (Salford: Working Class Movement Library).

Wiggershaus, Rolf (1994 [1986]) *The Frankfurt School: Its History, Theories and Political Significance* (Cambridge: Polity Press).

Winch, Peter (1958) *The Idea of a Social Science* (London: Routledge and Kegan Paul).

Williams, Alastair (2001) *Constructing Musicology* (Aldershot: Ashgate).

Willis, Paul (1990) *Common Culture* (Milton Keynes: Open University Press).

Witkin, Robert (1998) *Adorno on Music* (London: Routledge).

Wittgenstein, Ludwig (1972 [1953]) *Philosophical Investigations* (Oxford: Blackwell).

Woideck, Carl (ed.) (1998) *The Charlie Parker Companion: Six Decades of Commentary* (New York: Schirmer Books).

Woideck, Carl (1996) *Charlie Parker: His Music and Life* (Ann Arbor: University of Michigan Press).

Wynne, Derek, and O'Connor, Justin (1998) 'Consumption and the postmodern city', pp. 841–864 in *Urban Studies* (35/5–6).

Zangwill, Nick (2002) 'Against the sociology of art', pp. 206–218 in *Philosophy of the Social Sciences* (32/2).

Zuidervaart, Lambert (1991) *Adorno's Aesthetic Theory: The Redemption of Illusion* Cambridge, MA, and London: MIT Press).

# Index